Public Relations Campaigns

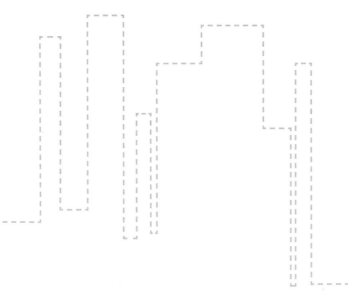

Public Relations Campaigns

Edited by **Mark Sheehan and Robina Xavier**

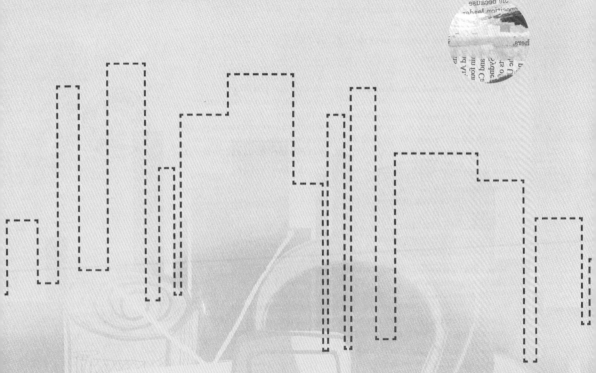

OXFORD
UNIVERSITY PRESS
AUSTRALIA & NEW ZEALAND

OXFORD
UNIVERSITY PRESS
AUSTRALIA & NEW ZEALAND

253 Normanby Road, South Melbourne, Victoria 3205, Australia

Oxford University Press is a department of the University of Oxford.
It furthers the University's objective of excellence in research,
scholarship, and education by publishing worldwide in

Oxford New York

Auckland Cape Town Dar es Salaam Hong Kong Karachi
Kuala Lumpur Madrid Melbourne Mexico City Nairobi
New Delhi Shanghai Taipei Toronto

With offices in

Argentina Austria Brazil Chile Czech Republic France Greece
Guatemala Hungary Italy Japan Poland Portugal Singapore
South Korea Switzerland Thailand Turkey Ukraine Vietnam

OXFORD is a trademark of Oxford University Press
in the UK and in certain other countries

First published 2009
Reprinted 2009

National Library of Australia Cataloguing-in-Publication data

Sheehan, Mark.
Public relations campaigns/Mark Sheehan, Robina Xavier.

9780195559101 (pbk.)

Includes index.
Bibliography.
Mass media and business.
Public relations—Management.
Xavier, Robina.

659.2

Edited by Natasha Broadstock
Cover and text design by Caitlin Ziegler
Typeset by diacriTech, Chennai, India
Indexed by Jeanne Rudd
Printed in Hong Kong by Sheck Wah Tong Printing Press Ltd

Contents

Author Profiles

COORDINATING AUTHORS

MARK SHEEHAN combines almost twenty-five years of middle and senior management experience in the private sector with more recent academic experience in the School of Communication and Creative Arts at Deakin University. He was the founding Postgraduate Course Director of the Master of Arts (Professional Communication) program and is currently an Associate Head of School and Undergraduate Course Director. He is also a Senior Associate and Honorary Life Member of the Financial Services Institute of Australia and an Associate Fellow of the Australian Institute of Management. Mark's high-profile positions in the private sector have included being the Director of Public Relations at the Australian Institute of Banking and Finance and the National Public Affairs Manager for the Insurance Council of Australia.

Mark is the editor of the *Asia Pacific Public Relations Journal* and a member of the Public Relations Institute of Australia (PRIA) National Education Committee. He has presented at national and international conferences in his chosen research areas of the growth of public relations in Australia, the role of public relations in the finance sector, and risk communication.

ROBINA XAVIER is a senior faculty member at the Queensland University of Technology (QUT) and has more than twenty years' experience in public relations practice and education. After starting her career with the federal government in Canberra, Robina moved to consulting, working primarily on investor relations and issues management. Prior to joining QUT, she managed the Corporate and Finance Division for Turnbull Fox Phillips in Queensland. Her excellence in teaching and learning has seen her receive numerous university awards and be selected as a QUT Teaching Fellow.

Robina's research interests include crisis management, investor relations and public relations planning and evaluation, and her research work has been showcased at national and international conferences, and in academic and industry journals. She plays an active role in the PRIA, having been a State President and National Vice President. She is currently the National Deputy President and chairs the National Education Committee. She is a Fellow of PRIA and the Financial Services Institute of Australasia.

CONTRIBUTORS

DONALD ALEXANDER is a Senior Lecturer in Public Relations and Organisational Communication at Charles Sturt University. He has had senior corporate affairs management experience in the mining, manufacturing and finance sectors, and has managed two consultancies, with clients in information technology and management consulting. Prior to his position at Charles Sturt, he was a Lecturer in Public Relations and Professional Communication at Central Queensland University.

DR JOY CHIA is a Senior Lecturer, a Program Director, a PRIA Fellow, an active member of PRIA's National Education Committee and a former South Australian PRIA President. Joy began the public relations degree in South Australia and developed strong industry partnerships, facilitating many new public relations positions.

DR KRISTIN DEMETRIOUS is a Lecturer in Public Relations at Deakin University. An experienced communication practitioner and media specialist, Kristin has worked in house and has operated her own communication consultancy. Kristin's research interests include communication in sub-political movements or activism, and public relations and ethics. Her work is published in Australia and the United Kingdom.

CHRIS GALLOWAY is the Discipline Leader, Public Relations and Program Coordinator, Bachelor of Communications, at Swinburne University. He was a journalist and then a senior public relations practitioner before becoming an academic. His research focuses on public relations and risk communication.

DR GWYNETH V. J. HOWELL is a Senior Lecturer at the University of Western Sydney (UWS). She has ten years' experience in corporate marketing and management roles, and extensive experience in the development, implementation and analysis of a range of traditional and non-traditional communication projects. Gwyneth has been head of the public relations major at UWS for the last five years. Her research profile includes crisis and issues management, and her current research focuses on how organisations may best maximise the impact of new communication channels such as websites, blogs and Really Simple Syndication (RSS).

BRONWYN KIRBY has more than eighteen years' experience in professional and management roles with a strategic corporate communications focus. Since

2002 Bronwyn has enjoyed the challenge of providing a real-life perspective for her public relations students at Deakin University. She is a member of PRIA and maintains a strong link with the local business community through various activities and associations.

DR KATHERINE MIZERSKI is a Senior Lecturer in the School of Marketing, Tourism and Leisure at Edith Cowan University. With a background in small business retailing and communications, Katherine conducts research in the area of effective communication strategies aimed at diverse populations. She also works with small businesses to develop effective marketing strategies for a sustainable competitive advantage.

JOSEPH PEART is the Program Leader, Communication and Public Relations at AUT University, and the New Zealand editor for *Asia Pacific Public Relations Review.* He contributed two chapters to *Public Relations Issues and Crisis Management* (2005), having earlier authored the *NZ Public Relations Handbook* (1996).

DEIRDRE QUINN-ALLAN is an Associate Lecturer in the School of Communication and Creative Arts at Deakin University. She has been teaching public relations full-time at Deakin since 2005. Prior to joining Deakin, Deirdre worked for both non-profit and commercial organisations in a range of managerial, marketing and public relations roles.

DR RICHARD C. STANTON is a Senior Lecturer in the Department of Media and Communication at The University of Sydney. He is a former journalist, editor, publisher and public relations practitioner, and the author of a variety of books including *Media Relations* (2006) and *All News is Local: The Failure of the Media to Reflect World Events in a Globalized Age* (2007). He is the editor of *Political Communication Report.*

Preface

Public relations campaigns are the lifeblood of our profession, challenging practitioners every day to achieve more for the betterment of individuals, organisations and the societies in which we live. The successful design and implementation of public relations campaigns require creativity, flexibility and strong organisational skills. They require practitioners who can deal with short-term issues while keeping their eye firmly fixed on the long-term imperatives; who know why and not just how to do things; and who provide evidence of their achievements through effective evaluation.

This book is designed to guide current and aspiring practitioners through the campaign development and implementation process. It recognises the strong and excellent practice currently happening in Australia and New Zealand, and our desire to share this expertise with others.

Many campaigns share a set of key elements (these are outlined in Chapter 1), which provide a framework by which we can analyse the campaigns in this book. While many campaigns share these elements, the specific techniques used to achieve the desired outcomes often vary. Professionals within the specialist practice areas need to map strategies and tactics to meet the needs of key publics and their sponsoring organisations.

Like all successful professions, public relations needs to know where it has been to know where it is going. Chapter 2 starts this process, describing some seminal campaigns in Australia and New Zealand that shaped our profession and our countries. Chapters 3–5 outline the foundations on which successful campaigns are built: theory, research and evaluation. Regardless of the type of campaign being undertaken, these three areas are integral to achieving effective outcomes.

Chapters 6–15 showcase a series of contemporary campaigns that highlight specialist areas of public relations practice in Australia and New Zealand. Two major approaches are taken in these chapters:

1   The first gives the reader an inside view, mapping the elements of the campaign step by step. This enables new and future practitioners to understand how a campaign is built.

2   The second focuses on campaign analysis, comparing and contrasting the competing interests represented as campaigns are put in place, and showing the external perspective of the campaign impact. This helps the reader to enhance their analytical skills while also constructing alternative processes for the campaign development.

Some campaigns featured in this book were more successful than others, emphasising for public relations practitioners the importance of learning from our mistakes. In some of the chapters we also hear from those who implemented the campaigns. Their reflections help us understand the challenges they faced and the lessons learnt.

Chapter 6 starts the community relations chapters, outlining the grassroots campaign used by a not-for-profit organisation to build community awareness and support for disability services. Chapter 7 expands on this theme, demonstrating a successful example of organisations and communities working together through the public participation process involved in a major infrastructure project, the Wivenhoe Dam Upgrade.

Chapters 8–10 examine key campaigns within the corporate communication framework. Chapter 8 charts the major challenges involved in an employee communication campaign for AMP. Chapter 9 explores the growing field of financial public relations, demonstrating how practitioners take the principles of general public relations and apply them to specialist financial audiences. The two case studies in this chapter highlight the breadth of the practice, from listing Domino's Pizza on the Australian Stock Exchange to launching the new Elders Rural Bank. Chapter 10 shows the creativity and flexibility needed to market a start-up company's products online. This campaign for FUndies demonstrates the need to persevere to achieve the stated objectives, and the need to adapt what works in one environment to another.

Chapter 11 outlines the campaign undertaken by New Zealand to win the rights to host the 2011 Rugby World Cup. Blending sports promotion and events management, this campaign involved both political and community activities to achieve its goals.

Chapters 12–14 showcase different aspects of risk, issues and crisis management approaches. Chapter 12 compares the risk communication campaigns involved in the public debate about introducing recycled water to the residents of the Queensland city of Toowoomba. Chapter 13 focuses on issues and crisis management, highlighting the positive and negatives steps taken by James Hardie Industries in its long battle to protect its corporate reputation in the face of government and community condemnation. Chapter 14 looks at the more immediate processes of emergency crisis communication, explaining the successful campaign to return power to a regional Queensland city— and illustrating the creativity needed when you have to communicate without using electricity.

To finish, Chapter 15 focuses on the important area of media relations in public relations campaigns, outlining the different approaches taken by the governments of Australia and New Zealand in dealing with a potential outbreak of avian influenza.

Just as most effective public relations campaigns are the result of significant teamwork, this book has required the work and commitment of a range of academics, practitioners and experts in the publishing world. First, we would like to thank all of the contributing authors whose hard work has made this publication possible. As they are recognised experts in their fields, we encourage you to seek out more of their published work in other forums to progress your learning.

We would also like to thank the commissioning editors at Oxford University Press, Lucy McLoughlin and Karen Hildebrandt, for their guidance and support.

As educators, we have our many students to thank for making us challenge our assumptions of public relations practice and for inspiring our search for new and better ways in learning and teaching practice.

And finally, we would like to thank our families for their support and understanding over the past eighteen months as we spent more time at our computers than we should.

Mark Sheehan and Robina Xavier

June 2008

1 Introduction to Public Relations Campaigns

Mark Sheehan

AIMS OF THIS CHAPTER

- To define a public relations campaign

- To demonstrate the key sections of a campaign and how it is developed through a hypothetical case study

INTRODUCTION

As noted in the Preface, 'The successful design and implementation of public relations campaigns require creativity, flexibility and strong organisational skills.' It is the design aspect of the public relations campaign that we will examine in this chapter.

Just as there are many definitions for the term 'public relations', it is important at the outset to make clear in our mind what a 'campaign' is. Harrison (2006, p. 82) distinguishes the different types of public relations activities and notes that a campaign is:

> a systematic set of communication activities, each with a specific defined purpose, continued over a set period of time and dealing with objectives relating to a particular issue, e.g. a campaign to increase industrial safety.

While situations and circumstances will vary from campaign to campaign, as you will read from later case studies, there are some essential elements common to all public relations campaign planning.

The Public Relations Institutes of both Australia and New Zealand (PRIA and PRINZ) annually give awards to campaigns conducted by public, corporate and consultancy practitioners. The criteria for these awards, in both countries, recognise the common elements necessary in planning a successful campaign. These criteria are broadly employed in the case study below.

AN APPROACH TO CAMPAIGN PLANNING

The following is a hypothetical example of the steps involved in designing, planning and implementing a public relations campaign. It should be noted that this particular campaign would fall into the marketing communications area within the arts industry.

Renewing a reputation

Jenny Ross has been employed by the local council as the Public Relations Manager for the Council Performing Arts Centre (CPAC). Also new to CPAC is the Artistic Director, Stefan Orlowski. Stefan has dropped into Jenny's office to talk about the first CPAC production for the new performing year.

'Look Jenny, the previous season was a dismal failure. The plays were unpopular and poorly produced. CPAC's reputation is at rock bottom,' Stefan said.

Jenny nodded in agreement. 'The subscriber base of 2500 is holding, but we're going to need a real hit to hang on to them this season, Stefan.'

'I know and I've got a real winner. You know at my previous theatre in New York, we staged *Freedom*.'

'I remember reading about it,' said Jenny. 'The critics were in raptures and the press labelled it as the most controversial play of the decade.'

'It is,' replied Stefan. 'I took it on a tour of Europe late last year and we had the same success. I've managed to secure the rights. So the Australian premiere will be here at CPAC—it's our opportunity to restore CPAC's reputation, Jenny. Can you draft a comprehensive public relations campaign to fill the house for our opening night?'

Constructing a plan for a campaign

Jenny will need to identify the challenges and problems CPAC faces in this situation. To assist her in developing the campaign, Jenny is using a plan that covers the major elements of public relations strategic campaign planning. While different terms may be used or interchanged with the ones here, the following are the key steps in public relations campaign planning:

1 Problem statements

2 Research

3 Target publics

4 Goals and objectives

5 Strategy and tactics

6 Evaluation.

The CPAC case study lays out an example of the steps a practitioner may go through in planning a campaign. Included in this plan are rationales for each step undertaken by the practitioner. The other case studies in this book provide further examples of campaign planning and will enlarge the understanding of this most important public relations activity.

1 PROBLEM STATEMENTS

The problem (or opportunity) statements identify a target public, and state both the problem and the reason for the problem. Jenny must state *communication* problems/opportunities that can be solved using public relations tactics, for example:

- Patrons view CPAC as likely to produce disappointing plays because they have either attended or heard about one or more of the past year's poor productions.

- Few patrons plan to attend the new production because they believe that it is likely to be a disappointment.

Problems/opportunities must be cast in terms of either the *thoughts* or the *actions* of *target publics*. Defining the problem as a production design fault, for example, would not be relevant to a public relations practitioner (unless they were involved in cross-functional management problem-solving). This would be a more appropriate problem for an engineering manager.

The guiding principle is that Jenny cannot write a problem/opportunity statement without knowing who the target publics are, and what they think or feel, or what they may do. It is also useful to prioritise the problems.

2 RESEARCH

Jenny must now contemplate the research she needs to undertake to plan the campaign. She would most likely divide her pre-campaign research into 'secondary' and 'primary'.

In this instance, Jenny has started with desk (or secondary) research. She will undertake an analysis of organisational materials, library research, research of online databases, the internet and so forth. This research may provide her with information on all aspects of the CPAC campaign, plus any relevant economic, social or regulatory issues, and current information regarding target publics.

Jenny has also broadly examined existing sources relating to contemporary theatre, the previous reviews of *Freedom* and media reaction to its debut. Existing CPAC files allow her to analyse subscriber demographics, psychographics and attitudes.

Now Jenny wants to gather primary data. She interviews Stephen to get more information on his experience of staging *Freedom* overseas. She also considers undertaking some qualitative research using focus groups to:

1   Define target publics

2   Unearth information to help develop a range of questions for subsequent formal quantitative questionnaire construction

3   Test effectiveness of planned key messages.

Jenny also decides to undertake primary quantitative research that would involve a method of random sampling (e.g. random telephone sampling) to help establish a baseline of the subscribers' attitudes/behaviours regarding the subject of her plan.

This baseline allows Jenny to undertake evaluative research. At evaluation points during—and particularly after—the campaign, the baseline can be measured against changes in target publics' opinions or behaviours. It will help her measure the success or otherwise of her campaign.

3 TARGET PUBLICS

The target publics are those groups or individuals with whom Jenny must communicate to overcome the problems faced by CPAC:

- Existing subscribers

- Potential subscribers

- Theatre reviewers

- Local media.

Jenny's key target public are the existing subscribers. Her secondary research, from existing files, has told her that the subscribers are males and females, predominantly aged eighteen to thirty, who reside in the inner-city area. Most are university students or workers in their first jobs, one to three years out of university.

Jenny's primary research focus groups, based on the above subscriber profile, revealed the following:

- Subscribers respond to the 'latest thing'—such as restaurants, cafés and bars that have a reputation for being fashionable—then abandon them when the next latest thing comes along. They are beginning to believe that, following the recent run of disappointing plays, CPAC 'has had its day'.

- CPAC's subscribers are social liberals, sympathetic to Aboriginal, gay and environmental issues. They see themselves as inner-city sophisticates, tuned in to international trends in music, art and fashion.

4 GOALS AND OBJECTIVES

Goals are generalised ends that can provide a framework for decision-making. Objectives are derived from goals, but they are specific and measurable. A goal is often the flip side of a problem or opportunity, because the purpose of most goals is to solve a problem or take advantage of an opportunity.

A goal is often relatively abstract and may be difficult to quantify—for example, 'We want to improve our reputation.' An objective, on the other hand, is something that can be documented—it is observable. For example a broadly stated objective could be: 'We need to get 20 per cent more people into our theatre.'

A set of goals is achieved only by achieving a subset of interrelated objectives. An objective is a strategic step along the way towards achieving a desired goal.

Most often, public relations objectives describe ways to implement various components of the overall campaign. For example a goal might be to increase public awareness, and a related set of objectives might be to prepare and distribute media releases, hold a media conference and contact community opinion leaders.

Good objectives should:

- Solve the problems or exploit the opportunities defined

- Be consistent with the broader goals and objectives of the organisation

- Be achievable with chosen public relations tactical devices

- Be specific and measurable

- Be governed by a deadline

- Specify the means by which they will be measured.

So, given the two problems facing CPAC, Jenny's objectives will be something like the following:

1   To convince 75 per cent of the 2500 subscribers that the new play is distinct from—and better than—the past year's disappointing productions, and to have done so a week before *Freedom* opens; the achievement of this objective will be measured by a random sample telephone survey undertaken seven days before the play opens.

2   To convince 15 per cent of the subscribers to attend opening night and a further 50 per cent to attend the balance of performances over the scheduled two-week run of the play (the achievement dates will obviously line up with the performance dates of the play); the achievement of this objective will be measured by monitoring ticket sales.

Note how the objectives flow out of the problems on a one-for-one basis and are target-public-focused. Also note that Jenny must make a reasoned guess at what percentage of the target public she will, in practical terms, be able to convince.

5 STRATEGY AND TACTICS

Given (1) the problems identified at CPAC, (2) the objectives Jenny is pursuing based on these problems, and (3) the facts she has uncovered about her key target public, she must now develop an argument to win that target public over. A persuasive strategy is the means by which she will convince the subscribers to think or do what the campaign requires.

Jenny's strategy is to change the existing attitudes of the CPAC subscribers. She must demonstrate to patrons that attending the play is in their self-interest because it is a 'must' for those who want to be up-to-date with the latest international theatre trends. She must also demonstrate that it is in their interest to support CPAC, so she will appeal to their need to be seen to belong to the social group with whom they identify (young sophisticates).

To determine the best tactics to use, Jenny should ask the following questions:

1   Is the medium selected the best available to deliver the key messages to my target public, or would an alternative be more effective?

2   What back-up tactical devices would be effective to repeat and/or reinforce my key messages?

In this particular scenario, a direct mail letter is just one of many possible tactics for delivering messages. The question is: Is this the most effective tactical device at Jenny's disposal?

Let us suppose that, in the course of the focus group research, Jenny recalls that this target public does not want to read lots of information and would prefer communications to have an air of sophistication. She might therefore decide to send stylised postcards, rather than letters.

She might also feel that a spread of tactics would be better than relying on the postcard alone. So as back-up tactics she could decide to use news releases and adverts targeting the media that are popular with the target public. This means, for example, quality newspapers, arts programs on radio and television, and perhaps news and current affairs magazines.

6 EVALUATION

Although Jenny will have already provided deadlines and identified means of measurement for objectives, this segment allows Jenny to expand on the rationale for the selected measurement.

She may need to consider the relative merits of quantitative as opposed to qualitative surveying. Remember, in this scenario one of the objectives called for random sample telephone surveying (quantitative) for evaluation. While sufficient time needs to be allowed to construct quantitative surveys, they have the advantage of providing—via a relatively small sample—an accurate indication (within the set margin for error) of the views of a large population.

As discussed earlier, another benefit of this approach is the ability to compare results against the baseline of target public attitudes obtained at the research stage. Jenny will be able to see what level of impact her campaign had on the total population of subscribers. Note that, over the course of a lengthy campaign, a number of quantitative 'tracking surveys' may be used to enable the public relations practitioner to alter the frequency or distribution of tactics.

Then again, sometimes qualitative surveying may be more appropriate where an indicative snapshot of attitudes is required (e.g. intercept surveying) or where in-depth information on the motivations of behaviour is required (e.g. focus groups).

Jenny will also remember that the second objective called for actual ticket sales to be used for evaluation. Care needs to be taken with this type of measure if it is used in isolation. While it does provide a true bottom line of success or failure, unless it is used in conjunction with survey methods it will not provide data as to *why* the result is what it is.

Note that many of the methods described above are further explained in Chapter 5: Campaign Evaluation. Accordingly it may be worthwhile to re-read this case study when you have familiarised yourself with the types of research that can be employed in pre-campaign research and campaign evaluation.

ETHICAL IMPLICATIONS OF CAMPAIGNS

Grunig wrote in 1992 that, 'Although scholars of public relations agree that ethics should be a priority when teaching and practising, the literature of our field (as evidenced, largely, in the body of knowledge) reflects little familiarity with ethical theory' (p. 80). In subsequent years, many academics and practitioners have sought to emphasise, through texts and scholarly publishing, the ethical dilemmas that public relations practitioners often face. How can they reach a morally right course of action? One suggestion for ethical public relations decision-making is by 'implementing and maintaining inter-organisational communication systems which question, discuss and validate these and other claims' (Pearson 1988, cited in Grunig 1992, p. 81).

Many moral values originate from personal and religious beliefs, and provide some basis for determining appropriate behaviours towards others in professional practice. Harrison notes that, 'Every profession has a moral purpose. Medicine has health. Law has justice. Public relations has harmony—social harmony. Public relations professionals keep information flowing among their employers and clients and stakeholders' (Harrison 2006, p. 187).

Public relations practitioners will also be bound by the ethics of their organisation. An organisation may express its ethical personality through a code of conduct, or state it in its mission and values statement.

Professional associations—such as the PRIA and PRINZ—emphasise, through their codes of ethics, the importance of guiding their members' behaviours. However, not all public relations practitioners are members of professional associations or work for organisations that have a code of conduct.

A public relations campaign involves practitioners making decisions that affect key publics for the organisation's or client's betterment. While the practitioner may engage in a campaign that is technically competent, it could also be the case that such a campaign is ethically inappropriate. For public relations to be considered a profession, its individual practitioners must display at all times both technical competence and ethically justifiable behaviour.

How can the public relations practitioner approach the challenge of acting ethically? The law requires every citizen to act in accordance with it, in society generally, in the workplace and in professional relationships. The law is therefore not necessarily a strong basis for acting ethically.

Professional codes of ethics and organisational codes of conducts require public relations practitioners to examine further ethical principles, rules, models and standards that can help guide competent practice. These concepts will assist the practitioner in making ethical judgments and in their moral reasoning.

REFERENCES

Grunig J. E., 1992, 'Toward a Philosophy of Public Relations' in Toth E. L. & Heath R. L. (eds), 1992, *Rhetorical and Critical and Approaches to Public Relations*, LEA, Hillsdale, NJ, pp. 74–88

Harrison K., 2006, *Strategic Public Relations—A Practical Guide to Success*, 4th edn, Century Consulting, Perth, WA

2 Overview of Twentieth-century Campaigns

Mark Sheehan

AIMS OF THIS CHAPTER

- To understand the early foundations of public relations in Australia and New Zealand

- To examine the development of public relations through a campaign perspective

INTRODUCTION

Designing and implementing campaigns fills the lives of public relations professionals around the world; however the work that they do varies widely. It would be impossible to cover in one chapter the public relations campaigns of the twentieth century. Rather, this chapter will highlight some of the major events in Australia and New Zealand, and the role that public relations campaigns played in helping organisations achieve their goals—whether these goals be political, social or commercial.

Public relations campaigns have changed throughout history, reflecting the emphasis of the time and the dominance of particular skills in the practitioner base. In the opening decades of the twentieth century, the communication tools available to public relations practitioners were exploited to influence or persuade the chosen target publics in attempting to attain an organisation's goals. Over the years, these tools became more sophisticated, assuring the growth of public relations as a profession and as a function of many aspects of Australian and New Zealand life.

We can assume that the development of mass media—from newspapers in the nineteenth century, to radio in the early twentieth century and then to television in the 1950s—increased the opportunity for public relations campaigns. However, the case studies in this chapter illustrate that other methods of communication existed prior to the expansion of the mass media market and that these were utilised by early practitioners.

Campaigns can be short or long. The themes may exist for decades, or they may be supplemented during the campaign's lifetime, or take a deviation as new issues arise that impact on the campaign's original purpose. Some campaigns are conducted to fit a specified time period. In 1938, for example, Australia celebrated the 150th anniversary of white settlement. As a lead-up to the sesquicentenary, the nation also celebrated the coronation of King George VI. Both of these campaigns had a certain date that dictated their culmination. In these instances, the goal setting is time related.

Other campaigns have an ongoing brief. The 1987 National Advisory Committee on AIDS's (NACAIDS) 'Grim Reaper' campaign, launched to prevent a national epidemic, met a short-term goal of making the community aware that AIDS was 'no longer someone else's problem'. However it also served as a 'flying start' to the campaign's next step, the NACAIDS National Education Programme (Patterson 1987).

In some instances campaigns may continue for years. The Petroleum Information Bureau (Australia) was established in 1951 with the goal of 'gaining public approval and public understanding' of how Australia stood to benefit from oil industry operations (Flower 2007). With this criterion the bureau set about designing and implementing several campaigns over its twenty-five-year history; however each campaign returned to this central theme.

HISTORICAL PERSPECTIVES

Many authors writing on the history of public relations in Australia tend to suggest that public relations existed only in the form of publicity until the 1940s (Johnson & Zawawi 2004; Tymson & Sherman 1987; Cunningham & Turner 2006; Potts 1976). For example in Australia between the wars, according to Potts:

> there were press agents, publicity officers, publicity managers ... [their] attempt to influence public thinking through the media or the press or early radio was regarded more often as an act to obtain publicity rather than a planned move to condition the thought processes of readers and listeners (Potts 1976, p. 355).

Similarly, in New Zealand, the pre-war practitioner Geoff Bentley suggested that the earliest form of public relations was press agency work. He also noted the role of the journalist in residence (Peart 1994, p. 4).

Many of these authors suggest that the arrival of the US General Douglas MacArthur in 1942, with his public relations entourage of thirty-five, changed the existing perception of public relations (as publicity) to be one 'about messages and how these were conveyed' (Zawawi 2004, p. 29). MacArthur may have been the first to use the term 'public relations', but just as the public relations function today exists under a variety of titles and roles, and in many organisational functions, this was also the case prior to MacArthur's arrival. Indeed, the case studies presented in this chapter demonstrate that the intentions of public relations professionals may well have been the mobilisation of public opinion in favour of their organisation, policy, product or service, clearly illustrating a much more developed approach to public relations than was previously considered.

Newsom et al. (2007, p. 25) state that, 'Various functions and uses of public relations have certainly existed throughout civilised history.' Sometimes campaigns were waged by a government trying to persuade voters, as in the First World War conscription referenda; sometimes causes were espoused for reasons above politics and commerce, as with the building of the Shrine of Remembrance in Melbourne; and sometimes the intent was commercial, as in the Comalco example at Lake Manapouri. Whatever the case in question, note that attempts to alter public opinion often rely on a number of concerted activities that can be identified as a public relations campaign.

CAMPAIGNS 1899–1939
Building a nation

Raising awareness of significant events was often the work of public relations campaigns during the forty-year period beginning in 1899. Such work was still labelled as 'publicity', and a primary function of public relations campaigns was centred around gaining publicity. Recognition of this major function was signalled by the founding of the Sydney Publicity Club in 1929 (Reekie). However publicity directors, managers or officers working in a variety of organisations were involved in seeking more than publicity, as there were many campaigns in these years that also sought to change public opinion on a number of issues.

A number of major campaigns focused on building the young nation of Australia. The early campaigns of Australian public relations pioneer Asher Joel, for example, included the 1938 celebrations for the 150th anniversary of the first white settlement, on the shores of Sydney Cove (Joel 1973).

The 1938 sesquicentenary celebration mainly focused on New South Wales (NSW). Apart from the extensive number of events held in the state, the NSW Government commissioned the forty-six-minute film *A Nation is Built*. This 'patriotic documentary uses historical footage, fictionalised scenes and propaganda to chronicle Australia's development and progress as a nation' (Smythe 1998). The film's release and associated activities were promoted and recorded by the use of publicity, but also exhibit a more focused message approach and a deliberate attempt to plan and manage the celebration on behalf of a coordinating body. Coming out of the depths of the Great Depression, the sesquicentenary celebration can be viewed as a morale booster for the young Commonwealth.

In pre–World War II New Zealand, an appreciation of the role of PR was acknowledged when in 1939 the Scotsman John Grierson accepted an invitation from the New Zealand Public Relations Council to assist the Ministry of Lands in promoting tourism. As a documentary film maker, Grierson's work with Sir Stephen Tallents in the UK was seen as 'highly significant in elaborating principles and practice of public relations' (L'Etang 2006, p. 148).

CONSCRIPTION REFERENDA OF THE FIRST WORLD WAR

In the years prior to 1938, the most significant event to affect Australia was the First World War, often referred to as the 'Great War'. This conflict created many challenges for communicators. The Creel Committee in the USA, founded by President Wilson to mobilise public opinion in support of the war, was seen by Bernays as the first time information was used as a weapon of war (Seitel 2007, p. 24). This was also to be the case in Australia.

In Australia, national leaders used public relations tools to persuade the public of the need to win the war. This was never more evident than in the two referenda conducted in 1916 and 1917 to change Australia's volunteer army to a conscripted fighting force.

In the early stages of the war, enthusiasm for the 'great adventure' drove recruitment numbers and the noble failure that was Gallipoli also increased the number of volunteers in 1915. However by 1916 the stalemate and muddy misery of the Western Front saw recruitment numbers dwindle. In October of that year, Prime Minister Billy Hughes sought a mandate from voters to conscript men aged between eighteen and forty-five for service.

The campaign to persuade voters and sway public opinion differed from the methods used in recruitment drives. Government-supported grassroots groups were established in communities. These groups, such as the United Services League, pushed for conscription as Australia's duty to the Empire. Opinion leaders were used to persuade the voters of the value of offering up their sons or husbands in the most noble of fights. Among the many to throw their weight behind the cause were the Premier of New South Wales, a former Prime Minister, the Anglican Primate of Australia and the Roman Catholic Archbishop of Sydney (Carlyon 2006, p. 268). Dame Nellie Melba sang at events organised to publicise the 'Yes' vote, and the 'mainstream press, city and country' (Carlyon 2006, p. 258) fell in behind Prime Minister Hughes' call for conscription powers for the federal government.

Despite the extensive efforts of the Prime Minister and his agents, the 1916 referendum failed. In a second attempt in 1917, Hughes broadened the use of persuasive tactics and seconded Claude McKay, a former journalist and writer, to work on the promotion of the campaign. McKay had been the successful Publicity Director for War Loans. He set up recruiting committees, held public meetings and produced a handbook for the conduct of these committees and meetings. The handbook, *The Speaker's Companion*, contained template speeches and featured one section called 'Sister Susie's Creed'. This creed exhorted women to die an old maid rather than 'flirt with men who did not enlist' (Carlyon 2006, p. 525). Again Dame Nellie Melba sang at events, both to publicise the 'Yes' vote and to influence women (Robson 1970, p. 107)—Hughes had identified women as highly persuasive, with their ability to urge doubtful enlisters and 'shame the shirker'.

Once again, however, the referendum failed, and by a larger majority than the first. Despite the support of the press and most of the nation's institutions, Hughes had been unable to persuade the Australian people to support his vision—proof of the fact that, despite the best endeavours, public opinion may not always be persuaded of the virtues or otherwise of a public relations campaign.

THE SHRINE OF REMEMBRANCE

After the war the Australian public sought to remember the fallen. In country towns, halls and hospitals were built and statues of diggers were erected in their memory. In Melbourne, however, there was a stalemate as to what was to be done to record Victoria's thanks to those who served and died in the war.

In 1924, a proposal to construct a Shrine of Remembrance had been agreed upon and a competition had chosen a winning design. However there were detractors who took advantage of bureaucratic delays to question such a development and, as time advanced, alternative proposals came forward. By 1926 the state government, the Returned Soldiers League (RSL) and the Melbourne City Council (MCC) favoured a city square. The city's newspaper, *The Herald*, declared that the time had passed for shrines and that the money could be better spent (Russell 1980).

The returned servicemen's organisation Legacy—highly respected and influential in the debate—took a stand, arguing for a shrine rather than a city square. Their opinion was crucial, but it still had to gain support from all quarters. Legacy gave its resolution 'the widest publicity in Press and Radio and in personal discussion with the War Memorial Committee and Members of Parliament' (Russell 1980, p. 39). While *The Herald* stormed against the resolution of the Legacy committee, other press outlets and radio stations gave support. Legacy began its campaign to persuade the power brokers to build a Shrine of Remembrance as originally planned. However the key parties, the MCC and the Victorian Parliament, had already made provision for a city square.

Over the next year Legacy lobbied and campaigned for a shrine. They secured leading opinion makers such as the former wartime general Sir John Monash who, in an Anzac Day speech before the Duke of York and state dignitaries, lent his considerable prestige to the plan.

Legacy's campaign paid off as the state government and the MCC eventually lent their support to a shrine. The public, who had followed the debate closely, finally had an opportunity to show their own opinions. On the day the campaign fundraising office opened, the queue stretched into the distance. It remained that way for more than four weeks. Even *The Herald* came to the party, offering the services of a leading journalist as the publicity officer for the campaign (Russell 1980, p. 47).

The campaign to build the shrine, now a landmark in Melbourne, was a powerful grassroots effort that took on the entrenched powerbrokers of Melbourne. Planned and coordinated public relations activities persuaded the general populous of the merit of the argument.

IMMIGRATION

Scott M. Cutlip writes in *Public Relations History* that public relations commenced in the USA:

> in the 17th century with the efforts of land promoters and colonists to lure settlers from Europe—mainly England—to this primitive land along the Atlantic coast. They used publicity, tracts, sermons and letters to disseminate rosy, glowing accounts of life and opportunity in the new land (Cutlip 1995, p. ix).

It is no coincidence that one of Australia's earliest forays into public relations campaigns was to attract new settlers to a strange and foreign land.

The fight to build the Australian population was a constant national goal of the twentieth century for commercial, political and social reasons. In the late 1940s, the desperate message of Immigration Minister Arthur Calwell was 'Populate or Perish'. While advertising was a feature of the many immigration programs, public relations also played an important part.

As one would expect of a new nation such as Australia, in the early 1900s traditional public relations tools of 'publicity, tracts, sermons and letters' were supplemented with the latest. In particular, newsreels were a common feature of Australian information campaigns from the early twentieth century onwards. While Zawawi (2004, p. 29) notes that during the Second World War newsreels were an important tool for 'building morale and garnering support', newsreels were used to achieve these aims well before then.

Film was increasingly used as a promotional tool. Smythe (1998) states: 'probably the first government film-making in the world occurred in Australia in 1899 when a Queensland government filmed thirty subjects including street scenes in Sydney and Brisbane with the aim of attracting immigrants'. After Federation, the Commonwealth took over responsibility for immigration from the states, and in 1911 the Australia House Publicity Officer, H.C. Smart, urged the Commonwealth to produce films. Over the coming decades the value of using film was increasingly recognised 'as a means of illustrating to intending migrants the features, industries and potentialities of Australia', and by 1927 it was reported that the films were achieving 'valuable publicity for Australia in Great Britain and the Commonwealth' (Smythe 1998).

With all public relations campaigns, historic or contemporary, it is often not the exposure of the message but its distribution to the target publics that delivers the desired outcome. The films produced for the Commonwealth were not only shown in cinemas, they were also used as tourism promotion on board ships, to be viewed by the wealthy travelling classes of the 1930s, and were screened at Australia House in London. In 1932 the official Commonwealth cinematographer, Bert Ive, recorded that, 'In the last two years 269,000 people in Britain' had attended films on Australia and its products, and that this film propaganda had extended around the world and had been 'of immense value in conducting Australian publicity abroad'. He went on to record the intention of producing film in 16 mm format 'to broaden the penetration of this film propaganda' (Smythe 1998).

The largest campaign to attract migrants was after the Second World War. The government, having learnt the value of public relations during the war, embarked on a publicity campaign in Britain and in other centres of potential immigration on the

European continent (Kiernan 1978). However, public opinion in Australia was against the immigration of 'aliens' (Europeans), so a major campaign was launched to try and change this opinion as well. Hirst (2007, p. 44) writes that Calwell 'came home and organised the first large-scale government advertising and public relations campaign to ensure that Australians accepted what he had done'.

CAMPAIGNS 1940–89
From publicity to strategy

The public relations development brought about by the Second World War has been covered in brief here, and in greater detail by others. It is recognised that it was General Douglas MacArthur who formally introduced the term 'public relations'. In both Australia and New Zealand, the military established public relations sections with soldiers, sailors and air personnel taking on the role of public relations officers. Peart (1994, p. 3) notes that both the New Zealand Army and the Royal New Zealand Air Force were major users of the press agentry model of public relations. After the war, these men and women formed the nucleus of the public relations profession and it is their experience that drove the profession forward.

It is interesting to note that in 1948 the New Zealand Post Office established a public relations section which, among the expected functions, included a 'damage control' role to deal with problems as they arose—early shadows of crisis management.

While achieving publicity was seen as a major role for these early practitioners, once again Zawawi stresses it was recognised that 'any organisation—especially the Army—could not afford to ignore public opinion', and that there was a need to 'work assiduously to ensure that public opinion remained on their side' (2004, p. 29).

Various public relations campaigns were conducted during the Second World War and with these came an increasing knowledge of the practice of public relations and its role in assisting organisations.

While the public relations role on the domestic front was developing, the Australian News and Information Bureau (NIB) was established in New York 'to publicise the country's contribution to the allied cause' (Northey 1993). In 1943 a London NIB was opened, with the aim of being 'an organised centre of reference on Australian problems, and a distributing house for Australian official statements, photographs, and films with the intention of making Australia and Australians better known to people overseas' (Northey 1993, pp. 594–5).

While it is considered that MacArthur's arrival 'gave birth' to public relations in Australia, it was a departure in Victoria in the 1950s that would influence the role of public relations for the next forty years. The closure of *The Argus* newspaper in January 1957 saw 'journalists emerge[d] as PR and PA [public affairs] managers in numerous corporations, associations and government agencies' (Usher 2007, p. 144).

SNOWY MOUNTAINS HYDRO-ELECTRIC SCHEME

In the postwar period, Australia sought to rebuild itself as a modern nation. The immigration campaigns, mentioned previously, were part of this rebuilding. Driving the need for immigrants were some of the massive postwar undertakings by the government, the biggest of which was the Snowy Mountains Hydro-Electric Scheme (HES). Two-thirds of the HES's 100,000 workers were immigrants, and the HES had successive campaigns of a political and social nature dealing with a variety of target publics. Potts notes: 'The Snowy was a tourist magnet, and its PR staff, as well as working in what could be termed routine PR, also had to develop techniques for ... visitors' (1976, p. 200).

Over fifteen newsreel documentaries were produced over the life of the HES, from 1948 to 1974. The first, *Where Giants Meet*, was made for the manufacturer of the International Bulldozer but also contained messages for domestic recruitment promotion, including a genuine man from the Snowy who is going to 'quit the saddle and lend a hand'. Clearly the film was addressing potential scepticism about the Snowy and countering criticism on the loss of livelihood of bush workers and high country graziers (Australian Screen website).

But the HES had to counter other critics. A change of government in 1949 meant that the HES could be easily terminated early in its development. The incoming Prime Minister Robert Menzies thought the HES was too closely associated with the former Prime Minister, Ben Chifley, and his Labor government, and so politically there was little to be gained in maintaining the scheme. Aubrey Hosking, an engineer on the HES, recalled the scheme's Commissioner, William Hudson, deciding in 1953 'to get the people of Australia on his side. And that's when he set up a huge, highly efficient public relations organisation with tours of the Scheme' (McHugh 1989, p. 118). In the first year of Hudson's campaign, more than 80,000 people visited the Snowy. Menzies soon realised he could turn the HES to his own political advantage and used every major milestone in the construction as a high-profile event for his own purposes.

Hudson used images of the bushfires and blizzards, the exotic mix of nationalities and of course the towering engineering tasks associated with the HES to keep it at the forefront of Australians' minds. The constant reference to this great 'achievement' meant that Australians' opinion of the scheme remained positive about the value to the nation of the exploit. McHugh notes that: 'In the days when public relations was in its infancy ... the Snowy attracted an extraordinary response from ordinary Australians' (1989, p. 198).

BANK NATIONALISATION

As Prime Minister Chifley was finalising the legislation that would enable the Commonwealth to commence the HES, he was also involved in a legislative goal that would have the ability to change the face of Australian finance forever. His ambition to nationalise the private banks would give Menzies the opportunity not only to recreate himself, but also to sell a vastly different brand of political philosophy to the Australian people.

At the time there was little sympathy for banks among Australians. It was only fifteen years since the Great Depression, when the collapse of the banks had lead to extreme hardship and financial misfortune for many. To create a positive opinion climate for the banking industry was a major public relations undertaking, but for the banks to include in their strategy the defeat of a popular government and leader was a very bold initiative.

The political scene in Australia had changed dramatically in the postwar period. Robert Menzies had established a new conservative party in 1944, the Liberal Party. Work started to 'repackage Menzies as its [the Liberal Party's] leader and to persuade the electorate that he was an acceptable alternative to Chifley as Prime Minister' (Golding 2004, p. 179). Also, despite losing the 1946 election, Menzies had been supported by the private banks' campaign to fight Chifley's Bank Nationalisation Scheme from 1947 to 1949.

The campaign to defeat the nationalisation of private banking and ultimately the Labor government commenced after the 1946 election.

The private banks had deep pockets for the campaign. Historian Ross McMullin notes that 'funds for this campaign were unlimited'. Others observed that it was 'the longest and most lavishly funded political campaign ever seen in Australia ... a campaign estimated to cost several hundred thousand pounds' (Goot 2002, pp. 144–6). Apart from traditional advertising, radio serials were broadcast from February 1948 to December 1949. One featured the fictional John Henry Austral, a 'neighbourly but knowledgable' political observer, 'able to see through sham and pretence'. The serials, which had no acknowledged provenance, emphasised the threat of Labor's policies (Goot 2002). While the banks funded the mass media campaigns, their employees founded the Bank Employees Protest Committee (BEPC), a spontaneous grassroots effort to stop nationalisation. They were of course financially backed by the banking corporations.

The success of John Henry Austral led to more dramatised serials in print and broadcast media. Once again many had no attribution to the banks. The *Freeland Family* (the name states the message!) was a newspaper serial. On radio there was *Star Pupil, Musical Families, Musical Comedy Stage, The Mantle of Greatness*—based on the achievements of free enterprise—and in Victoria *The Watchman*, a weekly news commentary program (May 1968). All delivered carefully crafted messages without identifying a specific party, but the bias was unmistakeable.

'By 1947 the banks had committed to a two-year publicity campaign' leading up to the 1949 election (May 1968, p. 18). In the final stages of the election campaign, the banks spared nothing in their attempt to defeat Chifley and his government:

> The bank had 'an army of over four hundred men to command in the last few weeks of the campaign ... and outside the full time forces was a reserve of some thousands of men and women, employees and wives of employees (May 1968, p. 123).

One bank employee active in the campaign was Bob White who, forty years later in the 1980s, was Managing Director of Westpac. In his biography White states that the BEPC 'distributed to us [bank employees] brown-covered handbooks ... [which] were invaluable because they contained possible questions which we were likely to encounter when canvassing voters or leading discussions' (White 1995, p. 24). White supports May's earlier comments when he observes that 'the way in which bank officers and their relatives worked on their campaign indicated their value as publicity agents' (White 1995, p. 25).

Some of the communication methods engaged in by bank staff included visits to 60,000 householders (34,000 in the six weeks prior to the election) in Victoria alone. The banks also distributed literature to over 300,000 homes in that state. The brochures and leaflets, cartoon pamphlets (notably one called *What Happened to Sam?*—a children's issue) had a print run of half a million. Reprints of newspaper articles, booklets of information and circulars were prepared and distributed.

May also lists the activities of New South Wales-based BEPC members in the final month of the campaign 'speaking at street meetings; door-to-door canvassing; distribution of pamphlets, How to Vote Cards etc; organising teams to ask awkward questions at Labor meetings; acting as campaign managers for Liberal/C.P. [Country Party—now National Party] candidates; writing newspaper articles and Letters to the Editor; giving talks in factories' (1968, p. 123).

Labor members of parliament were not immune from the distribution of banking information. Fred Daly termed the banks' mail campaigns a 'Frightening propaganda deluge' (McMullin 2001, p. 264). The banks, however, reasoned that 'a moderate sized press advertisement seen once a fortnight, a radio commercial heard weekly, a film or pamphlet seen occasionally are not of themselves sufficient to create an impression of excessive publicity on the part of the banks' (May 1968, p. 102).

This was, at the time and for many years to come, the most expensive and largest public relations campaign waged in Australia. May notes that advertising accounted for exactly half of the expenditure, so we can assume that public relations activities accounted for a reasonable amount of the remainder. After such a campaign there could be few Australians who could claim that they had not been exposed to the powers of persuasion in a modern world. Every existing communication tool, one-way and two-way, had been exploited and exploited successfully.

The outcome of the election was a foregone conclusion. White states with pride that, 'Ultimately we achieved our objective with the fall of the Chifley Government in December 1949 and the reaffirmation of the right of private trading banks to exist' (White 1995, p. 29).

THE LONG CAMPAIGN

It is a hallmark of many campaigns of the time that the process was long and arduous. The long-term view was considered appropriate and change was viewed with suspicion. Campaigns became strategic in their outcomes and it was recognised that organisations may work for years to achieve their ends.

There are examples where whole industries have sponsored open-ended campaigns to persuade the public of the merits of their work. In fact in some instances, industries funded whole organisations to undertake their public relations functions and run continuous campaigns.

The Petroleum Information Bureau (PIB) was established by Australia's oil-refining giants, including Shell and Mobil, in 1951. Its unofficial charter was to develop 'a range of activities aimed at gaining public approval—or at least public understanding—of how Australia stood to benefit from oil industry operations' (Flower 2007, p. 181). Initially there were specific communication campaigns undertaken by the PIB, for instance the building of positive public opinion about the construction of massive oil refineries in three states in outer suburban metropolitan areas, and the announcement of the resurgence of oil exploration in Australia.

Flower notes that the staff of the PIB in Victoria, New South Wales, Queensland and Western Australia 'used every opportunity to give talks about oil and how the industry works, often supplemented by dramatic photographic enlargements or screenings of 16 mm films' (2007, p. 181).

From 1951 to its demise in the mid-1970s, the PIB took on many public relations campaigns on behalf of the oil industry. Chiefly the aim of the initiative was to counteract much of the blame directed at oil producers for the state of the environment. The PIB established a separate body, the Petroleum Industry Environmental Conservation Executive (PIECE), which undertook various public education campaigns. These included the publication of the booklet *Respect for our Environment*, which was widely distributed after being initially published in the *Reader's Digest*. It focused on the good work the oil industry was doing in caring for the environment (Flower 2007).

The growth in campaign research

From the 1950s onwards, it becomes increasingly obvious that research began to play a more significant role in campaigns.

In 1961 the private banks:

> felt that the favourable climate of public opinion towards them [generated by the Labor Party's 1949 proposed banking legislation] was giving way to indifference, if not downright antagonism ... [brought about by among other things] public misconceptions about ... profit ratios, lending practices; alleged political intrigues and accusations of monopoly practices (Walker 1967, p. 352).

They decided to establish a 'research directorate', much like the PIB, to 'counter criticism and channel information, literature, speakers' etc. By 1964 the campaign by the directorate recorded that 'attacks had become less frequent; criticism on profits ... had virtually ceased' (Walker 1967, p. 353). These campaigns by PIB and the banks indicate the use of research to gauge and monitor public opinion, and the use of public relations campaigns to influence that public opinion.

From the 1950s onwards, organisations turned more frequently to public relations solutions. Many campaigns were conducted with publics unaware of the campaigns' activities—indeed the very nature of a public relations campaign may mean the public is completely unaware of it (unlike an advertising campaign which relies on exposure and delivery in unsubtle ways).

LAKE MANAPOURI

Former New Zealand Comalco public relations executive Don Alexander has recounted one of the most seminal campaigns in New Zealand's public relations history (personal communication with author, 2007).

To provide extra power for a major new industry-aluminium smelter, it was necessary to raise the level of Lake Manapouri in the South Island. In 1970, over 70,000 people from a local population of quarter of a million signed a petition aimed at preventing the lake level from being changed. This populist movement caused a by-election loss for the ruling Government Party in 1971. Analysts agreed that conservationist votes changed the electoral tide, and this was further reinforced in 1972 when the Labour Party won the general election on a promise not to raise the level of the lake.

Comalco Limited was initially unprepared for the surge in support for leaving the lake alone. The company had negotiated an agreement, which became a New Zealand Act of Parliament, for substantial quantities of power to be supplied to the smelter. In return, Comalco would build a world-class plant, employ a large number of technically skilled workers in an area that suffered from seasonal closures (freezing works) and contribute to New Zealand's export earnings (at the time these were diminishing due to the loss of European agricultural markets). These economic arguments were known to the government and the company, but were never deemed of interest to the public.

When the conservation movement started to raise questions about the need to produce more power from Lake Manapouri, the company view was simply that it had been invited to establish the industry and had negotiated a legitimate agreement.

The 'protect the lake' movement grew from very small beginnings, with local farmers, hikers and bird lovers concerned that the lake raising might destroy valuable nesting sites of rare birds and reduce the scenic utility of the area. In early 1970, Comalco's public relations manager organised a visit to the lake for some Australian engineers and the party was very surprised when, on the 3 kilometre road from the airport to the boat ramp, there was a person holding a sign with a series of anti-company slogans every 100 metres.

It was this event that stimulated a response from the organisation, which in retrospect was the wrong choice. Because Comalco was an engineer-dominated firm, it was decided to mount an education campaign to 'sell' the economic benefits of the project. First, a survey of public opinion on the project was made—primarily to test the level of awareness of the project among the voting population of the project and aspects of its economic impact. This showed that there was close to 20 per cent support for it, 60 per cent had very low awareness, and the balance was very opposed.

The next step was to commission the country's eminent research group, the New Zealand Institute of Economic Research, to report on the value of the project to the national economy. This document was very positive about export earnings, impact on the local economy and a boost to the employment opportunities for graduates from a range of disciplines. After its national launch in the capital, Wellington, with the Prime Minister and key ministers attending, the public relations manager toured the country and personally spoke to every newspaper editor and to local radio news journalists about the report. This generated substantial and positive media coverage.

After nine months, the national awareness survey was replicated and the level of support had moved from 20 to over 45 per cent. Those opposed had increased by a further 5 per cent, with a consequent reduction in the numbers of those who were unaware.

It was at this stage that the various special conservation groups started to coalesce and create a larger and more powerful movement that then attracted the attention of media on a more regular basis. Some of the more radical fringe groups started spreading distorted information about the price the company was paying for the power it was to receive from the Manapouri power station for the Tiwai Point aluminium smelter, and the amount of tax being paid by the company; also negative stories about the environmental impact on the lake started to spread, including photographs of damaged overseas lakes. The government retreated further from answering many of the specious claims, and the company office in Wellington was inundated with calls from concerned citizens asking if the conservationists' claims were true. A national print advertising campaign was arranged to spell out the key economic facts, but by this stage the campaign had become emotional and the media were highly supportive of many of the conservationist leaders.

Following the 1972 election, the new Labour government announced that the lake level would not be raised and appointed six independent individuals who had been prominent in the campaign as Guardians of Lakes Manapouri, Monowai and Te Anau. Their task was to oversee the management of the lake levels.

The end result was that in 1986 the company was unsuccessful when it took the government to court to enforce the contract. The contract was then abrogated by the government and new legislation was passed. This legislation included a new contract that reduced the term of the agreement and also escalated the amount of tax the company had to pay. Another outcome was the creation of a national environmental group, ECO.

1960–89

From the early 1950s onwards, the number and nature of public relations campaigns spread, so that by the 1960s the function was losing some of its mystery.

In New Zealand, by the early 1960s, the government had a large centralised public relations function and handled numerous campaigns (personal communication between the author and Grant Common, former New Zealand public relations practitioner, 14 February 2007). Potts' 1976 publication, *Public Relations Practice in Australia*, includes more than forty case studies of campaigns in a variety of practice areas undertaken in the previous decade. All of these case studies give a good overview of the development of public relations practice. The linking of public relations campaigns to work with advertising revealed a growing awareness in business, government and not-for-profit organisations that advertising alone cannot deliver the message or influence and persuade.

Of particular interest is the chapter in Potts' book on attitude research by Ian McNair. While few of the case studies carry any evaluative research, the ones in this chapter emphasise the role and value of preliminary research in developing messages. One example is a campaign undertaken by Australian and New Zealand authors. The campaign's primary goal was author compensation 'from public circulation of books through lending libraries' (Potts 1976, p. 54). Statistical data were collected to prove to the target public—politicians and the reading public—that authors in both countries suffered economic hardship. The campaign commenced in Australia in 1969, and in New Zealand in 1971. Research proved the low wages of authors and 'much hard public relations work on the part of the authors themselves, eventually resulted in the granting of public lending rights in New Zealand and in Australia' (Potts 1976, p. 54). A secondary goal was also achieved in 1975 with the establishment and improvement of literary grants in both countries.

THE GRIM REAPER—AIDS AWARENESS CAMPAIGN, 1987

The most widely recognised and controversial Australian campaign of the 1980s was the public education for Acquired Immune Deficiency Syndrome (AIDS), known by its powerful advertising image of the Grim Reaper. In the 1980s, AIDS was one of the largest health issues facing the Western world. While many people in Australia were aware of the disease, research showed that most people in the heterosexual community were 'hopelessly misinformed' (Patterson 1987).

Before the launch of the advertising, the National Advisory Committee on AIDS (NACAIDS) sought a public relations campaign that would 'create the most receptive communications environment possible for the launch of a major advertising campaign' (Patterson 1987, p. 2).

The campaign was characterised by the results of extensive research conducted by the consultancy Lee Patterson and Associates and by NACAIDS. At no stage did the powerful television advertisement set out to educate the public about AIDS—this was made clear by the Chair of NACAIDS. In addition, the campaign was directed at a large target public—sexually active Australians. It was essential for such Australians to realise that transmission was as much a reality among heterosexuals as homosexuals.

The public relations campaign identified eight crucial strategies for success, including the cooperation of the media. While the advertising blitz was driving a heightened awareness, Patterson realised that without 'active editorial support the NACAIDS was doomed' (Patterson 1987, p. 6). Specialist briefings made senior media decision-makers realise the need for such a confronting campaign and ensured that the negativity of the images was kept to a minimum.

The decision to have NACAIDS Chair Ita Buttrose as the spokesperson was a signature of the campaign's use of opinion leadership. In the week following the launch, 'peer group and opinion leaders in capital cities and provincial cities' were briefed on the campaign's aims. In addition, specialist briefings were delivered to medical and health (consumer press) reporters, and over 2000 press kits were distributed to other media, including ethnic, community and parliamentary.

The NACAIDS campaign displayed a focused approach that ensured blanket media coverage while delivering tailored messages to specialist media outlets.

CONCLUSION

As stated at the outset, it would be impossible to review or even mention all the public relations campaigns undertaken in Australia and New Zealand in one volume, let alone one chapter. Rather, this chapter has attempted to examine the nature of public relations in Australia and New Zealand, and the nature of public relations as it is viewed within our society through an historical perspective.

This historical perspective has illustrated that the common perception that the arrival of US forces in 1942 brought about the arrival of public relations is more of an interpretative notion than a fact. One view is that the arrival of MacArthur was the arrival of US public relations, and that Australian public relations practitioners had already been carrying out public relations that were appropriate to the existing communications environment. However, as Australian society in the post-Second World War period increasingly moved away from the British colonial influence and absorbed much of the US culture, the practice of public relations in Australia made the same change.

As we have seen, it is difficult when dealing with something as pervasive as public relations to find a commencing date. If we extrapolate the interpretative notion that public relations is as fundamental as persuasion, it could be then argued (as some authors have) that the Epistles of St Paul were a successful public relations campaign; that the image-making methods of Phillip II of Macedonia—juxtaposing his statue with those of the gods—was a foray into image management; and that the 'Monuments and other art forms of the ancient world ... Pyramids, statues, temples, tombs, paintings announc[ing] the early divinity of rulers' (Newsom et al. 2007, p. 22) all mean that public relations is as old as civilisation itself.

No matter how we define public relations, it is clear that early practitioners used communication techniques and these are recognisable through history. In the context of this book we can claim that early practitioners were pioneers in using what were the latest methods of communication. More importantly, we can also claim that there was not a random use of these techniques, but that they were organised and methodically executed. No matter when these campaigns were implemented, it is clear in their execution that they sought to 'address an issue ... solve a problem ... or correct or improve a situation' (Newsom et al. 2007, p. 301).

PRACTITIONER PROFILE

Former journalist Peter Golding joined Eric White and Associates (EWA) in the 1950s and was later CEO before setting up his own public relations consultancy, Public Affairs Management. In these excerpts from his autobiography, Just a Chattel of the Sale, *he recounts his first experience as a public relations practitioner.*

'Back in the middle 50s when I first ventured on the scene, public relations in Australia was still in its comparative infancy. Most people, including many who practised it, thought its sole purpose was to achieve "free" publicity in the news media. Eric White was an exception. He saw PR as having a much broader role.'

In 1957 Golding had his first lesson in the 'science of influencing public opinion'. The Commonwealth Aircraft Corporation was facing closure unless it could secure a government contract, but Australian government policy favoured purchasing foreign aircraft. EWA's brief was to convince the public, media and politicians of all persuasions of the value of a home-grown defence industry.

EWA's campaign approach was built on detailed research, the strategic use of media and the involvement of key stakeholder groups and opinion leaders on defence matters. The campaign successfully altered the view of government. Golding was amazed at 'how relatively easily and quickly it had been possible, with determination and efficient organisation to marshal public opinion and force a change in government policy.'

REFERENCES

Australian Screen, australianscreen.com.au

Carlyon L., 2006, *The Great War*, Macmillan, Sydney

Cunningham S. & Turner G. (eds), 2006, *The Media and Communications in Australia*, 2nd edn, Allen & Unwin, Crows Nest

Cutlip S. M., 1995, *Public Relations History: From the 17th to the 20th Century*, LEA, Hillsdale, NJ

Daly F., 1977, *From Curtin to Kerr*, Sun Books, Melbourne

Dwyer T. J. (ed.), 1961, *The Australian Public Relations Handbook: A Guide to the Principles and Practice of Public Relations in Australia*, Ruskin, Melbourne

Flower J., 2007, 'The Birth and Growth of an Information Agency' in *Asia Pacific Public Relations Journal*, Vol. 8, Deakin University, Victoria

Golding P., 2004, *Just a Chattel of the Sale*, Peter Golding, Spit Junction, NSW

Goot M., 2002, *Australian Dictionary of Biography*, Vol. 16, Melbourne University Press, pp. 144–6

Hirst J., 2007, 'Political Courage—Some Australian Examples' in *The Monthly*, July 2007, Issue 25, Melbourne

Joel A., Oral History Interview, 4 June 1973, de Berg tapes, National Library of Australia, Canberra, pp. 8, 493–512

Johnston J. & Zawawi C. (eds), 2004, *Public Relations Theory and Practice*, 2nd edn, Allen & Unwin, Crows Nest

Kiernan C., 1978, *Calwell—A Personal and Political History*, Nelson, Melbourne

L'etang J. & Pieczka M. (eds), 2006, *Public Relations: Critical Debates and Contemporary Practice*, LEA, Mahwah, NJ

May A. L., 1968, *The Battle for the Banks*, Sydney University Press, Sydney

McHugh S., 1989, *The Snowy—The People Behind the Power*, WHA, Port Melbourne

McMullin R. in Grattan M. (ed.), 2001, *Australian Prime Ministers*, New Holland, Sydney

McNair I. in Potts J. D. S., 1976, *Public Relations Practice in Australia*, McGraw-Hill, Sydney

Newsom D., Turk V. J. & Kruckberg D., 2007, *This is PR—The Realities of Public Relations*, 9th edn, Thomson, Belmont, CA

Northey R., 1993, *Australian Dictionary of Biography*, Vol. 13, Melbourne University Press, pp. 594–5

Patterson L., 1987, 'The National Advisory Council on AIDS (NACAIDS) National Education Programme (NEP)', Golden Target Awards Competition Entry

Peart J., 1994, *The Growing Pains of Professional Public Relations—A Study in the Sociology of Occupations*, University of Auckland

Potts J. D. S., 1976, *Public Relations Practice in Australia*, McGraw-Hill, Sydney

Reekie G., *Australian Dictionary of Biography—Online Edition*, Stanley C. R. (1899–1954), www.adb.online.anu.edu.au/biogs/A120060b.htm, accessed 7 March 2007

Robson L., 1970, *The First AIF: A Study of its Recruitment, 1914–1918*, Melbourne University Press

Russell W. B., 1980, *We Will Remember Them—The Story of the Shrine of Remembrance*, The Dominion Press, Victoria

Seitel F. P., 2007, *The Practice of Public Relations*, 10th edn, Pearson Education International, NJ

Smythe R., 1998, 'From the Empire's Second Greatest White City to ...' in *Historical Journal of Film, Television and Radio*, Vol. 18, Issue 2, p. 237 26pp, ebscohost.com database, accessed 1 March 2007

Tymson C. & Sherman W., 1987, *The Australian Public Relations Manual*, Millennium Books, Sydney

Tymson C., Lazar P. & Lazar R., 2002, *The New Australian and New Zealand Public Relations Manual*, Tymson Communications, Chatswood

Usher J. (ed.), 2007, *The Argus—Life and Death of a Newspaper*, Australian Scholarly Publishing, North Melbourne

Walker R. R., 1967, *Communicators—People, Practices, Philosophies in Australian Advertising, Media and Marketing*, Lansdowne Press, Melbourne

White B. & Clarke C., 1995, *Cheques and Balances—Memoirs of a Banker*, Viking, Ringwood

Zawawi C. in Johnston J. & Zawawi C. (eds), 2004, *Public Relations Theory and Practice, A History of Public Relations in Australia*, 2nd edn, Allen & Unwin, Crows Nest

3

Overview of Contemporary Public Relations Theory

Bronwyn Kirby

AIMS OF THIS CHAPTER

- To outline key theoretical frames that inform campaign development

- To demonstrate the challenges of applying certain theories

- To illustrate the application of theory in practice

INTRODUCTION

All public relations programs and campaigns should be based on theories (McElreath 1997, p. 161). Coombs holds that a good theory goes beyond description to prediction (2001, p. 106), while Mackey suggests theories can be thought of as imaginary road maps that can be used to gain understanding (2004, p. 43).

Theories provide direction and can signpost possible problems. They serve to underpin sound public relations practice by helping to predict and explain. Importantly, through public relations education, theories inform the profession's future. Tench and Yeomans (2006, p. 53) state that education plays a key part in establishing any profession, and L'Etang (2002, p. 47) agrees, saying education is the 'crucial plank in PR's quest for professional status'. As a public relations educator, the author of this chapter uses these theoretical maps as a vital step in the learning process, aiming to provide a logical cognitive path for students—the public relations professionals of the future.

Public relations is a comparatively new discipline; the Public Relations Institute of Australia (PRIA) was only established in 1951 and the first Australian degree courses were introduced in the 1960s. Given their relative infancy, public relations practice and theory have been informed by the knowledge base and theoretical foundations of other disciplines, such as business and management, communication, culture, sociology, psychology, media and politics. However over more recent decades, and with the drive for the professionalisation of public relations, visionaries such as Grunig, Hunt and others have developed specific theories from within the field of public relations itself. The development of theory and the associated growth of ethical frameworks specifically for public relations is vital, given its use by powerful entities (governments and large organisations) and its ability to influence opinion and behaviour. Academic research in the area is now plentiful and diverse, providing a rich pool of information from which practitioners and academics alike can draw as the profession strives for continually improved effective and ethical practice.

Tench and Yeomans state that the value of theory in underpinning practice has been a discussion point in the past:

> Some practitioners will have managed very well for many years without theory, or rather they will have relied on their own version of common sense theory. Others have taken postgraduate courses, like a masters degree ... Increasingly, public relations graduates who have studied theoretical modules in their degree courses are joining the profession and shaping the expectations of the next generation. The theory that practitioners have been exposed to will inform the role they play (2006, p. 51).

Many theories are short-lived, making way for new schools of thought grown out of academic debate. Most theories evolve through modifications and revisions which keep them relevant and contemporary. Theories do not fit a 'one size fits all' mould; some aspects of a theory may suit a particular application, while other aspects seem not to relate at all. Students and practitioners alike must learn to be discerning in dealing with theoretical concepts.

This chapter sets out to give a brief overview of the more commonly used theories in public relations education and those that are particularly pertinent for current professional practice. The theories have been grouped into three sections:

1   Theories of communication

2   Theories of receiver response

3   Theories of practice.

The theories of communication are concerned with the process of communication whereby a message is relayed from sender to receiver, identifying participants in the process and effects that impact on the communication flow. The theories of receiver response build on the communication theories but focus on the receivers of the message. Receiver response theories are concerned with the communication process in terms of the receiver's cognitive (thought processes), affective (feelings and emotions) and behavioural (actions) responses. Finally, the theories of practice section introduces theories used in organisational settings and includes examples of planning models which provide structure and underpin public relations practice.

The theories represented here are mere shells, intended as an introduction to the concepts only—they offer a 'toe in the water' approach to the vast array of theoretical platforms that inform contemporary public relations. (There is a wealth of information available for the reader who wishes to delve deeper, and the sources referred to at the conclusion of this chapter are an excellent place to start.) The 'Consider ...' sections serve to alert the reader to some of the aforementioned shortcomings associated with each, and/or to highlight issues for further thought.

At the chapter's conclusion is an example of student work. The piece illustrates how theory is integrated into the study of public relations. It is indicative of the very real way in which theoretical concepts are related to professional public relations practice by contemporary public relations students.

SECTION 1: THEORIES OF COMMUNICATION
Shannon and Weaver model of communication

IN BRIEF

In 1948, mathematicians Claude Shannon and Warren Weaver developed a model as a basis for communication theories. Their book, *The Mathematical Theory of Communication* (1949), had a major impact on information technology, and its effect on the understanding of communication theory still has value today. The concept involves a *message* being disseminated by a *sender*, via a *channel of communication*, to a *receiver*, thereby producing an *effect*. The model was modified to include the notions of feedback from the receiver (which can in turn be used to modify the message), and *noise*.

Noise is an important concept, referring to external interference that may affect or distort the message. Noise refers to the barrage of advertising, news and events that compete with the sender's message for the receiver's attention. For instance, noise could be a political announcement that draws media attention away from a charitable event; alternatively it could be a national scandal involving a major financial organisation which in turn reflects poorly on the activities of an unrelated locally based firm.

CONSIDER ...

Several problems can impact on this communication model. It relies on the effective operations of the channel—any kind of malfunction can have an adverse affect on the message. The characteristics of the sender can also influence the effectiveness of the message—if the source does not appeal to the receiver, the message simply will not get through. Characteristics can refer to the particular medium chosen (for example one magazine over another) or the choice of 'face' used to convey the message (for example a model, celebrity or accredited professional). Sometimes problems are encountered because of personality traits of the receiver—different people interpret messages differently—which points to the importance of researching target publics. And sometimes there are problems with 'influence'—the message simply does not have the desired persuasive effect on the receiver (Tench & Yeomans 2006, p. 145).

Hierarchy of effects

IN BRIEF

Behaviour change is the goal of public relations activity. Having the target audience listen to a message, consider it, comprehend it and agree with it is generally the accepted path to achieving behaviour change. The public relations hierarchy of effects model builds on earlier designs that concentrated on the message's receiver and assumed that 'learning new behaviours occurred logically through a hierarchy of effects: first, awareness; then, comprehension; next, acceptance; and finally, retention' (McElreath 1997, p. 159).

From a management perspective, a more relevant model for public relations is one that is 'producer oriented', thereby acknowledging the role of public relations in the process. Using a stepped design, the public relations hierarchy of effects model begins with message formulation and works through to the desired behaviour change:

1 Formulating the message

2 Disseminating the message

3 Receiving the message

4 Comprehending the message

5   Changing or reinforcing attitudes and/or opinions

6   Changing or reinforcing behaviour.

CONSIDER ...

The hierarchy of effects is limited in its assumption of a consecutive, sequential process. In reality, the process of receiving and acting on a message is complex and will often not occur in such a prescribed manner. The way in which a message is received is also infinitely complex, being influenced by personal biases which can be nurtured by a myriad of factors, including stereotypes, symbols, semantics, peer influence and media (Seitel 2007, pp. 53–5).

Situational theory

IN BRIEF

Grunig and Hunt's (1984) situational theory provides a tool to categorise publics' perceptions of a situation and their subsequent behaviour. It is used to identify and segment an organisation's publics into three categories:

1   **Latent publics**

Groups that face a particular situation due to the organisation's activities, but do not recognise the fact

2   **Aware publics**

Groups that recognise the situation exists

3   **Active publics**

Groups that recognise the situation exists, assess it as being worthy of their involvement and decide to act upon it.

Further categorisations are also proposed: *apathetic publics* do not care about any issues or problems); *single-issue publics* are active on one particular issue that has limited popular appeal (activist groups often fall into this category); *hot-issue publics* are active on an appealing or popular issue; while *all-issue publics* become involved in a wide range of issues or problems.

Situational theory holds that predictions can be made about a public's involvement based on three independent variables in the publics' psyche:

1   **Problem recognition**

Recognising that a problem exists

2   **Constraint recognition**

Recognising that they are limited in their ability to create change

3 Level of involvement

Recognising that they are affected by the problem, regardless of whether they feel able to affect change.

It is wise public relations practice to address a situation when publics are at the latent or aware stage, rather than wait until the active publics have begun to react.

CONSIDER ...

Situational theory allows the identification of vulnerable groups that are unlikely to protest an organisation's actions due to their high levels of constraint recognition. This fact could be exploited by powerful organisations over minority or disadvantaged groups. Springston (2001, p. 616) points to the theory's limitation in its assumption that an organisation and its publics are discrete entities, rather than acknowledging that there is a recursive relationship between the two.

The public sphere

IN BRIEF

While many critical theorists have shaped the direction of ethical public relations practice, of particular influence is the work of German philosopher, Jürgen Habermas. Habermas (1989) proposed the notion of the 'public sphere', where citizens are able to rationally discuss and debate in a social, mediating environment. The public sphere operates between the 'political sphere' and the 'private sphere'. Threatening citizens' rights to the discursive realm of the public sphere is the rhetoric of powerful organisations such as big business and governments. These entities can overwhelm the public sphere, dominating communication. The need for discussants to be as equals in terms of power relations is a key aspect of the theory. Without this balance, communication can become 'strategic'; that is, used as an instrument of force (Mackey 2004, p. 52).

The public sphere is inextricably linked with relationship building, that most important of concepts for public relations. Stanton (2006, p. 16) says the public sphere embodies the good in a society. Ethical implications arise for public relations when communication is distorted or manipulated by those in power.

CONSIDER ...

Some say the public sphere is an ideal that has never existed (Moloney 2000). Certainly Habermas makes societal judgments that have far-reaching implications for public relations. Mackey encapsulates this notion by stating: 'The implication is that public relations is an integral expression of the contemporary capitalist style of society, a style of society which is unfair and unbalanced' (2004, p. 53).

SECTION 2: THEORIES OF RECEIVER RESPONSE
Behavioural public relations model

IN BRIEF

The behavioural public relations model is based on the premise that behaviour change is the ultimate evaluation in any public relations activity. The model in itself is simple, consisting of four stages: *awareness* moves through *latent readiness to act* and *triggering event* to the final objective, *behaviour*. Jackson considers the communication process—that is, the tactics proposed by public relations practitioners—to fit into the awareness phase. Depending on the influence of the communication, people then begin to formulate readiness to act, which is then affected by the triggering event. Wilson says this event could be an election day or a sale at a clothing store—the event transforms the readiness to act into actual behaviour change (1997, pp. 20–1).

CONSIDER ...

Behaviour is based on values, beliefs and attitudes. As such, being able to affect behaviour change is no easy task, usually requiring far more than just information dissemination. For public relations to influence behaviour, there must be an understanding of how to influence human cognitive elements, basing any action firmly on ethical and responsible grounding (Wilson 1997, p. 32).

Social exchange theory

IN BRIEF

Social exchange theory has roots in sociology, economics and psychology, and was proposed by Hormans (1958) to understand the social behaviour of humans in economic dealings. The theory was developed in the 1970s and 1980s by sociologists Emerson and Cook ('Social Exchange Theory' 1978).

Social exchange theory revolves around equity in relationships. In public relations, social exchange theory is based on the premise that people crave balanced relationships, and do not like to feel they 'owe' others. People make judgments about the comparison of alternatives based on a subjective cost–benefit analysis. When there is a perceived imbalance in a relationship, rational entities—be they individuals, groups or organisations—will communicate in some way to regain balance. Knapp explains that social relationships involve the exchange of 'resources', which can include status, information, goods, services, money, security and love (1984, p. 44).

The social exchange perspective has been projected onto community/organisational relationships. For instance, social exchange theory can be seen at work in community liaison committees that represent community views. It is anticipated that members of the committee, and those over whom they have influence, will respect an organisation in return for the opportunity to have their opinions attended to.

CONSIDER ...

According to Mackey, social exchange theory has been criticised by theorists for its inability to account for social peculiarities such as tradition, political dominance and gender discrimination. However, he contends, the notion that relationships beg reciprocity works at the most base of levels and is useful in public relations practice (Mackey 2004, p. 67).

Social learning theory

IN BRIEF

The assumption of social learning theory, as first proposed by Canadian psychologist Albert Bandura in 1977, is that we learn by modelling our behaviour after others (McElreath 1996, p. 155). The theory posits that identification with a model increases learning—people attune their behaviour and attitudes to fit in with those of others, be they friends, family, teachers or peers. However the concepts of social learning extend to others who are not accessible on a personal level, but whose behaviour people admire, such as celebrities, spokespeople and movie stars.

Social learning theory assumes a sequence of events: we notice a certain behaviour, we admire it, we wish to emulate the behaviour, so we adopt it. If we like the new behaviour, we integrate it into our being. The use of celebrities by organisations to endorse products is a prime example of social learning theory, as is much of the television advertising we are exposed to (McElreath 1996, p. 155).

CONSIDER ...

Burgoon, Dunbar and Segrin (2002, p. 450) point to evidence regarding physical appearance and its relation to persuasion, providing an interesting aside to social learning theory. For example findings have suggested that people may be inclined to comply with sources who are dressed similarly to themselves:

> For instance, all social groups—from street gangs, to work groups, to entire cultures—rely on clothing, insignias, ownership of certain brand-name products, and the like to symbolize their in-group status. In other cases, high-status clothing, attractive facial features, and conventional appearance have been shown to increase persuasiveness (Bickman, 1971, 1974; Brownlow & Zebrowitz, 1990; Pallak, 1983; Pallak, Murroni, & Koch, 1983). In these latter cases, attractive appearance may be persuasive in itself, or it may relate to violations of expectations ... (Burgoon et al. 2002, pp. 450–1).

Maslow's hierarchy of needs

IN BRIEF

Public relations is involved with issues of self-interest, a basic premise being that people pay attention to messages that appeal to their psychological or economic needs. Humans are driven by different motivations, observed US psychologist Abraham Maslow (1954). Maslow proposed a hierarchy of needs, a scale upon which appeals to self-interest could be based.

The hierarchy of needs theory can be used to predict and explain publics' behaviour in public relations campaigns, and is thereby valuable as a planning tool. The hierarchy of needs is often depicted as a triangle or a staircase with five levels of human needs which move from the bottom to the top. The lowest level is *physiological* (water, sleep, food etc.), then come *safety* (security, shelter, protection), *social* (love, friendship, belonging) and *esteem* (self-esteem, status). The final stage in the hierarchy is *self-actualisation* (self-development, enrichment). People can only move 'up' to the next level of needs once their lower level needs are satisfied; that is, basic physiological needs must be met before people can consider higher level needs (Belch & Belch 2004, pp. 109–10; Seitel 2007, p. 69; Wilcox et al. 1998, pp. 219–20).

Wilcox, Ault and Agee effectively illustrate the hierarchy of needs through the example of the early AIDS public information campaigns in the USA, where there were difficulties disseminating information to minorities and low-income groups: 'For these groups, the potential danger of AIDS is less compelling than the day-to-day problems of poverty and satisfying the basic needs of food and shelter' (1998, p. 220).

CONSIDER ...

While Maslow's hierarchy of needs is useful, the success of public relations ultimately depends on the accurate assessment of the wants, needs, lifestyles and opinions of target audiences. Belch and Belch (2004) state that in reality it is unlikely that people move through the hierarchy in a 'stairstep' manner. Providing a marketer's perspective, Belch and Belch also note the fact that in most developed countries the lower levels of physiological needs are already met. This has led to appeals for social needs being employed to promote products that fill basic physiological requirements. This strategy can be seen through the depiction of mother–child love in advertisements for children's nappies or food.

Agenda setting theory

IN BRIEF

although the news media do not tell you *what* to think, they do strongly influence what you think *about* (Mackey 2004).

In contributing to public opinion research, agenda setting theory was first suggested in the early 1970s by University of Texas journalism academic Maxwell McCombs and University of North Carolina mass communication professor Donald L. Shaw (McCombs & Shaw 2001). Agenda setting theory is concerned with the media and the way news is selected by media outlets for consumption by the public. Some issues are presented while others are not, impacting on which issues assume prominence.

There are several agendas at work behind this theory:

- The media agenda, which is inextricably influenced by news values

- The public agenda, which is undeniably influenced by the media agenda

- The policy agenda, brought about by pressure groups and politicians

- The corporate agenda.

The media, policy and corporate agendas are each trying to sway the public agenda. In addition, each agenda relates to the others, as well as to outside influences, including—importantly—public relations (Watson 2003, p. 131; Tench & Yeomans 2006, p. 118).

Public relations is often concerned with gaining media attention for clients and organisations. Practitioners must understand news values as well as media policies and routines. They need to be able to recognise conflicting issues that may divert attention from their message, and they even need to understand the personalities of those with whom they are dealing in the media. All of these factors contribute to public relations' ability to achieve the best media coverage possible.

CONSIDER ...

While the media is a powerful persuasive tool, research shows that people do not automatically form opinions from media coverage. Thought processes are much more complicated than that (see, for example, the section on social learning theory, above). Consider also the effect new technologies have had on the traditional media. The internet has prompted vast changes in the way newspapers and television are consumed, providing a whole new way to access news and opinions, often bypassing the traditional outlets.

Elaboration-likelihood model

IN BRIEF

The elaboration-likelihood model, developed by Ohio State University psychologists Petty and Cacioppo in 1986, integrates the literature on source, message, receiver and context effects in persuasion. It brings together what can appear to be the many disparate research findings in the field. The model differs from other theories in its process-oriented approach, where the focus is not on source, message or receiver variables in themselves, but rather on the processes by which these aspects of a message influence people to change their attitudes.

The theory suggests that two routes to persuasion can be identified when looking at how messages are processed. The *central* route involves processing arguments contained in a message using reason and consideration, while using the *peripheral* route results in emotional reactions. The theory proposes that the central route is more likely to lead to long-lasting attitude change, while the peripheral route works best for short-term messages.

To understand when people will engage in each type of processing, this theory posits the 'elaboration-likelihood continuum':

- When a message has a high elaboration likelihood, people will be more inclined to engage in central route processing, whereas

- When elaboration likelihood is low, peripheral processing is more probable.

CONSIDER ...

Elaboration likelihood is not a simple thing to predict. As well as the more manageable source and message variables, elaboration likelihood is also influenced by a number of receiver and context factors, such as personal relevance and the message's complexity. A behavioural or attitudinal change is most likely when the receiver is able to relate the message to their own personal experience. These factors will determine whether persuasion will be based on message scrutiny or peripheral cues.

Another complexity in the theory's practical application is the fact that a single persuasion variable (such as the source's attractiveness) can take on multiple persuasive roles depending on the specific circumstances in which it is encountered.

SECTION 3: THEORIES OF PRACTICE
The four models of public relations

IN BRIEF

Perhaps the theory that has had the most influence over contemporary public relations is Grunig and Hunt's (1984) four models of public relations. A set of public relations typologies, the following four models were developed through observation of professional practice in the USA:

BRONWYN KIRBY

1   **Press agentry/publicity**

Epitomised by P. T. Barnum's approach to promoting his circus acts, this model is concerned only with one-way communication (which may or may not be truthfully based).

Example: Publicity stunts used to draw attention to a product launch or coming event.

2   **Public information**

Also a one-way mode of communication, this model is concerned with disseminating factual (truthful) information. The public relations practitioner operating in this manner can be depicted as a journalist-in-residence, objectively providing information to the public.

Example: Government departments issuing information, for instance about a change in policy or a crisis situation.

3   **Two-way asymmetric**

While this model encourages feedback from publics, it is primarily concerned with providing persuasive communication. The feedback gathered is used to tailor the message in order to better persuade, rather than to alter the organisation's position.

Example: Credible charitable organisations that rely on feedback from publics when selecting messages and communication modes. The organisations seek to be as persuasive and ethical as possible, while maintaining their original stance.

4   **Two-way symmetric**

The two-way symmetric model is proposed by Grunig and Hunt as being the ideal. The aim is to achieve mutual understanding; the views of both the publics and the organisation adjusting as a result of the flow of two-way communication. The two-way symmetric approach advocates relationship building through dialogue, listening and gained mutual understanding.

Example: A large manufacturer that alters plans to a proposed development project due to objections from neighbouring residents. In return for this concession, the residents cease complaining about the manufacturer to local government and the media.

CONSIDER ...

The two-way symmetric model of public relations has been criticised for being too idealistic and unrealistic to the point of naïvety. This is particularly so given the role of public relations as a paid advocate/representative of an organisation. L'Etang (2006, p. 414) states that corporate social responsibility, as promoted through the symmetrical approach, can be motivated by organisational self-interest—it simply makes good business sense.

Tench and Yeomans (2006, p. 148) also warn that the four models of public relations are culturally specific and thus may not be relevant in some countries.

Systems theory

IN BRIEF

Systems theory (also known as general systems theory) is widely applied to the field of public relations, helping to explain and predict organisational behaviour, and explain how the public relations role contributes to the entity as a whole. A complex web of theories, the systems approach holds that organisations are dynamic and living, made up of a series of interacting subsystems, each with boundaries, inputs, outputs and 'through-puts'. Feedback, both internal and external, allows appropriate adjustments to be made for the organisation's continued well-being.

Systems theory as proposed by biologist Ludwig von Bertalanffy (1968) sought to explain the arrangements and relations between parts that connect them to a whole. Systems theory has since been extensively researched and modified by public relations academics to help explain contemporary practice.

Systems theory introduces the notion of public relations practitioners as 'boundary spanners'—people who support other subsystems by communicating across the organisational boundaries, internally and externally. Systems theory also introduces the concept of 'open' and 'closed' systems. The closed system organisation operates as if in a vacuum, not adapting to external conditions and communicating only within specific departments. On the other hand, open system organisations are able to adapt their activities to suit the environment, the public relations role allowing effective communication between all departments, at all levels, and promoting interactions with the external environment. An organisation's major decision-makers, the 'dominant coalition', ultimately set the agenda. Therefore, as McElreath states, 'If public relations is able to influence an organization's view of itself and its relationships with others, it can only do so by significantly changing the views of the dominant coalition' (1997, p. 15).

CONSIDER ...

Systems theory offers a variety of theoretical perspectives, each with its strengths and weaknesses, however none can truly reflect the complexity of most real organisations. Mackey (2004) states that systems theory is limited in its lack of attention to the psychology and power relations of discussants. Systems theory does not take into account any analysis of content, validity or ethics of the messages that are circulated (2004, p. 48). Neither does it credit individual endeavour such as leadership, upholding the assumption that the complexity of the organisation is greater than any individual input (McElreath 1997, p. 15).

BRONWYN KIRBY

Planning models

IN BRIEF

Public relations practice is informed by models that guide the planning process. While there are several of these models, and healthy debate continues about their relative attributes, they all advocate similar planning elements and are generally referred to by acronyms. Perhaps the best-known of these is Marston's RACE model (*Research, Action, Communication, Evaluation*), whereby the 'action' step calls for the identification of the action of the client in the public interest. Action is the heart of the process in the RACE model: 'You can't have effective communication or positive publicity without proper action. Stated another way, performance must precede publicity' (Seitel 2007, p. 5).

Crifasi's ROSIE model (*Research, Objectives, Strategies, Implementation, Evaluation*) advocates the identification of objectives and the setting of strategies prior to the work of actual implementation (Seitel 2007, p. 5). Hendrix's practical ROPE model (*Research, Objectives, Programming, Evaluation*) has been widely adopted (Hendrix 2001, p. 45). Focusing on relationship management, Kelly uses the ROPE model as the basis of ROPES, where the 'S' stands for the crucial step of *Stewardship*. Through stewardship, Kelly advocates the importance of maintaining relationships with all publics, stating: 'It is easier to keep a friend than to make a new friend' (Kelly 2001, p. 279).

CONSIDER ...

Models offer a way forward in public relations planning. However in the professional world, public relations practitioners must work in a flexible manner to adapt quickly to the demands of a dynamic environment. This often means that adhering to a hard-and-fast model can be unrealistic. Guth and Marsh (2006, p. 15) recognise the demands this environment places on the public relations role, requiring it to be more flexible than a traditional four-step model. For instance, rather than evaluation occurring at the end of the model cycle, it may be better practice to evaluate throughout every phase, the rest of the program adjusting and altering itself to fit the evaluation findings and the current environment.

CONCLUSION

The theories included in this chapter help to explain the nature and practice of public relations. Effective public relations practice is inextricably tied to understanding communication, cognitive processes, emotional responses and behaviour patterns. As seen here, many theories overlap—some take up where others leave off. Theories evolve to explain specialised situations, relationships and behaviours. As formal public relations practice matures, existing models will be adapted and new theories will be established, helping to define the profession further.

CASE STUDY

Theory applied: the student perspective

Public relations students in tertiary institutions in Australia and New Zealand are well versed in the theoretical concepts related to their studies. This example of work from a third-year Deakin University student is based on the unit 'Public Relations Campaigns and Practice', through which students are required to develop a public relations campaign proposal on behalf of a real-world client. As a first step they are asked to reflect on the theoretical platforms that may underpin the campaign's planning process. This piece illustrates the way in which students learn to identify theoretical principles and apply them in a discerning manner. It also indicates the level of understanding students have of the junction between theory and practice.

This work is gratefully reproduced by kind permission of the Lighthouse Foundation and Tim Browne.

Like any successful public relations activity, the public relations campaign is underpinned and guided by careful planning and strategic direction. Working with a fellow Deakin student and colleague, we are undertaking the End of Financial Year Campaign for the Melbourne-based charity, Lighthouse Foundation. Our campaign will be built upon the recommendations and direction provided in many of the theories taught in our studies at Deakin. This essay outlines the role of the theories in each part of our campaign, including research, communication models, persuasion techniques and implementation within an organisation. Like most campaigns, our End of Financial Year Campaign will not solely nor strictly rely on just two or three theories, but draw features from relevant theories such as ROPES, Hunt and Grunig's four models of communication, Social Exchange Theory, Jackson's Behavioural Public Relations Model, Maslow's Hierarchy of Needs, Elaboration Likelihood Theory and Hierarchy of Effects.

Lighthouse Foundation is a not-for-profit organisation that provides a home environment for young people aged 15–22 who would otherwise be homeless. Often these young people come from a background of abuse and have poor social, education and emotional coping skills. Recent statistics suggest that on any given night there are 26,000 homeless young people on the streets in Australia. Lighthouse seeks to address this problem by engaging the community to build and support Lighthouse homes where the young people can live safely and are supported by live-in carers 24 hours a day, 7 days a week. There are currently ten Lighthouse homes across Victoria, with up to six young people in each home. Lighthouse receives no recurrent operational funding from any level of government. This is because Lighthouse offers shelter and support to young people even after they turn 18. Current guidelines for funding do not allow youth accommodation programs to operate under these terms. The cost of operating a home is around $100,000 per year, while the organisation requires a total of around $2 million to provide services and programs to the young people in the homes and on its outreach program.

To raise funds, Lighthouse engages members of the community, the corporate sector and the philanthropic trusts and foundations to fund its operation. Traditionally the end of the financial year has been a key time for campaigning for tax-deductible donations. Lighthouse has a database of around 5000 donors and supporters with whom they communicate regularly. Lighthouse needs to target this public with a fundraising campaign to help generate enough funds to support the homes through the next financial year.

A fundraising campaign is an excellent example of a public relations campaign because it ultimately relies on strategic and effective communication between an organisation and its target publics. Ideally this communication will continue to develop mutually beneficial relationships between the organisation and these publics. This is particularly crucial in our campaign as Lighthouse's supporters are a key stakeholder and are responsible for providing funding for the organisation's survival.

Hunt and Grunig (1994) identify four different models or ways that communication can be managed by a public relations practitioner. Our campaign will employ tactics that encourage two-way symmetric communication between Lighthouse and its target publics, however, we will also use tactics that fall within the more traditional models of press agentry and public information. Some of these tactics will serve only to raise the profile of the organisation and generate awareness of current issues such as youth homelessness. However, in order to develop and maintain mutually beneficial relationships with its supporters we will be encouraging Lighthouse to engage in dialogues and be open to feedback.

The basis for our campaign strategy is closely aligned with some of Lighthouse's key values. Much of the written material about Lighthouse describes their commitment to treasuring and nurturing individual relationships: with the young people, the community, the volunteers and their supporters. This is, perhaps, a practical demonstration of the social exchange theory outlined in Kendall (1996, p. 19). Social exchange theory describes the transactions that occur between two parties as they develop and then maintain a stable relationship. Indeed some Lighthouse employees often describe their organisation as a 'social-profit' rather than a 'not-for-profit' organisation, focusing on the return they offer their supporters and contributors in the form of 'building social capital'. We will identify and address the 'needs' of the target public in our strategy. We do not assume that Lighthouse will receive donations in exchange for nothing. Indeed we will demonstrate the impact of the donation and the 'return on investment' donors can expect.

Another key theory that will underpin our campaign is Jackson's Behavioural Public Relations Model. Wilson (1997, p. 20) explains Jackson's focus in a four-stage process that easily translates to our fundraising campaign. In order to elicit a certain behaviour from our target public (making a donation) we aim to raise awareness through communication tactics and build a latent readiness to act through aligning the target public with Lighthouse objectives. We will then produce a triggering event, or a 'call to action', and provide a transaction opportunity for the desired behaviour to take place. Jackson's model is strongly based on public opinion and perception, and argues that it is imperative practitioners attempt to understand their target publics' 'frame of reference' when delivering their messages.

Public opinion has the potential to hinder or help a particular campaign. The recent controversy surrounding the distribution of funds raised for the Tsunami disaster has fuelled a public perception that not-for-profit organisations are not necessarily trustworthy or financially transparent. It is essential that we are aware of public opinion on this and other issues. While we may not be able to, nor should we aim to, change public opinion about charities generally, we can at least acknowledge it and attempt to include key messages that demonstrate Lighthouse as a financially responsible and transparent organisation.

The strategic planning and structure of our campaign draws features from a number of different models and theories. Wilcox, Ault and Agee (1998) offer four main ingredients of a public relations campaign, and all are relevant to our campaign: Research, Action and Planning, Communication and Evaluation. While all these components are crucial, Kelly's (2001) ROPES model is a more appropriate theory and acknowledges the need to aim for other long-term, sustainable outcomes. Kelly's model builds on the model proposed by Hendrix (1998) and suggests that effective stewardship of previous donors 'is essential to raising future gifts' (2001, p. 80). Indeed the relationships Lighthouse has with its donors are possibly one of its most treasured assets. Kelly also quotes Grunig (1992) who emphasises the importance of 'building relationships with publics that constrain or enhance the ability of the organisation to meet its mission'.

In all models of effective public relations, research is paramount to the successful implementation of a campaign. Despite operating for fifteen years, Lighthouse has a relatively poor collection of quantifiable data and information for constructing benchmarks or measurable objectives. This unfortunately restricts the amount of written archival or historical research available. This type of research is designed to provide a backbone for other research techniques (Kendall 1996, p. 63). Instead the majority of information about previous campaigns, donor details and successful tactics is located within the minds and memories of key staff members. This would suggest that in order to collect and collate data we will need to employ a series of qualitative research techniques. These would include a focus group, interviews and a public relations audit that may include a sample phone survey of a number of supporters who have previously donated to Lighthouse. The audit will be particularly useful in measuring the organisation's standing and as a 'research tool used specifically to describe, measure and assess ... and to provide guidelines for future public relations programming' (Wimmer & Dommick 1997, p. 333).

The lack of quantifiable or accurate primary research dictates that we must investigate some secondary sources of information. Here too, however, there is also a lack of tried and tested benchmarks or research within the not-for-profit sector. Perhaps this is due to poor resources or a poor understanding of the importance of post-campaign evaluation. However, in 2004 Philanthropy Australia conducted an extensive research project on giving trends in Australia which provides some valuable insight on who gives to charitable causes and why. We have also located some excellent secondary research on websites such as <ourcommunity.org.au> and the Australian Charities Fund websites, which will help set benchmarks and realistic objectives.

Eliciting a desired behaviour through persuasion is not an easy thing. As well as using concepts and strategies outlined in the Social Exchange Theory and Jackson's Behavioural Model, a number of other theories and approaches will influence our strategy and in particular, the composition of different tactics. These theories include Maslow's Hierarchy of Needs, Elaboration Likelihood Theory and Hierarchy of Effects (Smyth & Sheehan 2002, p. 37).

Maslow's Hierarchy of Needs helps outline and prioritise the various needs of a particular public. Public relations practitioners employ this theory to connect with and appeal to a target public. Because our primary target public for this campaign has some level of disposable income, we can assume that the majority of them will have their basic needs, such as shelter, food and safety, met. Instead we will appeal to their social needs (a sense of community and belonging), their higher ego needs, such as the desire to feel important, and their self-actualising needs (Newsom & Haymes 2005, p. 43).

The Australian Philanthropy Report on Giving in Australia identifies a person's personal experience of a situation or close personal connection to a cause as a major motivation for giving. This evidence supports one of the founding principles of Elaboration Likelihood Theory that suggests a change in attitude or behaviour is more likely to occur when the situation or call to action can be related to their own experience or life (Smyth & Sheehan 2002, p. 37). While none of our target publics are likely to be future victims of youth homelessness (as opposed to cancer etc.) the key messages of our campaign will be aimed at prompting a personal recognition and connection to youth homelessness. We will focus on values such as family, love, warmth and safety. Our target public will hopefully identify with some of our messages, apply them to their lives and consequently feel motivated to give. This theory will form part of our emotive persuasive strategy.

Newsom and Haymes (2005, p. 39) suggest that effective persuasion relies on both factual and emotional arguments. Our persuasive strategy will also use cognitive arguments designed to appeal to rational and logical thought processes. This will utilise the Hierarchy of Effects Theory that expands upon the Shannon-Weaver Model of Communication (Ruben & Stewart 1998, p. 26). Put simply, communication in the form of a message, is sent from a sender to a receiver who decodes the message. However, this process in itself does not guarantee successful communication, let alone elicit a desired behaviour. The Hierarchy of Effects Theory argues that the receiver must understand the message, agree with the message and act accordingly. This means the content and formation of our communication must be understandable, relevant and persuasive for our target public to become aware and interested in the message and then adopt the desired behaviour (Smyth & Sheehan 2002, p. 37). If our target public does not know why Lighthouse needs funds urgently or is not interested in helping, they will not be motivated to give.

While Kendall (1996, p. 217) suggests that the major motivation underpinning charitable donations is guilt, a strategy based around this and communications that seek to elicit this emotion would be in contrast to Lighthouse values. The Lighthouse 'Model of Care' (Lighthouse Foundation 2006) places a strong emphasis on empowerment and validation of the young people, the community and its supporters. This means that the young people cannot be used as 'sob stories', nor can the community be made to feel guilty for not giving. This is a prime example of how a campaign must be adapted to fit the values and culture of an organisation to be successfully implemented (Kendall 1996, p. 223). It also demonstrates the need for public relations practitioners to take a considered and ethical approach to campaigns and communications. Deal and Kennedy describe practitioners as often being 'charged with the duty of ... maintaining the corporate code of ethics and almost invariably with disseminating the code of ethics within the organisation' and indeed without (Kendall 1996, p. 32).

Lighthouse has a very distinct corporate culture that may well be, as described by Kendall (1996), 'a product of mythic interpretations rather than objective or factual history'. In truth Lighthouse operates within a very open and transparent system. The lack of a rigid hierarchical organisational structure contributes to the organic and relaxed nature of the organisation. Many employees job-share and 'pitch in' when needed on an urgent project. Lighthouse is passionate about its values, its heroes, its rites and rituals, yet it also struggles to establish and maintain effective systems of communication.

The theories outlined above will provide valuable direction towards the successful implementation of our campaign both internally and externally. Running through all these theories is a strong emphasis on 'knowing our target public'. While it would be nice to believe that a solid theory-based strategy alone will ensure a successful campaign, this is not the case. An ongoing process of evaluation throughout the planning and implementation stages of the campaign will allow us to adjust our messages and tactics accordingly to improve the campaign's effectiveness.

REFERENCES

Belch G. E. & Belch M. A., 2004, *Advertising and Promotion: An Integrated Marketing Communications Perspective*, 6th edn, McGraw-Hill/Irwin, NY

Bertalanffy L. von, 1968, *General System Theory: Foundations, Development, Applications*, George Braziller, NY

Burgoon J. K., Dunbar N. E. & Segrin C., 2004, 'Nonverbal Influence' in Dillard J. P. & Pfau M. (eds), 2004, *The Persuasion Handbook—Developments in Theory and Practice*, Sage Publications, Thousand Oaks, CA

Coombs W. T., 2001, 'Interpersonal Communication and Public Relations' in Heath R. L. (ed.), *Handbook of Public Relations*, Sage Publications, Inc., Thousand Oaks, CA

Festinger L., 1957, *The Theory of Cognitive Dissonance*, Harper Row, NY

Grunig J. E. & Hunt T., 1984, *Managing Public Relations*, Holt, Rinehart & Winston, NY

Grunig L. A., Grunig J. E. & Dozier D. M., 2002, *Excellent Public Relations and Effective Organizations: A Study of Communication Management in Three Countries*, Lawrence Erlbaum Associates, Inc., Mahwah, NJ

Guth D. W. & Marsh C., 2006, *Public Relations: A Values-driven Approach*, Pearson Education Inc., Boston, MA

Habermas J., 1989, *The Structural Transformation of the Public Sphere: An Inquiry into a Category of Bourgeois Society*, Polity, Cambridge

Harmon-Jones E., 2002, 'A Cognitive Dissonance Theory Perspective on Persuasion' in Dillard J. P. & Pfau M. (eds), 2002, *The Persuasion Handbook: Developments in Theory and Practice*, Sage Publications, Inc., Thousand Oaks, CA

Hormans G. C., 1958, 'Social Behavior as Exchange' in *American Journal of Sociology*, Vol. 63, Issue 6, pp. 597–606

Johnston J. & Zawawi C. (eds), 2004, *Public Relations Theory and Practice,* 2nd edn, Allen & Unwin, Crows Nest, NSW

Knapp M. L., 1984, *Interpersonal Relationships: Their Structures and Processes*, Allyn & Bacon, Boston, MA

L'Etang J., 2002, 'Public Relations Education in Britain: A Review at the Outset of the Millennium and Thoughts for a Different Research Agenda' in *Journal of Communication Management*, Vol. 7, Issue 1, pp. 43–53

L'Etang J., 2006, 'Corporate Responsibility and PR Ethics' in L'Etang J. & Pieczka M. (eds), 2006, *Public Relations: Critical Debates and Contemporary Practice*, Lawrence Erlbaum Associates Inc., Mahwah, NJ

McCombs M. & Shaw D. L., 2001, 'Mass Communication Context' in *Honors: Communication Capstone Spring 2001 Theory Workbook*, www.uky.edu/~drlane/capstone/mass/agenda.htm, accessed 4 October 2007

McElreath M. P., 1997, *Managing Systematic and Ethical Public Relations Campaigns,* 2nd edn, McGraw-Hill, Boston, MA

Mackey S., 2004, 'Theoretical Perspectives' in Johnston J. & Zawawi C. (eds), *Public Relations Theory and Practice,* 2nd edn, Allen & Unwin, Crows Nest, NSW

Marston J. E., 1979, *Modern Public Relations*, McGraw-Hill, NY

Maslow A., 1954, *Motivation and Personality,* Harper & Row, NY

Moloney K., 2000, *Rethinking Public Relations: The Spin and the Substance*, Routledge, London

Petty R. E. & Cacioppo J. T., 1986, *Communication and Persuasion: Control and Peripheral Routes to Attitude Change*, Springer-Verlag, New York

Pieczka M., 2006, 'Paradigms, Systems Theory and Public Relations' in L'Etang J. & Pieczka M. (eds), *Public Relations: Critical Debates and Contemporary Practice*, Lawrence Erlbaum Associates Inc., Mahwah, NJ

Seitel F. P., 2007, *The Practice of Public Relations*, 10th edn, Pearson Education International, NJ

Shannon C. E. & Weaver W., 1949, *The Mathematical Theory of Communication*, University of Illinois Press, Urbana, IL

'Social Exchange Theory', 1978, in *Pathbreakers*, www.washington.edu/research/pathbreakers/1978a.html, accessed 3 October 2007

Springston J. K., 2001, 'Public Relations and New Media Technology' in Heath R. (ed.), *Handbook of Public Relations*, Sage Publications, Inc., Thousand Oaks, CA

Stanton R., 2006, *Media Relations*, Oxford University Press, South Melbourne

Tench R. & Yeomans L., 2006, *Exploring Public Relations*, Pearson Education Limited, Essex

Watson J., 2003, *Media Communication. An Introduction to Theory and Process*, 2nd edn, Palgrave, London

REFERENCES: CASE STUDY

Cutlip S., Center A. & Broom G., 2000, *Effective Public Relations,* Prentice Hall, NJ

Hendrix J. A., 2001, *Public Relations Cases,* 5th edn, Wadsworth/Thomson Learning, Belmont, CA

Hunt T. & Grunig J. E., 1994, *Public Relations Techniques,* Harcourt Brace, Fort Worth, TX

Kelly K. S., 2001, 'Stewardship: The Fifth Step in the Public Relations Process' in Heath R. L. (ed.), *Handbook of Public Relations,* Sage, CA, pp. 279–83

Kendall R., 1996, *Public Relations Campaign Strategies,* 2nd edn, Longman Publishers, New York, p. 56

Lighthouse Foundation, 2003, *Annual Report,* Cleveland Printing, Melbourne

Lighthouse Foundation, 2006, *About Us,* www.lighthousefoundation.org.au, accessed 4 April 2006

Newsom D. & Haymes J., 2005, *Public Relations Writing, Form and Style,* Thomson/Wadsworth, Belmont, CA

Ruben B. D. & Stewart L. P., 1998, *Communication and Human Behaviour,* 4th edn, Allyn & Bacon, Boston, MA

Seitel F. P., 2001, *The Practice of Public Relations,* Prentice Hall, NJ

Smyth R. & Sheehan M., 2002, *Public Relations Management (ALR279) Study Guide,* Deakin University, Geelong

'Social Learning Theory' in *A First Look at Communication Theory,* 2006, www.afirstlook.com/main.cfm, accessed 5 April 2006

Wilcox D. L., Ault P. H. & Agee W. K., 1998, *Public Relations: Strategies and Tactics,* Longman, NY

Wilson L. J., 1997, *Strategic Program Planning for Effective Public Relations,* 2nd edn, Kendall Hunt, Dubuque, IA

Wimmer R. D. & Dominick J. R., 1997, *Mass Media Research: An Introduction,* 5th edn, Wadsorth Publishing Company, Belmont, CA

4

Understanding Research

Methodology and Terminology

Mark Sheehan

AIMS OF THIS CHAPTER

- To examine the role of research in public relations campaigns

- To evaluate the different types of research methods and their use in campaigns

INTRODUCTION

Today's public relations function is underpinned clearly by research. In previous decades, many public relations practitioners responded to issues/situations by summoning up their 'gut feeling' and reaching into their bag of favoured tactical responses. But over time, management has sought more accountability and justification for decision-making based on the systematic examination of the relevant issues and target publics, supported by data and findings obtained using the principles and methodologies of social research.

Public relations theorists Cutlip, Center and Broom (2006, p. 285) observe that 'when the public relations aspect of organisational problems must be brought home ... the research-based approach is most effective'.

Research is used to understand various situations better, to test assumptions about a program's publics and to help anticipate public relations consequences for a program. It cannot answer all questions or clarify all issues, but it provides a firm basis from which to commence the planning process. Put simply, research is an attempt to reduce uncertainty and increase our understanding of a situation—because all research findings are, after all, simply estimations.

There is a variety of research activities that can be employed when preparing a public relations campaign. The type of research should vary depending on the situation or problem, resources and skills available, and the time in which action must be taken. This chapter will look at conducting pre-campaign research that:

- Defines the problem, issue or opportunity
- Determines the organisation's current position and where it wants to be
- Identifies the stakeholders and target audiences
- Contributes to the planning of what action to take.

This process can go by many names, such as background research, preliminary research etc.

In the next chapter you will read about evaluative research. Evaluative research in public relations campaigns involves measuring the results against the objectives of the campaign, tracking research during campaigns to ensure you are heading in the right direction, and undertaking post-campaign research that measures the success or otherwise of a campaign. This research judges the performance against the objectives you have made based on your pre-campaign research. So these two chapters are the two halves of the research implemented prior to and during a campaign.

The importance of these two roles can be gauged by examining planning acronyms used in public relations campaign management. As outlined in Chapter 3, there are a number of different models including ROPE (Hendrix 2000), RACE (Marston 1963),

ROSIE (Seitel 2006) and RAISE (Kendall 1997). These acronyms all feature a step-by-step planning method that covers:

1 Defining the problem or opportunity

2 Planning and programming

3 Taking action and communicating

4 Evaluating the program.

The common factors in all of these is research and evaluation—these are the beginning and end of every public relations activity. So we must first define our problem or opportunity by research.

Given the complexity of research in public relations, this chapter seeks only to give a summary of the application of social research methods in public relations. Those seeking a more in-depth examination of this area can refer to texts dedicated specifically to research. Authors such as Baxter and Babbie (2004), Wimmer and Dominick (2006) and Stacks (2002), for example, have covered research and its application to communication and public relations.

THE ROLE OF RESEARCH

Often public relations campaigns are constructed when a problem or opportunity arises, is perceived to exist, or has the potential to arise; for example someone makes a value judgment that something is wrong or could be wrong in the near future. Once such a judgment is made, the process becomes an objective, systematic research task designed to note:

• The dimensions of the problem

• The factors contributing to it

• The publics involved in or affected by the situation.

In essence, research is used to 'define the problem situation' and determine what is happening at that time. Inherent in this is an understanding of the publics both inside, and external to, the organisation in question. Undertaking research before planning is necessary to test the accuracy of assumptions about:

• Who the publics are

• What the publics know about the situation, or think they know

• How they feel about the situation (and their attitudes toward it)

• What information they see as important

• How they will use that information

• How they will receive that information.

A thorough study of the publics who are important in a program also serves to determine priorities. As public relations practitioners rarely have enough money to mount campaigns that will reach all publics, systematic research assists in determining who are the most important audiences to reach and who might have the greatest impact on the situation. Certain questions need to be answered, such as, 'Which publics are central to the problem?' By gaining an understanding of the answers to such questions, it follows that practitioners can then determine the most effective ways of delivering their messages.

PLANNING THE RESEARCH PROCESS

In planning the research process, the generally accepted approach is to begin with a clear statement of the problem or situation to be investigated. This can be phrased as a research question or a hypothetical statement. Basically, it is a tentative generalisation about the relationship between variables (measurable features of the unit of analysis). For example if a unit of analysis is a person, then their characteristics—such as age, height, weight and so on—will vary and that variation can be measured. A hypothesis might then be: 'As people age they get taller and heavier.' The next step in the process is to develop a research design. To do this, you will need to consider how best to collect the data necessary to answer your research question. The approach and methods used will depend on a combination of the extent of the problem, and the time and resources available.

Figure 4.1: Early identification of solution

METHODS OF RESEARCH

Once we have decided what needs to be researched, we need to ascertain the best methods to gather the data. Research methods can be categorised as quantitative/qualitative and primary/secondary. In describing these two categories, the practitioner will always be mindful of selecting what is appropriate and necessary for their particular campaign.

Primary research

Stated simply, primary research is when the researcher collects original data, while secondary research is when the researcher uses existing data, to examine an issue for example. It could be that this existing data has been gathered from a different perspective than that required by the researcher; accordingly allowances may have to be made in using secondary research.

Both quantitative (numerical) and qualitative (non-numerical) research can be referred to as primary research. A basic differentiation between the two is that while the former measurement tool is used for description and prediction, the latter provides understanding.

QUANTITATIVE RESEARCH

One of the most common forms of quantitative research in public relations is a survey using a set questionnaire with close-ended questions. The people selected to complete the survey will vary depending on the sampling strategy used by the researcher. A random sample means everyone in a target public (population) has an equal chance of being surveyed. This is called a probability sample. So if the chosen population are Australian public relations students, then the researcher would ensure that each student has the potential to be surveyed and not choose (for example) those from a specific state, or first-year students only.

At times it can be impossible to survey the entire population, due to time or resource constraints, so a sample is chosen. The validity of the results is contingent on the size of sample—predictability improves with the size of the sample. So 1000 is more reliable than 500 which is more reliable than 100. The larger the population, the larger the sample required. However once a certain number is reached, historical statistical analysis shows that the research accuracy will only improve minutely. For example voter intention polls published periodically in Australian newspapers will typically have a sample size of approximately 1500, while the population of voters is in the millions. Cameron et al. (2008, pp. 124–5) observe that, in a probability sample of 1500, 'a national poll sample of 1500 people provides a margin of error within 3 percentage points 95 percent of the time. In other words, 19 out of 20 times that the same questionnaire is administered, the results should be within the same 3 percentage points and reflect the whole population accurately'.

The following are methods by which quantitative surveys collect data:

- **Telephone surveys**

  Respondents are surveyed by phone based on a standard listing such as the *White Pages* entries in Australia. This method is not as favourable currently due to the unpopularity of telemarketing and the growth of unlisted and mobile phone users excluded from standard listings.

- **Mail questionnaires**

  A letter and survey is mailed to respondents.

- **Intercept surveys or face-to-face surveys**

  Researchers randomly interview respondents in, for example, shopping centres.

- **Piggyback or omnibus surveys**

  An organisation buys a series of questions in a larger survey undertaken by a national survey or research company, such as Quantum, Newspoll or Roy Morgan.

- **Online surveys**

  Web and email surveys are the most recent way to reach respondents and have the advantage of immediate response, however controlling the sample can be difficult given the almost universal access of the web. Those who do not fit into the population surveyed may also respond.

All forms of data collection have certain advantages and disadvantages. It is worth examining the most widely used methods for their strengths and weaknesses.

Mailed or internet-based

The advantages of mailed or internet-based surveys include greater assurance of anonymity for the respondent and minimal interviewer bias (although even so, bias may appear in the actual survey questions). Another advantage is that there is greater access to respondents living or working in isolated areas or in geographic regions outside the researcher's location. In addition, telephone and face-to-face methods are more expensive than mailed or internet-based ones. However, the response rate to mailed or internet-based surveys is normally low, which could lead to a skewed and unrepresentative sample, and there is no guarantee that the answers have been completed by the targeted respondent.

In person or over the phone

Advantages of researcher-administered surveys are that there is increased influence on the sample, as there is greater flexibility in dealing with respondents personally and more control over the conditions under which the questions are answered. The research process can be quickly implemented and ensures a larger response rate. A face-to-face interview also provides an opportunity to observe and record some non-verbal reactions to the questions.

As with all survey methods, there are disadvantages here too. Respondents are not anonymous, there may be difficulty in contacting selected individuals, and there is more chance of the interviewer's own biases being expressed in the course of the interview process. In addition, respondents may say what they think the interviewer wants to hear, rather than what they really think—a fault that can also occur in mailed and internet-based surveys.

SURVEY PREPARATION

In preparing a questionnaire for either self- or interviewer-administered survey interviews, it is imperative that a decision is made at the outset to determine what type of reaction you anticipate. For instance, do you want a spontaneous statement, or an answer that has been deliberated upon?

The questions you pose will dictate the answers you are given. Researchers identify two types of questions—close-ended and open-ended:

- An open-ended question is where the respondent supplies their own answer, written or verbal, for example: 'What is the major issue facing Australians today?'

- A close-ended question asks respondents to choose an answer from those presented by the interviewer.

Babbie (1999, p. 127) notes that close-ended questions are popular because 'they provide a greater uniformity of responses and are more easily processed than open-ended responses, which must be coded before they can be processed'.

Be mindful, however, that close-ended questions are often not broad enough to elicit a meaningful range of responses, and be wary of making assumptions about the ability of the respondents to understand and adequately answer the questions.

Generally, open-ended questions collect qualitative data while close-ended questions collect quantitative data.

QUALITATIVE RESEARCH

While the results for quantitative research can be expressed in numbers, qualitative research mostly relies on non-numerical elements such as words, visuals, behaviour etc to deliver its results. This type of research will assist in understanding—in some detail—the opinion and attitudes of a chosen target public.

Focus groups

A focus group usually meets in a conference room setting and consists of a small group of eight to ten individuals drawn from the target public. A skilful facilitator will conduct the session using open-ended questions, keeping the group 'focused', and ensuring that participants contribute and that the topic under discussion receives as many opinions as possible in the hour or two available. One technique is to show the group a video as stimulus material to get the discussion started.

This method is widely used and favoured for returning results quickly and cheaply. Bobbitt and Sullivan (2005) note that, among other focus group objectives, public relations departments use this research to measure public perception and employee morale, and to evaluate publications. Wilcox et al. (2007) note the potential of conducting focus groups online and web-casting focus groups to clients where 'the focus groups files remained available for review via password on the Web'. This development has meant that 'time and location are becoming less relevant to conducting focus groups' (Wilcox et al. 2007, pp. 137–8).

However, as Harrison (2003, p. 141) warns, 'practitioners need to be mindful that ... results can't be extrapolated as representing the views of the total population in question'.

Media content analysis

Media content analysis can be an effective method of analysing a company's image, as presented in the media. Most organisations monitor what is being said, printed or televised about them, as well as issues of importance to them or their industry in general. A media monitoring service can collect relevant copies of newspaper articles and transcripts of electronic media coverage, and so provides an insight into what is on the public agenda. However this is simply data collection. Without some form of analysis, it gives little indication of readership or impact.

It has been argued that content analysis can be applied using quantitative and qualitative methods. Quantitative content analysis provides figures on the total audience reached and percentages about what is being published or broadcast in various types of media on various topics. If, however, we wish to know whether those comments are positive or negative, then the research needs to involve qualitative analysis.

Reflecting on media content analysis as a quantitative method, Newsom et al. (2007, p. 78) state that public relations content analysis is usually concerned 'with the time or space given to an organisation and its spokespersons. In broadcasting, the concern is whether the spokesperson does the talking, the announcer describes the situation, or the two work in combination.'

This method tells the researcher what has been said or written about the organisation, mainly in the mass media. It informs the researcher on the type of information to which target publics are being exposed.

Today, sophisticated full-text newspaper databases allow keyword searches on particular topics and themes. Software tools such as Leximancer are available to analyse material and gain a fuller understanding of the chosen text.

However, Newbold et al. (2002, p. 84) note that quantitative content analysis 'has not been able to capture the context within which a media text becomes meaningful', and advocate attention to qualitative approaches as well. Qualitative content analysis draws on text analysis, discourse analysis, narratology and semiotics to identify the tone, key messages and likely impact of media coverage (Macnamara 2005).

Secondary research

This method of research goes by many names—library research, desk research, informal research etc. It has the advantages of being quick and relatively inexpensive to conduct. The often-made claim—that public relations research is a 'gut' response and not a scientific appraisal of the situation and stakeholders—could stem from some of the informal research methods employed by public relations practitioners.

An examination of a specific category of the Public Relations Institute of Australia (PRIA) Golden Target Awards for 2007 revealed that informal methods were twice as likely to be used as quantitative methods. A combination of qualitative and informal was the most commonly used form of research.

Austin and Pinkelton (2006) list fourteen informal research methods, including personal contacts, professional contacts, advisory committees or boards, field reports, community forums, telephone calls, mail and email, library research, internet research, clip files and media tracking, real-time responses to media messages and survey questions, and in-depth interviews. The following are some of the more common methods used in campaign research.

DESK RESEARCH/LIBRARY RESEARCH/ HISTORICAL RESEARCH

This is often the first form of research undertaken when exploring the situation faced by an organisation, and provides a quick response to an issue at hand. It is a way of obtaining information from internal records and published sources such as official statistics (in other words, information that can be read at the desk). Many large organisations, government departments, and professional and industry associations maintain libraries that carry information pertaining to their particular area. Libraries will, for instance, supply company reports, brochures and directories, all of which provide published information on an organisation. A profile can then be extended by seeking further printed information about a company's contribution to an industry. Annual reports, for example, list sponsors.

Organisational files and archive websites can also provide the type of information needed at this stage of preliminary research.

PROFESSIONAL CONTACTS, EXPERTS AND OPINION LEADERS

This form of in-depth interview involves selecting someone who is trusted to gather the data and/or who is knowledgeable about the subject area. The basis for selecting key informants is their understanding of an issue, as well as their ability to represent other people's views on a subject. Austin and Pinkleton (2006) include in this list members of state and local government, newspaper editors and reporters, leaders of special interest groups, teachers and educational leaders, leaders of community groups, union leaders and trade association managers. As this will often be a one-on-one exchange, it could also be termed an in-depth semi-structured interview between the public relations practitioner and their contact.

ADVISORY COMMITTEES AND BOARDS

This type of research is recommended in cases where long-term strategies are to be evaluated. Rather than a one-off group session, ongoing committees can provide advice that is updated on a regular basis. However it is important to remember that the objectivity of such a group might be compromised by knowing too much about the history of an issue or about the wider situation. Cutlip et al. (2006, p. 296) advise that such boards 'provide valuable information and guidance, but they cannot substitute for formal approaches to determining the distribution of opinions and reactions among target publics'.

CALL-IN LINES/MAIL ANALYSIS

Both of these methods are practical for in-house practitioners wishing to analyse how publics view an organisation and its operations. Organisations that have monitored their mail or phone calls (through 1800 or 1300 telephone numbers) will be able to provide statistics and information about problems or about how their publics feel about other areas. For single programs, some market analysis might be used. For example organisations can measure the impact of a program by building into it a component whereby the target publics are requested to respond to certain messages. Organisations that arrange advertising for a particular product might ask that interested parties phone to place an order or to gain more information about that product.

FIELD REPORTS

Sales representatives or field agents who visit customers and clients are often valid sources of information who can provide an objective analysis of the views that a public holds about an organisation. These representatives may be pleased to discuss their observations and provide feedback to the organisation. Like other informal research methods, they act as radars in detecting early warnings or situations that require further investigation; but, as with advisory committees and boards, they are not a substitute to the breadth of target public opinions.

ONLINE SOURCES

Public relations professionals monitor what is being said about their organisations online. Rumours on the internet have the potential to influence industrial action, attract regulatory attention, and increase or decrease not only share prices but product sales. Various search engines can be used for detecting what is being said on the internet; however they cannot produce profiles of public opinion.

Importantly, public relations professionals should remember that monitoring online sources can help them tap into the rapidly expanding channels of interactive communication and to intervene in virtual conversations.

Organised activist sites such as <mcspotlight.com> are constantly representing alternative views on the activities of organisations, which can damage reputation and influence target publics. To a lesser extent, blogs (web-logs—online diaries maintained by individuals recording their daily activities and opinions) can confer prominence or notoriety on an organisation.

SECONDARY ANALYSIS AND ONLINE DATABASES

It is not always feasible to collect data first-hand and therefore secondary analysis is helpful. Basically, this is data already collected by an outside source such as the Australian Bureau of Statistics, Statistics New Zealand, Roy Morgan Polls or market researchers. The media regularly conduct and report survey results that can be used by the public relations practitioner. Public relations and communication journals also publish research findings.

One of the most popular approaches to information gathering is through online databases. Public relations professionals use a variety of online databases to access and search through news and technical publications, business information services, market research, government records and broadcast transcripts (e.g. the ABC's Radio National provides transcripts and downloads of many of its programs).

CONCLUSION

It is not appropriate for public relations practitioners to rely on gut feelings when implementing strategy. Research is the most powerful tool in the public relations practitioner's armoury. It gives credibility to public relations strategy and means that the public relations advice is based soundly in objectively sought opinions. Research allows the public relations practitioner to come to the board table with a contribution to strategy and planning as relevant and measurable as that of finance or operations. In the campaign case studies in this book you will see that we have focused on the research undertaken by organisations and public relations consultancies to provide information and measure the success of their campaigns.

Apart from providing credibility to public relations strategies and knowing how to collect research information, it is vitally important that public relations practitioners know what to do with the research they collect. The foundation of a twenty-first-century public relations campaign's success is dependent on implementing strategies identified using systematic research findings.

REFERENCES

Austin E. & Pinkleton B., 2006, *Strategic Public Relations Management—Planning and Managing Effective Communication Programs*, 2nd edn, LEA, Mahwah, NJ

Babbie E., 1999, *The Basics of Social Research*, Wadsworth, Belmont, CA

Baxter L. & Babbie E., 2004, *The Basics of Communication Research*, Wadsworth Thomson, Belmont, CA

Bobbit R. & Sullivan R., 2005, *Developing the Public Relations Campaign—A Team Based Approach, Pearson*, Boston, MA

Cameron G., Wilcox D., Reber B. & Shin J.-W., 2008, *Public Relations Today—Managing Competition and Conflict*, Pearson, Boston, MA

Cutlip S., Center A. & Broom G., 2006, *Effective Public Relations*, 9th edn, Pearson, Upper Saddle River, NJ

Harrison K., 2003, *Strategic Public Relations*, 3rd edn, Century Ventures, Perth

Heath R. L., 1997, *Strategic Issues Management—Organizations and Public Policy Challenges*, Sage, Thousand Oaks

Kendall R., 1996, *Public Relations Campaign Strategies Planning for Implementation*, 2nd edn, Longman, NY

Lerbinger O., 1988, 'Corporate Uses of Research in Public Relations' in Hiebert R. (ed.), *Precision Public Relations*, Longman, NY

Macnamara J., 2005, 'Media Content Analysis: Its Uses, Benefits and Best Practice Methodology' in *Asia Pacific Public Relations Journal*, Vol. 6, No. 1, pp. 1–34

Newbold C., Boyd-Barrett O. & Van Den Bulck H., 2002, *The Media Book*, Arnold (Hodder Headline), London

Newsom D., Turk J. & Kruckeberg D., 2007, *This is PR—The Realities of Public Relations*, 9th edn, Thomson, Belmont, CA

Seitel F., 2007, *The Practice of Public Relations*, 10th edn, Pearson, Upper Saddle River, NJ

Smith R., 2005, *Strategic Planning for Public Relations*, 2nd edn, LEA, Mahwah, NJ

Stacks D., 2002, *Primer of Public Relations Research*, Guildford Press, NY

Wilcox D., Cameron G., Ault P. & Agee W., 2007, *Public Relations—Strategies and Tactics*, 8th edn, Pearson, Boston, MA

Wimmer R. & Dominick J., 2006, *Mass Media Research: An Introduction*, 8th edn, Thomson Wadsworth, Belmont, CA

Zikmund W. G., 2003, *Exploring Marketing Research*, 8th edn, Thomson Southwestern, Mason, OH

5 Campaign Evaluation

Deirdre Quinn-Allan

AIMS OF THIS CHAPTER

- To situate the role of evaluation within the public relations campaign and examine approaches to evaluation

- To identify common barriers to campaign evaluation and consider how these can be addressed

INTRODUCTION

Public relations campaign evaluation provides practitioners with the data and information they need to demonstrate the value of their work to management or their clients. Without evaluation they can only guess whether the campaign is on track, that the campaign budget is being well spent and resources used wisely, and—when the campaign is over—that the campaign achieved its objectives.

Research into evaluation practice and attitudes during the 1980s, 1990s and early part of the twenty-first century clearly highlights that few practitioners and academics believe evaluation is not important. Evaluation is a quality control and campaign-tracking mechanism, and provides lessons for future campaigns. Although evaluation of public relations campaigns can be problematic and uncertain, evaluation problems must be resolved if public relations is to be taken seriously and have a role to play in strategic management.

This chapter presents an overview of the evaluation process, and offers starting points and considerations for developing a systematic approach to evaluation. The chapter concludes with a discussion of some common barriers to evaluation that must be acknowledged and addressed, because it is clearly too easy for evaluation tasks to be ignored.

EVALUATION—WHAT IS IT?

The distinction between evaluation and research can be confusing. The problem is compounded by the way practitioners and academics use these terms (often interchangeably). In this chapter, research is treated as a function that has multiple uses (Lattimore et al. 2007, p. 152), and the particular use that concerns us is for the evaluation of public relations campaigns.

It is important to understand that evaluation is a process involving research, measurement and analysis—it is not a single task. The goal of evaluation is to be able to measure the efficiency and effectiveness of public relations efforts in achieving campaign objectives. Thus evaluation relies on research to help answer questions about whether a campaign is headed in the right direction, or to identify when objectives have been met— but research is not in and of itself evaluation.

Planning and evaluation

Evaluation is an integral part of the planning process; this is expressed clearly by Hon (1998, p. 106) when she says the 'systemization of public relations planning is a necessary precursor to meaningful public relations evaluation'. Evaluation points, tasks and process need to be interwoven into planning and planning decisions.

The previous chapter presented various planning models, all of which place evaluation at the end of their acronyms. Close analysis of these models would not suggest that evaluation is a final end stage in campaign planning; but the linear placement of evaluation at the end can lead to confusion for students who may believe evaluation is something that happens when a campaign concludes, to determine if the campaign objectives were met (summative evaluation).

While summative evaluation is clearly important, it is only half the story. Formative evaluation also needs to be part of a systematic evaluation process. Formative evaluation is best thought of as ongoing monitoring and control throughout a campaign to ensure the campaign will achieve the planned objectives.

To make the distinction between formative and summative evaluation clear, consider Ahmed who has to travel to an unfamiliar city for a business meeting. Ahmed's objectives for the trip are to arrive safely at a predetermined but unfamiliar destination at a specific time.

Formative evaluation takes place throughout his journey. Ahmed will monitor factors such as road conditions, his engine's performance and fuel consumption, road signs and elapsed time to make sure he is making satisfactory progress towards the destination. Throughout this process Ahmed will assess his situation and make any necessary changes or course corrections along the way to overcome problems encountered. For example a traffic accident may block his planned route. Ahmed will need to decide, given the time constraints, whether to risk waiting for the road to clear, or to change course and take a different route. If Ahmed does not have a map, he might realise he now needs to telephone someone to seek advice on the best alternative route. He might also find he needs to inform those waiting for him at the other end that he will be late.

Summative evaluation, on the other hand, will take place when Ahmed's trip is over. At this point he will consider whether or not he arrived safely, on time and at the correct destination. And in evaluating his trip and its conclusion Ahmed will (hopefully) be better prepared the next time he makes a car journey—by taking a map with him, working out an alternative route in case of roadblocks, allowing more time for the trip and so on.

It is important to remember that both formative and summative evaluations provide useful input into future campaigns so that we can improve our performance, reduce uncertainty and increase the likelihood of campaign success.

A framework for evaluation: inputs, outputs and outcomes

Of course a car trip is not a public relations campaign and is much more easily evaluated. Jim Macnamara's (2006, p. 19) pyramid model of public relations research is a useful model for presenting a simple but clear conception of the process and levels of evaluation. His model provides evaluation points at three levels: inputs, outputs and outcomes. As one moves through these levels, the complexity and costs associated with evaluation increase. However this does not mean that evaluation at the lower levels is any less important. Related to this point, Macnamara (2006, p. 17) argues that 'more research should be done at the beginning and in the early stages of communication than at the end'. Evaluation of input and output decisions and performance provides vital information to help track progress towards the campaign goals and objectives (outcomes), and allows for correction before costly mistakes are made.

So what are the campaign inputs, outputs and outcomes in Macnamara's model and how do we evaluate them?

INPUTS

Inputs occur at the first level of Macnamara's (2006, p. 17) pyramid model, which he describes as 'the strategic and physical components of communication programs or projects'. Essentially, inputs are the decisions and choices made about medium, content and format.

The *medium* refers to the mix of communication channels selected for the campaign, which can be personal or non-personal channels:

- *Personal channels* are those channels that deliver communication in a face-to-face context. Delivering a speech, telephoning a journalist and conducting a meeting are all examples of personal communication.

- *Non-personal channels* include channels that do not rely on face-to-face interpersonal communication between an organisation and its target audiences. For example television, radio, the internet and mobile devices are all examples of non-personal communication channels.

The *content* is the arrangement of elements—such as text, images and the spoken word—that are used to deliver the message. It should be noted that content is therefore a function of medium and format. For example one cannot deliver an image to a journalist via a phone conversation; so if an image is a key element of the message, then an alternative or supplementary channel is needed, such as email.

The *format* refers to the presentation of content, not the channel used. For example a brochure can be delivered to an audience in print form or made available electronically via email or the organisation's website. Email and the website are channels; however the brochure could be made available for download in a PDF or a MS Word document: these are formats. Likewise a speech can be delivered in person to an audience or made available for download from a website as a podcast.

Evaluation at the input stage should answer questions about the relevance and suitability of selected media, content and formats for the target audience. Understanding the intended audience is crucial to the effective evaluation of inputs, to avoid mistakes

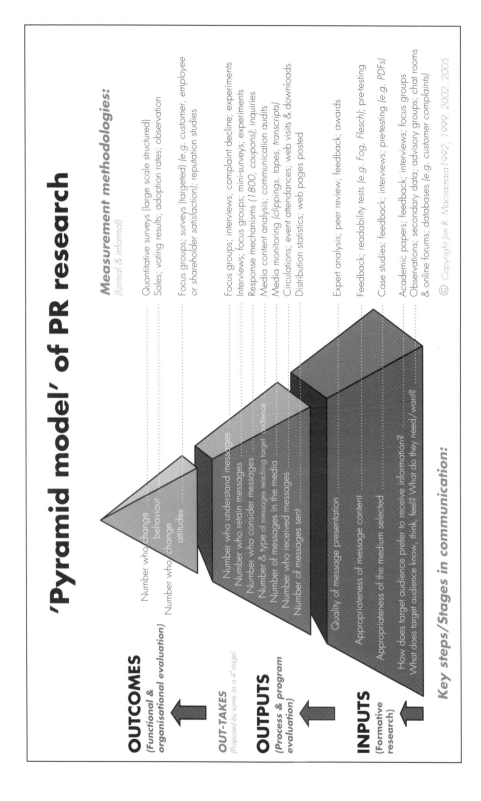

Figure 5.1: Pyramid model of public relations research

being made. Let us use a media release as an example. When deciding what content to include in a media release, you first need to know what the journalists you are targeting regard as newsworthy; you may believe your key messages are interesting and important, but these may not be relevant to your chosen journalists' rounds.

Research undertaken at this point can include both qualitative and quantitative methodologies, as well as secondary research. Evaluation from previous campaigns should also be integrated into input decisions.

OUTPUTS

Outputs occur at the second level of the pyramid model and are the end products of the input stage targeted at an audience. Outputs are the visible artefacts and events produced that make up the public relations campaign, and include tactics like websites, advertisements, publicity, brochures, media kits, newsletters, roadshows, lobbying and so on.

At face value, outputs might appear to be easy to evaluate. Take a brochure designed to inform the target audience about a new service being offered. We might be able to say the brochure looks good and has been designed well, with key messages clearly articulated and properly positioned for impact and comprehension. There might be a call to action, such that the audience is asked to seek more information or advice from the sponsoring organisation. These are all important, but output evaluation must be more comprehensive and be able to answer questions such as:

- *Have we defined the target audience correctly?* Diagnosing communication problems can be difficult and new data may suggest that the targeted audience is not actually the most important—or indeed the correct—audience. Both qualitative and quantitative research methods can be employed here.

- *Are we communicating with the target audience through appropriate channels?* In the period before the declaration of the 2007 Australian Federal Election, the Australian Prime Minister, John Howard, was criticised for his attempts to reach a Generation Y audience of voters through YouTube. At the time of writing, his video clip had received a two-star rating (out of a possible five stars), with 5423 views, indicating the audience did not rate the clip highly. By contrast, a spoof clip titled 'John Howard—Search for a Scapegoat Ep. 1' had 16,572 views and earned a more favourable four-star rating. Howard's clip was not consistent with the personality of the channel or indeed the entertainment values shared by many YouTube users.

- *Are we achieving the required level of reach and frequency, given our objectives and resources?*
    - *Reach* is a measure that refers to the percentage of the target audience exposed to a message at least once in a defined period of time (normally a four-week period).

♦ *Frequency* measures the number of times the target audience sees a message in a defined period (again this period is normally four weeks). Put simply, before a campaign can deliver communication effects such as awareness or comprehension and have an impact on outcomes like attitude or behaviour, the intended audience must see, hear or experience the intended message often enough for the message to have an effect.

Measuring reach and frequency will depend on the media channel used. Measuring the reach for a billboard is far more problematic, for example, than measuring the reach for a national magazine with audited circulation (the number of people who buy or subscribe to a magazine). In the case of the billboard, how can we measure the percentage of the target audience who have driven by the billboard, let alone seen or noticed the key message on it (reach)? How do we know how many times the audience has seen the billboard (frequency)? Given the campaign budget we may not be able to measure this accurately—and the true value of this tactic may only be inferred through the measurement of campaign outcomes.

Even though some media channels are difficult to measure, they still need to be evaluated. If we cannot find a way to measure or account for the contribution the billboard makes to the overall communication effect, then how can we justify its inclusion?

• *Are the key messages being received and understood as we intended?* Messages evaluated at the input stage are likely to have been tested using qualitative techniques, like focus groups. You will remember from the previous chapter that qualitative research results cannot be generalised to the population from which the sample is drawn. Focus group testing may suggest key messages are sound when in fact they are not. Ongoing monitoring needs to be done to ensure message recall, comprehension and acceptance. Research methods that you encountered in the previous chapter can be employed to answer these questions—methods like focus groups, surveys, the nature of calls to 1800 numbers, media content analysis, the numbers in attendance at roadshows and events, and so on. Your choice of methodology will be guided by what you need to know:

♦ If having accurate numbers is important, then quantitative methodologies are appropriate.

♦ If you want to know what the audience is thinking or feeling in response to outputs, then qualitative methods may be the better option.

♦ You may consider a mix of both qualitative and quantitative research is best where you need hard numbers, but also need to gauge sentiment and attitudes beyond the simple yes/no, or limited option responses such as those allowed for in Likert scales.

- *Have we selected the correct mix of media and tactics?* In today's fragmented media landscape, adopting a mass communication approach is becoming very difficult to manage and coordinate successfully. Segmentation of target publics and audiences should include an analysis of media consumption habits along with other relevant segmentation variables. It is likely that public relations tactics will need to be developed for delivery through multiple and complementary channels, including face-to-face where necessary. Both formal and informal research methods are relevant and secondary research will also be useful.

- *Are key messages being lost or distorted?* Negative publicity or publicity obtained in media not read, seen or heard by the target audience will not serve campaign objectives. Referring back to the Howard example above, we can see that Howard's key message on climate change and the Coalition's policy response was lost in the publicity that surrounded the clip's airing. Howard's video clip and use of YouTube became the message. So in the short term, we can say the key message was lost.

The above list is not exhaustive, and evaluation questions and research need to be tailored to the specific nature of the campaign, its objectives and the tactics employed. Answers must also be analysed in the context of responses to other evaluation questions. For example quantifying reach and frequency is useful, but unless you can prove that the reach and frequency figures pertain to your target audience (that is, the right one), they are just figures.

The sort of evaluation methods commonly used to evaluate outputs include activities such as media monitoring, media content analysis, readership and circulation statistics, and audience surveys, enquiries and feedback. However organisations routinely collect a wide range of data and information that can be used too, for example calls to customer complaint numbers or requests for more information. You should use and employ the methodologies that are appropriate and realistic, given resource constraints.

An important caution in relation to evaluating output is to avoid simplistic or unethical measurements. For example simply measuring column inches of publicity gained is neither a useful nor a valid measurement. Column inches do not tell us whether the target audience has read the publicity. This measure does not tell us whether the publicity was negative, positive or neutral. Nor does it shed light on whether the key messages were delivered intact or distorted in some way. Consider using column inches to answer some of the questions posed above, and you will see how ineffective a measure this is.

OUTCOMES

At the third level, Macnamara proposes that outcomes need to be evaluated. A campaign is designed to change a target audience in some way—most often, campaigns will seek to change behaviour or attitudes through communication. So at this level of evaluation, the campaign's communication effects will be judged against campaign objectives.

Communication effects manifest in awareness, comprehension, attitudes (development or change) and behaviour. Non-behavioural communication effects are not always easily observed. So measuring change in awareness, attitudes and comprehension with any certainty can really only be achieved through survey research methodologies that use probability sampling, or by conducting a census if the audience (sample frame) is small enough.

That caution aside, Macnamara's model allows for observation with the proviso of 'sometimes'. Behaviours can be observed, but the underlying reasons behind behaviours are not always obvious, or are masked. As Zikmund (2003, p. 61) points out: 'things of interest, such as attitudes, opinions, motivations, and other intangible states of mind, simply cannot be observed'. For example Juanita may choose to join her friends at the local fast food outlet while still holding negative attitudes towards that outlet and fast food in general. In such a situation, she ignores her negative attitudes because she is motivated to pursue her friendships and enjoy a social outing. However, in another situation Juanita may be very vocal in sharing her negative views on the subjects of fast food and the outlet. Observed behaviour must be used as a measure with caution.

CLOSED-SYSTEM AND OPEN-SYSTEM EVALUATION

Mark McElreath (cited in Lattimore et al. 2007, p. 161) proposed two evaluation approaches: open- and closed-system evaluation. A closed system is characterised by a short-term focus and effectively ignores internal and external factors beyond the control of campaign planners, but which may have had an impact on the achievement of campaign objectives. Lattimore et al. (2007, p. 161) say closed-system evaluation is the most commonly used approach, with the focus being on the pre- and post-test of key messages.

However, public relations does not occur in a vacuum, and simply integrating closed-system evaluations into a campaign will fail to account for factors other than public relations activities that influence campaign objectives. For example the organisation's marketing tactics may have a significant bearing on target public attitudes and behaviours.

Consider the organisation pursuing a profit-maximisation objective. The organisation's marketing mix will be tailored to achieve this strategy. In Australia, over the last decade or so, banks have demonstrated this type of behaviour, and rural and regional communities have witnessed the closure and loss of branches in their communities. Banks are the lifeblood of these communities—not just for personal customers, but also for local businesses and farmers. Businesses need to be able to bank the day's takings and ensure they have a constant supply of change in the float. Farmers want to be able to establish and maintain relationships with personal bankers who are familiar with the local farming conditions. And while banks have tried to provide alternative avenues for their customers to do business with them via online banking, the net effect has been the erosion of customer loyalty in the wake of reduced service from the banks.

In this scenario you can imagine the challenge for the public relations staff. Using an open system of evaluation provides public relations practitioners with an opportunity to identify and respond to factors beyond their control, as well being able to demonstrate the scope or limitations of the public relations impact. And so an open-system evaluation perspective is vitally important if public relations is to be able to argue the case for inclusion into strategic planning and decision-making.

Measurement by objectives

Evaluation needs a benchmark, a point of reference by which to assess performance for variance from the goal or goal attainment. Poorly stated or vague objectives are one of the most common problems the practitioner is faced with when setting about the business of evaluation. Such objectives cannot be evaluated. Furthermore the language used in objectives can be utter nonsense. How does one evaluate 'buzz', for example, and indeed what communication outcome does 'buzz' represent?

Wilcox and Cameron (2006, p. 158) also make the point that objectives must document 'ends' not 'means'. This is a common point of confusion for students (and some practitioners too), when inputs and outputs are presented as campaign objectives. For example to raise awareness is an 'end'; to distribute 5000 brochures is one tactic ('means') that can be used to support that end.

The SMART acronym of objective setting is well known and widely used by public relations educators, and with good reason. SMART provides a simple framework that can be used as a checklist for evaluating the quality and structure of an objective. The reader is very likely to be familiar with the acronym which, broken down into its constituent parts, is:

- Specific goal

- Measurable

- Achievable

- Realistic

- Time bound.

Why then do so many practitioners persist in ignoring this simple approach when setting objectives? It is not uncommon to see objectives that fail to quantify the goal, indicate the level of change expected or even specify the timeframe. These errors make it nearly impossible to determine if goals are achievable or realistic. Omitting a timeframe from an objective is dangerous—and potentially means measurement can be put off until whenever. 'Whenever' may be too late for evaluation to be useful.

Perhaps the answer lies in a lack of a systematic approach to objective setting. Lattimore et al. (2007, p. 157) identify five steps in the measurement by objectives process that can be employed. These are:

1 **Work group involvement**

Objectives are set and agreed on by the group after taking into account each group member's position and role. The dynamics and synergies of teamwork also come into play, capitalising on individual experience and expertise.

2 **Manager–subordinate involvement**

The manager assists the subordinate to develop a set of goals, which become personal objectives for that person. The advantage of this approach is that personal objectives are commensurate with skill and experience, as well as the individual's role in the campaign. So if a subordinate fulfils a technician role, then they are not being given responsibility for management and outcome objectives.

3 **Determination of intermediate objectives**

Intermediate objectives are lower-order objectives that support the overall campaign objectives. They are like 'building blocks' or milestones—they state some interim goal that must be achieved before a campaign can move closer to the end goal. So in this sense, they serve an important monitor and control function, alerting campaign staff to problems while there is still time for corrective action to be taken.

To illustrate, consider a not-for-profit organisation that has received government funding to provide a service to their community. In this scenario, one of the campaign objectives might be to build awareness within the community about the service provided. Intermediate objectives might be: to distribute 5000 brochures to letterboxes in the community; to obtain pre-launch publicity in the local press; to run an open day for the community and so on. In a sense, such intermediate objectives can be thought of as the outputs. However the point is, without these short-term tactical objectives, the campaign's awareness objective cannot be achieved.

4 **Determination of measures of achievement**

This is the point at which the SMART principles must be applied.

5 Review, evaluation and recycling

This step recognises that evaluation is a circular process and that prior lessons learnt should be fed into current planning in a virtual cycle of improvement. Lattimore et al. (2007, p. 157) point out that objectives may be neither perfect nor precise with 'absolute' certainty. In the previous chapter on research, the point was made that reducing uncertainty lies at the heart of research and evaluation in an effort to improve decision-making. Objectives are a form of decision-making, and they can only be improved through the systematic review and evaluation of past objectives.

Barriers to evaluation

Because of the problems associated with evaluation practices, our discussion would not be complete without a closer look at some of the barriers to evaluation. This final section looks at some of the common reasons cited for omitting evaluation from the campaign planning process. By recognising and acknowledging these barriers, the practitioner is better placed to develop strategies for dealing with them.

THE COST OF EVALUATING

You cannot afford not to evaluate, or so it is often claimed. Well if this is true, why do cost and budget restrictions continue to be cited as one of the leading reasons for clients or practitioners not evaluating their public relations activities? Certainly, expenditure on evaluation represents an opportunity cost—money spent on evaluation is money not spent on tactics and implementation. But such reasoning represents unsound logic—money spent on misdirected tactics or strategy that will ultimately fail is money wasted, because nothing is achieved; and in addition there is potential for actual harm if the implementation has the opposite or some other negative impact on the audience.

Some research methods underpinning evaluation can be expensive. Obviously the size of the overall campaign budget will moderate the scope and type of evaluation undertaken, but small or limited budgets are not justification for avoiding evaluation as being too expensive. Even campaigns with limited budgets can still build evaluation into the process—they will simply need to decide what evaluation techniques are affordable and feasible given financial constraints.

Another challenge is deciding what percentage of the overall campaign budget needs to be earmarked for evaluation. Academic and practitioner literature is vague on this score. Rockland and Puckett (2006), from public relations firm Ketchum, suggest 'spending about 4 to 7 per cent of the program budget [on evaluation] is typical'. However various studies in Western countries reviewed by Watson and Noble (2005) in their book *Evaluating Public Relations* suggest that anywhere between 0 and 5 per cent may be typical.

TABLE 5.1: THE COST OF EVALUATION

CAMPAIGN BUDGET ($)	EVALUATION AS A PERCENTAGE OF CAMPAIGN BUDGET ($)			
	2%	4%	5%	7%
10,000	200	400	500	700
50,000	1,000	2,000	2,500	3,500
100,000	2,000	4,000	5,000	7,000
500,000	10,000	20,000	25,000	35,000

The table above clearly demonstrates that the amount of money available for evaluation is a function of the size of the overall campaign budget. As a generalisation, using a rule-of-thumb percentage, campaigns with a budget under $100,000 will have limited funds available for evaluation, which presents real limitations in relation to the type of formal evaluative research that can be undertaken. However, this simply means that campaign managers and planners need to be clever (although this is actually true for any size of budget).

One of the problems of thinking too narrowly about budget is that it is easy to overlook other data routinely collected by organisations, or accounted for in marketing or other budget centres within an organisation. For example what market research has the firm conducted recently? Rockland and Puckett (2006) point out that: 'Most organizations usually have some type of measurement program evaluation in place (e.g., many brands routinely conduct awareness, attitude and usage studies).' Find out if such data exists and use it.

ORGANISATIONAL AND MANAGEMENT SUPPORT

While practitioners may voice support for evaluation, it can in fact often be overlooked. The likelihood of this happening increases if there is little top-down support for, or recognition of, the importance of evaluation. Within organisations, commitment to and respect for evaluation must start at the top—if senior managers treat evaluation as an afterthought, then staff under them will take their cue from the senior managers and 'gloss over' the role and application of evaluation. Integrating measurement by objects (MBO) into the campaign-planning process would help to encourage support from senior managers.

The situation is slightly different in the client–agency relationship. In such a relationship the agency may need to act as both advocate for evaluation and educator, in cases where the client demonstrates minimal or confused understanding of evaluation. In such circumstances agencies may find themselves facing an ethical dilemma too. What if the client does not want to pay for evaluation, or perhaps thinks evaluation of outputs is all that is required? If the client only wants to measure the level of publicity gained, should the agency provide this level of evaluation only? The answer is clearly no—evaluation would not be complete. The evaluation process needs to be completed by measuring and evaluating the overall campaign objectives, not just input and output objectives.

TECHNICIAN OR STRATEGIC FOCUS

The level of importance given to evaluation is dependent on the scope of the practitioner's role—technician or manager (Hon 1998, Macnamara 1997, Watson & Noble 2005):

- The public relations technician uses input to produce output, but may not have direct responsibility for outcomes.

- The public relations manager, on the other hand, is accountable for quality outcomes.

This has important implications for students—particularly at undergraduate level—who will start their career in a 'technician' capacity. In a technician role, new graduates may consider evaluation from a narrow personal perspective, rather than in terms of the overall campaign. Perhaps they may evaluate their ability to complete a task on time, rather than seeing the broader impact of their work. But if, as part of an MBO process, those in a technician role are assigned personal objectives designed to support campaign objectives, and are helped to understand how their role impacts on the successful campaign, then this focus ceases to be problematic.

TIME

A common reason given for the failure to attend to evaluation is that there was not enough time. Citing lack of time really suggests a lack of commitment to evaluation. A sound and scientific planning process should result in a clearly documented evaluation plan. This means articulating what is to be measured beyond campaign objectives, and declaring evaluation points, tasks and methodology within the formal campaign plan at the outset. And, most importantly, authority and responsibility for the evaluation process needs to be stated. In other words: Who takes ownership and drives the evaluation process? Simply documenting evaluation process and tasks without assigning responsibility is asking to have them ignored. Refer back to the section on MBO to see how this can be avoided.

Time can be a challenging factor when considering the role of public relations staff within public and private sector organisations. A United Kingdom study by the Department of Trade and Industry and the Institute of Public Relations (2003, p. 73) found that some public relations staff have other communication functions, which can take their attention away from their public relations roles. The report stated: 'This reinforces a common theme throughout the study that in many organisations PR is a part-time responsibility competing for time with other organisational roles.' In this situation support from senior managers is vital, as is a clearly articulated and documented evaluation plan.

UNDERSTANDING RESEARCH METHODOLOGY

Lack of understanding of scientific research methodologies has been cited as a significant factor underpinning poor evaluation practices. Although practitioners may believe evaluation is important, unless they are familiar with the language of research and research methods that underpin evaluation, then evaluation will continue to be regarded as a task that is difficult and ends up being avoided. Education is the only real solution to this problem. Many public relations students will be exposed to the basics of research methodology during their course of study. This foundation should be supplemented by ongoing reading on the topic of research, and by attending professional seminars and training sessions throughout one's career. This will be particularly important as the field of public relations research and evaluation matures.

CONCLUSION

Campaign evaluation must not be treated as an afterthought; it is an important component of the planning process which takes into account the skills and experience of public relations staff, the organisational resources available to achieve campaign objectives and the situational factors that present obstacles or opportunities. A structured approach to evaluation draws on lessons learnt in previous campaigns and applies them to present and future campaigns, so that past mistakes or misdirections are not repeated. In this respect, evaluation may be thought of as a form of quality control that allows the campaign planner to assess whether resources are being used effectively and efficiently towards achieving campaign goals.

Public relations evaluation is still in its infancy and some practitioners appear uncertain about evaluation. As a consequence, they are not really able to prove the strategic worth of public relations, preferring instead to rely on the easier task of measuring outputs to demonstrate the contribution public relations makes to an organisation or their clients. This chapter has presented a series of evaluation models and approaches that present a starting point for understanding how evaluation can be integrated into campaign planning, and that recognise that evaluation is a process comprised of research, measurement and analysis—a process both formative and summative. In the concluding section of the chapter, some of the most common reasons for not undertaking campaign evaluation are addressed. These reasons must be acknowledged and understood if they are to be overcome effectively.

The rewards for adopting a sound approach to campaign evaluation are many: improved campaign outcomes where objectives are achieved; organisational learning that can be applied to future campaigns; and wise and responsible use of resources, which makes it less likely for public relations budgets to be cut during lean times. And, importantly, evaluation will contribute to the improvement of the status of public relations as a strategic communication function, by means of which public relations professionals can demonstrate in concrete terms the value of public relations to an organisation or client.

REFERENCES

Department of Trade and Industry (DTI) & The Institute of Public Relations (IPR) (UK), 2003, *Unlocking the Potential of Public Relations: Developing Good Practice*, www.cipr.co.uk/unlockpr/Unlocking-Potential-Report.pdf, accessed 13 August 2007

Hon L. C., 1998, 'Demonstrating Effectiveness in Public Relations: Goals, Objectives, and Evaluation' in *Journal of Public Relations Research*, Vol. 10, No. 2, Lawrence Erlbaum Associates

Lattimore D., Baskin O., Heiman S. T. & Toth E. L., 2007, *Public Relations: The Profession and the Practice*, 2nd edn, McGraw-Hill, New York

Macnamara J., 1997, 'Research in Public Relations: A Review of the Use of Evaluation and Formative Research' in Public Relations Institute of Australia, www.pria.com.au/resources/cid/118/parent/0/t/resources, accessed 21 July 2007

Macnamara J., 2006, 'PR Metrics: Research for Planning and Evaluation of PR and Corporate Communication' in CARMA, www.carmaapac.com/downloads/PR%20Metrics%202006.pdf, accessed 13 August 2007

Rockland D. & Puckett J., 2006, 'Don't Be Scared: Having the ROI Conversation with Clients' in *PR Tactics*, July 2006, reprinted with permission by the Public Relations Society of America, www.ketchum.com/node/539, accessed 21 July 2007

Watson T. & Noble P., 2005, *Evaluating Public Relations: A Best Practice Guide to Public Relations Planning, Research and Evaluation*, Kogan Page, Sterling, VA

Wilcox D. L. & Cameron G. T., 2006, *Public Relations Strategies and Tactics*, 8th edn, Pearson, Allyn & Bacon, USA

Zikmund W. G., 2003, *Exploring Marketing Research*, 8th edn, Thomson South-Western, USA

6 Community Relations

Gateways Support Services 2005–06

Dr Kristin Demetrious

AIMS OF THIS CHAPTER

- To define the qualities of a sustained and effective community relations campaign that meets extended social, ethical and economic imperatives

- To demonstrate how organisations can choose communicative activities that holistically build community, cooperation and trust, as well as providing important funds

- To identify other trends in community relations and highlight their limitations

INTRODUCTION

The business of not making a profit

The concepts of community and 'enlightened' self-interest are prominent in a corporate social responsibility (CSR) approach to building strong, lateral relationships between the corporate, government and not-for-profit sectors. Indeed, the CSR approach claims that business can achieve an acceptable intersection between profit-making and its social, economic and environmental responsibilities, to create sustainability that has a 'positive social and environmental impact' (Birch 2001, p. 62).

This chapter presents a case study of community relations that reflects this innovative and interactive approach in the not-for-profit sector. It examines the 2005–06 communication campaign of Gateways Support Services—a small-to-medium not-for-profit disability support organisation that started ten years earlier when two grassroots community action groups merged. Operating in south-west Victoria and based in Geelong, Gateways is a network of volunteers and professionals that deals with the 'here and now' of disability in our society. In this, it communicates with the public to develop support, resources and social awareness of disability issues. In addition, Gateways pushes for longer-term changes in community values, attitudes and behaviour towards disability, in order to achieve greater equity and justice for all. However, its role as service provider and advocate is complicated by a social context where it is acknowledged that there is a 'crisis of unmet needs for services and support for people with disabilities, their carers and families' (*Funding and Operation of the Commonwealth State/Territory Disability Agreement [CSTDA]* 2007, p. 63).

This chapter analyses how Gateways, with limited financial resources, communicates to inform communities about public policy in ways that promote its local economic and socially based goals. It argues that for civil sector organisations, such as Gateways, a redefinition of 'value' and 'success' is vital in order to measure their complex contribution to the common good and to validate their legitimacy to advocate on behalf of others. The Gateways case study serves as a model for other not-for-profit organisations that seek to communicate without the support of big budgets, using an accountable approach that balances the politics of survival with ethics and a commitment to grassroots ideologies.

According to Mark Lyons (2001, p. 5), a leading Australian social researcher, third sector organisations (TSOs) can be defined as not-for-profits that exist outside the government and business sectors, and that provide many wide-ranging activities and services in our society. TSOs, such as clubs, societies, community groups, associations and cooperatives—all largely drawing on the support of volunteers—are centred on cultural, sporting, charitable and religious spheres, and work with issues such as humanitarianism, social justice and welfare, environmentalism, social planning, health, education and quality of life. Clearly, the intricate networking of the third sector throughout society is vast. However, Lyons (2001, p. xi) argues that despite this considerable activity, the third sector is 'generally overlooked' when most people think about how Australia is organised; rather they think of a duality of government and business sectors. Indeed, he argues that it is vital for citizens 'to be conscious of the important role the third sector has played and must continue to play if we are to remain a just, prosperous, diverse and democratic society' (Lyons 2001, p. xi). Thus it is essential to look beyond a single TSO and to analyse broad national socioeconomic factors that may impact on the sector as a whole. For example, Zappala (2000, p. 2) points out that such things as increases or decreases in rates of volunteering can depend on 'changing attitudes and motivations in people' and the impact of demographic, socioeconomic and government policy factors—such as income, population, education and aging trends—over which individual organisations have no control. The third sector should therefore be recognised for its important, but vulnerable, role in a democratic society.

To gain legitimacy, TSOs are expected to be accountable for their actions. But what precisely is the TSO accountable for and how can this be measured? TSOs, now estimated in Australia to number 700,000, are sometimes criticised as 'vocal minorities' that are 'unrepresentative', 'unaccountable' and 'self-serving' (Corey 2004). These criticisms highlight the need for TSOs to establish forms of accountability in the conduct of their activities that in turn validate a secure mandate to advocate on behalf of others. Onyx and Dalton (2006, pp. 10–11) claim that funders in contemporary Australia, such as governments and other donors, measure the accountability of a TSO by imposing a raft of compliance and governance measures, such as business plans and performance measurement. Significantly, however, they say that for the third sector, these measures can lead to the mimicking of corporate values that have compromising consequences, especially for the TSO's advocacy role. One consequence is a move away from volunteers to paid staff, which weakens a TSO's links to its grassroots support base. Another is that 'the demands of funders' are met 'at the expense of their constituency' (Onyx & Dalton 2006, p. 10).

Onyx and Dalton (2006, p. 12) make the point that the measurement of third sector groups' performance, especially for those concerned with advocacy, is 'difficult, long-term, and usually qualitative rather than quantitative'. Butcher (2006) furthers our understanding of the third sector's complex relationship to government by suggesting that, in Australia, the former Howard government's neo-liberal programs conflicted with the agendas of some TSOs that advocated social justice. He argues that this has resulted in the favouring of some TSOs over others and says that 'At times ... governments are willing to co-opt broadly sympathetic TSOs in order to further particular political or policy agendas' (Butcher 2006, p. 73).

Drawing on the views of Onyx and Dalton (2006) and Butcher (2006), it is reasonable to suggest that particular social and political conditions may directly and indirectly influence the ability of TSOs to establish acceptable forms of accountability and legitimacy in society. For example, a progressive TSO—or even coalition of TSOs—seeking reform in an area can publicly pressure governments to change policy that may impact adversely on an industry or corporate sector. This advocacy, independent of self-interest, establishes a TSO's values and legitimacy to advocate in society. On the other hand, by taking this action the TSO may risk being ignored or shunned by governments and other funders. More broadly, this situation may lead to an embedded culture where government and business funding bodies are more likely to bestow favour or 'mandate' on politically benign not-for-profit organisations, that adopt business approaches in line with their expectations of accountability.

Overall, the work of Lyons (2001), Onyx and Dalton (2006) and Butcher (2006) suggest that a robust, independent third sector is important to create a diverse, fair and democratic society; but to support its claim to do so, a TSO must be accountable. Further to this, Onyx and Dalton (2006, p. 13) argue that a number of distinct forms of accountability can be applied to TSOs. They claim that one form of accountability is the principal—agent relationship designed around such things as 'target outputs' set by the principal for the agent to achieve. A second form of accountability is a contractual relationship that they argue is not ideal for advocacy organisations. However, a third form of accountability 'entails a mutual relationship of equal trust, respect and influence, and involves a broad general commitment, usually based on the moral suasion of peer networks' (Onyx & Dalton 2006, p. 13). Under this form, a TSO must investigate its commitment, values and its 'broad, lateral and general' interactions with stakeholders' (Onyx & Dalton 2006, p. 14).

TSOs can measure this third form of accountability in three ways:

1 By participating in decision-making and 'the action of the organisation'

2 By the processes of representation in decision-making, such as election

3 By a guided democracy of professionals who act for the constituency, but are removed from direct involvement (Onyx & Dalton 2006, p. 14).

Moreover, accountability is most likely to follow in conditions where there is a culture of participation in decision-making:

> Where there is a strong culture of participation, accountability will occur naturally, at least in theory in that those most affected by the decision have been a part of making it, and will be immediately aware of its implementation (Onyx & Dalton 2006, p. 15).

The notion of 'social capital' is a key concept that also intersects with TSO accountability and legitimacy debates. Lyons (2001, pp. 135–6) defines social capital as a normative concept of 'trust and reciprocity that enable members of a group or community to work together'.

For Lyons, collective action is important because it draws on social capital and simultaneously renews it. In relation to TSOs, Lyons (2001, pp. 136–7) argues that the process of producing and reproducing social capital creates different criteria to measure and judge success. One criterion is to measure goals against client- or customer-based objectives, which he argues contribute little to social capital. Another criterion is to measure the extent of citizen participation in the organisation's decision-making—an approach Lyons argues does contribute to social capital. Social capital is a useful notion to further our understanding of what 'accountability' means for TSOs. In particular, it shows how an organisation must also account for the extent to which it participates and represents its constituency and society, as well as demonstrating that it acts lawfully and appropriately acquits its funds.

Further to this, specialist communicative approaches can help a TSO build a culture of participation in the community. Public communication is a form of communication used by some organisations—in particular, collective action groups, not-for-profits and non-governmental organisations (NGOs)—that meets social- as well as economic-based objectives. The principles of public communication are to:

- Work in ways guided by the principles of human dignity, truth telling and non-violence (Christians & Traber 1997)

- Contribute to citizen participation

- Create meaningful discussion and dialogue in public debates

- Track the organisation's ethical performance to maintain its integrity (Demetrious 2004).

The principles and practice of public communication articulate into Onyx and Dalton's (2006, p. 13) notion of public accountability as a form that requires mutuality, trust, respect and commitment within community networks; and into the notion of social capital as a benchmark in evaluating success (Lyons 2001). Public communication also adopts a stakeholder approach in determining how the organisation interacts with groups and individuals, rather than the narrow organisational-centred public relations and marketing concept of 'target public'. Freeman defines a stakeholder as 'any group or individual who can affect or is affected by the achievement of the organisation's objectives' (1984, p. 46). Therefore, the notion of stakeholders is anchored firmly to an understanding of participation and interdependency between business, government and civil sectors. However not all citizens have an equal ability to participate in society. In particular, Marks (in Stevenson 2001, pp. 170–2) argues that people with physical and mental disability are largely excluded from this ideal. Therefore organisations such as Gateways—centred on people with disabilities and complex behaviour—are presented with unusual challenges in facilitating a public communication approach of participation and representation of their constituents.

In summary, the accountability and mandate of TSOs can be measured by a range of methods, which are linked to different ways of thinking and validating knowledge. In particular, a method that is appropriate for the third sector is to show how a not-for-profit organisation seeks to encourage commitment, citizen participation and representation in decision-making to produce social capital. The next section describes and analyses the Gateways organisation and its communication campaign.

GATEWAYS SUPPORT SERVICE—SPEAKING FOR YOURSELF

Background

In 2005–06, Gateways supported more than 900 children and adults with disabilities and additional needs and their families, in the south-west Victorian region, to maximise their quality and enjoyment of life, potential and positive relationships within the community (Gateways 2006). The agency employed 180 staff and accessed support from over sixty volunteers. The organisation had a budget of A$5 million, with 80 per cent of funds from the state government and 8 per cent of funds from the Commonwealth—Gateways used fundraising to meet the 12 per cent shortfall.

Formed in 1997, Gateways is an incorporated association resulting from a merger of two grassroots community action groups (CAGs) in Geelong, Victoria. The Association for Autism and Allied Disorders (AAAD) and Interchange Barwon had formed in the 1980s to address the unmet needs of families caring for children with disabilities in the local region. According to Gateways' CEO Rosemary Malone (personal interview with the author, February 2007), 'The 1980s was a time of growth and innovation in disability services as "deinstitutionalisation" became government policy. AAAD and Interchange Barwon both took on the challenge of gaining government funding for local services and support. Both action groups represented partnerships of professionals and parents. While each organisation addressed different needs in relation to support for children with disabilities, they were similar in that they were both characterised by a strong culture of community inclusion— Interchange Barwon having a strong reliance on volunteers, with AAAD delivering most of its programs in mainstream community settings.' ('Deinstitutionalisation' is a term that refers to 'a shift in service delivery away from institutional care, towards care in the home and community' <www.health.gov.au/internet/wcms/publishing.nsf/Content/Glossary#n>.)

However, in the mid-1990s, an ethos of economic rationalism under a Coalition state government saw disability organisations—like schools, hospitals and councils— amalgamated for logistical reasons. At the time, the state government had used its strong electoral mandate to justify radical changes to public policy such as the privatisation and 'the contracting out of public services' (Alford & O'Neill 1994, p. 101). The amalgamation of AAAD and Interchange Barwon occurred at a critical time, when a merger of smaller organisations with compatible goals was necessary for survival.

Today, Gateways address three core areas of unmet community need:

1   **Child and Family Services**

Offering a range of supports to families, and mainstream early years services for young children with disabilities and/or additional needs

2   **Respite and Recreation Services**

Providing age-appropriate community activities for children and adults with disabilities, while giving families a much-valued break from their caring role

3   **Supported Community Living**

Supporting adolescents and adults with disabilities and complex needs to live in community residential units within the community.

For Gateways, empowerment is about supporting people with disabilities and their families to develop skills and confidence in themselves. This includes:

- Listening to and affirming their needs and wishes (person-centred and family-centred practice)

- Responding to their priorities (person-centred and family-centred practice)

- Assisting them to gain experience and skills through accessing information, education programs, mutual support activities and/or participating in community activities that maximise their ability to be self-reliant and self-confident (active support).

According to Malone, 'Gateways has fostered community inclusion and participation over many years. This is critical to us achieving our mission. Our current strategic plan includes a section on promoting positive community awareness and understanding of people with disabilities.' One example is called Interchange, where a host family develops a mutually enjoyable, beneficial and supportive relationship with a young person who has a disability. It can involve a child spending a day or a weekend with a host family. Malone says that 'families consistently say how valuing it is for them to know that another local family or individual chooses to spend time with their child, while they have some time out'.

Public communication campaign strategy and method

Gateways adopted an integrated focus to communications that was set in motion following a fragmented, short-term approach adopted several years earlier. Malone indicated that a turnaround in communication occurred after the organisation realised that it did not have an understanding of public communication and how to do it well. She stated that 'Gateways needed to coordinate an integrated approach where the messages were tailored to the organisational values and cooperation and support could be garnered from the wider organisation'.

According to Malone:

> As part of our strategic planning exercise in 2003 we reviewed our mission and objectives, and developed organisational values and a vision statement. Staff identified that Gateways is a positive organisation that does great work, but we are not well known in the community with confusion about our name, which is similar to some others.

She said that Gateways had made attempts to raise its profile when the organisation was formed and again in 2000, but these efforts were not sustained nor well integrated within the organisation's strategy and operations.

Kate Kent is Gateways' Communications and Promotions Officer. She stated that the developments in 2003 'were a major positive turning point. What it highlighted was the need for Gateways to now improve its profile within the community' (personal interview with the author, February 2007). To further this objective, Gateways linked an internal innovations program with its public communication activity. The Innovation Grants Program aims to promote original programs to extend Gateways' services to the community and to promote its mission. Gateways also sought to use public information via the media and to provide accurate and valuing messages about children and adults with disabilities and their families, for example in advertisements for volunteers and media articles.

Gateways also sought to network with other organisations where possible. Malone sums up the organisation's approach to partnerships in the key message: 'Together We Can'. This statement refers to the complex networking that underpins the organisational approach, both with the people it represents and the other individuals and groups that it must work with in order to be effective and far-reaching. Networking provides Gateways with the flexibility of a larger organisation but the responsiveness and connectedness of a smaller organisation, which is core to its profile.

To inform future policy direction and practices, in 2004 Gateways conducted a public profile survey of forty randomly selected respondents. Questions related to:

- The respondents' awareness of Gateways
- Their level of community concern about services and support for people with disabilities and additional needs
- What the key message 'Together We Can' meant to them
- Whether they would consider volunteering for Gateways.

Gateways' budgets for its programs are often under pressure. The problem it faced in the conduct of its 2006 campaign was to research and develop a public communication plan that did not rely heavily on costly advertising, which may not give a great return. Importantly, Gateways considered that the organisation should carry out its intentions in relation to building partnerships with internal and external key stakeholders.

Goals

In 2005–06 Gateways set a number of communication goals that were linked to its mission, vision and core values:

- Goal 1: To support people with disabilities to enjoy life in the community by building community awareness and understanding

- Goal 2: To promote financial support by building community awareness of Gateways' role, in high-quality service provision

- Goal 3: To promote future funding opportunities by building awareness of the needs of people with disabilities and their families, and Gateways' role in high-quality service provision

- Goal 4: To recruit skilled and committed staff with empowering and team-orientated attitudes

- Goal 5: To recruit volunteers for respite and recreation programs, board of management and auxiliary

- Goal 6: To increase the number of people selecting Gateways as their preferred service provider

- Goal 7: To increase new and existing funding

- Goal 8: To raise community awareness and gain in-kind and financial support and volunteers

- Goal 9: To ensure Gateways maintains its reputation as a high-quality, innovative and cooperative partner (*Gateways Support Services Promotional Plan 2004–06 Final Report*).

Stakeholders were identified as:

- Children and adults with disability/additional needs and their families

- Other regional health and social service agencies, peak industry bodies

- Funding bodies: state and federal governments, trusts/foundations, individual sponsors, service clubs, corporate groups

- Job seekers

- Corporate citizen programs

- Politicians/leaders/local MPs (state and federal)/local councillors and the nine local government areas in the south-west region of Victoria

- General community in the south-west region of Victoria.

Communication tactics

A range of communication tactics was used in the 2005–06 campaign. General tactics included:

- Local media liaison (media releases)

- Advertising features

- The *Way Ahead* newsletter

- Billboards

- Promotional materials such as signage, presentations, participation in key regional projects, information packs and the Gateways Resource Kit

- Events such as golf days and movie nights.

A website was also used to empower families and the broader community through its 'user-friendly' material. In particular, many tactics encouraged participation, representation and social capital; these are discussed in detail below.

INSPIRATIONAL CHILDREN POSTER SERIES

This poster series was funded under the Innovations Grants Program and encourages the pre-school community to value and support children with disabilities and their families. It grew out of a comment from a kindergarten teacher to a visiting Gateways staff member, who took up the challenge to address an unmet need.

The posters contain simple calls to action, such as the key message: 'It's about being invited to a birthday party: to be accepted.' They show how people can make a difference right now, and were distributed to every kindergarten in the region. According to Malone, the posters highlight that 'the organisation is listening to grassroots needs and will act to do something about it'.

WORKSHOPS IN AUTISM WEEK

Gateways is linked in various ways to other peak organisations. This allows it to join in and 'piggy-back' to respond to local unmet needs. During Autism Week, for example, Gateways conducted free workshops covering issues such as sensory processing, self-help skills and fine motor skills, in response to requests from families requiring this type of information.

HAPI AWARDS (HELPING ACHIEVE POSITIVE INCLUSION)

The HAPI Awards are a Gateways initiative, sponsored through a partnership with G-Force Recruitment, another local not-for-profit organisation. The HAPI Awards recognise kindergartens that develop inclusive programs for children with disabilities. Winners are presented with plaques and cash prizes donated by the sponsor. According to Malone, the HAPI Awards program both empowers families and values welcoming kindergartens. She said that it was important to provide recognition for community role models who demonstrate leadership in broader values and standards.

SUNNY DAY IN WINTER CAMPAIGN

The commitment of time and support from an individual or family to the Interchange program is significant, and the Sunny Day in Winter volunteer recruitment campaign seeks to involve more people in the program. While this state-wide campaign is facilitated through Interchange Victoria, the program is flexible and organisations such as Gateways are encouraged to act locally. To raise awareness of its own Interchange program, therefore, Gateways used this campaign to get more information to potential volunteers and host families through face-to-face communication, leaflets and brochures in the central shopping area of Geelong.

GRASSROOTS LOBBYING

Gateways and other disability agencies and self-help advocacy groups meet with local politicians regarding unmet needs and issues. The organisation has a particular interest in advocating with, and for, people with complex needs and their often stressed families.

HOT GOSS

The Hot Goss Dance parties were created at the request of young people with disabilities, due to the lack of affordable and fun night activities on the weekend. They were achieved with minimal funding but a great deal of goodwill between a range of partners within the project.

Hot Goss is a partnership between people with disabilities, who help to organise the event; a range of community agencies; the Kiwanis service club; and the Geelong Football Club. The dance parties could not have happened without the strong support of volunteers. Kate Kent said that 'underpinning the whole project is the view that to be a success the event must be of quality equal to other things done in the community'. Once again, this is an example of what can be done with limited financial resources.

LEADERSHIP ROLES FOR PEOPLE WITH DISABILITY

Gateways sought to facilitate opportunities for people with a disability to be represented in wider community activities, in order to achieve reciprocal benefits for both parties involved:

- **The 'Have Your Say' Conference, organised by Valid (a disability advocacy group)**

  Gateways supported people with an intellectual disability to participate in the organising committee of this state-wide conference, and in presenting at the conference. Hot Goss provided the entertainment. This was seen as an inclusive way for people with an intellectual disability to take on leadership roles and to develop the skills and confidence to communicate in their own words.

- **The City of Greater Geelong (CoGG) Disability Advisory Committee**

  Gateways supported people with an intellectual disability to apply for membership of the CoGG Disability Advisory Committee. In this way, Gateways is attempting to facilitate opportunities for people with disabilities:

  - To represent themselves
  - To be involved in decision-making that affects their lives
  - To educate community leaders about their priorities.

- **Participation of a guest speaker with a disability at the Gateways 2005 AGM.**

Evavluation

A number of qualitative and quantitative methods were used to evaluate the effectiveness of the Gateways public communication campaign. Quantitative methods included media content analysis, a small survey of responses to questions gauged over a two-year period, and the benchmarking of targets set out in Gateways' Promotional Plan. A qualitative analysis shed light on the organisation's relationship to the community using the criteria of participation and representation, commitment and the production of social capital that Lyons (2001), Onyx and Dalton (2006) and Butcher (2006) argue are indicators of accountability and legitimacy. The following results are aligned with the original goals established by Gateways in its 2005–06 plan:

- **Media coverage**

  This was outstanding. Positive media about Gateways went up from twenty-two positive news stories in 2004 to thirty-seven in 2005–06. This represents a 68 per cent increase over the period (Goals 1, 5 and 8).

- **Funding targets**

  These were exceeded. Sponsorship and funding objectives were attained with an increase of 30 per cent in community funding (Goals 3, 4, 7, 8 and 9).

- **Public profile survey**

  Random surveying of forty people in March 2006 showed that 42 per cent had heard of Gateways Support Services—benchmarked against 30 per cent in November 2004 (Goals 5 and 6).

- **Staff vacancies**

  These were successfully filled (Goal 4).

- **HAPI Awards**

  These are to be emulated by another region in Victoria, and anecdotal responses from participants has also been very positive. Rosemary Malone said that 'feedback from kindergartens has been that everyone nominated feels that they are already a winner because they have made an important difference for the children and families they support' (Goal 8).

- **Hot Goss**

  The entertainment at the 'Have Your Say conference' attracted 700 people (Goals 8 and 9).

- **Sunny Day in Winter campaign**

  This produced positive results via an increase in local volunteers for the Interchange program (although this cannot be benchmarked as the campaign was not conducted in 2004–05) (*Gateways Support Services Promotional Plan 2004–06 Final Report*) (Goals 5 and 9). However, more generally, the public profile survey revealed a decrease in the potential volunteer base in Geelong. Responses to the question 'would you consider volunteering for Gateways?' show that in 2004, 40 per cent of people said 'yes', while in 2006 the figure was only 27 per cent.

- **Participation and representation**

  Gateways communication activities—such as the Inspirational Children posters and workshops during Autism Week, along with Hot Goss and Leadership Roles for People with Disability—encourage participation and representation within both the community and the organisation (Goals 1 and 6). Malone said that:

  > Over the last two years we have focused more on promoting leadership opportunities for people with disabilities, for example inviting them to be the guest presenter at our AGM, supporting their participation on committees that organise events, supporting them to speak at conferences and supporting their involvement in community life (e.g. applying for membership of the

City of Greater Geelong Disability Advisory Committee). Given that we support people with complex needs, this does involve significant support but has proved to be well worthwhile.

- **Commitment**

Gateways encourages people to make a long-term commitment to the community and the organisation. This is evidenced by the increase in Interchange volunteers as a result of the Sunny Day in Winter campaign, and the fact that other organisations are planning to take up the HAPI Awards. Commitment is also evidenced by the fact that the Gateways Board of Management has two current members who were part of the Interchange formation group in 1983—one a professional and the other a parent. According to Malone:

> the Board has always had a clear vision for Gateways' role in contributing to a caring community, while ensuring that the organisation is responsive, innovative and well managed. This is a vital part of the organisation as it needs people who have skills to perform the governance roles and maintain a responsive, innovative, well-managed organisation (Goals Eight and Nine).

- **Social Capital**

Gateways created the 'social capital' that Lyons (2001) argues is necessary to enable members of a group or community to work together. In actioning inclusive and responsive programs—such as the Inspirational Children posters, the HAPI Awards, the Sunny Day in Winter campaign and Hot Goss—Gateways created trust and reciprocity in the community by responding in practical ways that provide the opportunity for mutual benefits to the organisation and the community and a rethinking of core assumptions surrounding disability.

The evaluation of Gateways' 2005–06 public communication campaign shows a raft of positive indicators in the achievement of its goals. Overall, the results showed that there was a significant change in community attitudes and behaviour towards supporting people with disability, and an increase in building community awareness and understanding of disability issues. In evidencing these quantitative and qualitative criteria of accountability, it is demonstrated that this small-to-medium grassroots organisation made a substantial contribution towards its social and economic goals by applying a public communication approach to campaigning, characterised by inclusion and empowerment of others to think and act for themselves.

However, the fact that volunteerism was more generally in decline was also evident in the small public profile survey sample. Given the success of the local Sunny Day in Winter campaign and other strong indicators of success for the organisation, this decline appears consistent with Zappala's (2000) contention that trends in volunteerism relate to a range of changing demographic, socioeconomic and policy factors outside the control of the organisation. For example a factor that may influence the extent of volunteerism in communities is time-poor workers struggling to service higher household debt, which in Australia, as a ratio to income over the last decade, 'has more than doubled to just over 150 per cent' (Reserve Bank of Australia 2006). Clearly, further investigation and analysis of data would be useful in determining the link between trends in volunteerism and broader socioeconomic conditions.

In summary, Gateways approached its public communication activities with a focus on building relationships and collaboration. Its activities emphasised creating opportunities and mutual benefits that linked to both its long-term business and social goals (Demetrious 2004).

SIGNS OF THE TIMES

This case study shows that for TSOs, being bigger does not necessarily mean being better. Rather success, accountability and legitimacy can depend on how 'better' is defined (Lyons 2001; Alessandrini 2006; Butcher 2006; Onyx & Dalton 2006). An emerging trend in TSOs is to conduct high-profile, expensive, corporate-style communication campaigns, but these have limitations. In some cases, the relationship between donor and TSO is primarily transactional; that is, the donor listens to a telemarketer's spiel and provides credit card details. While an interaction such as this may raise important capital, in line with free market doctrines, and may result in the TSO being favoured and funded by governments, it fails to produce and reproduce social capital of mutuality, trust, participation, representation and reciprocity. According to Rosemary Malone:

> Gateways' inclusive programs have always focused on giving mainstream services knowledge and confidence. Where necessary, modelling and practical support have also been provided to make inclusion successful for the child with the disability, the other children, the parent of the child with the disability, the staff and the families of the other children. We aim for a 'win—win' outcome for all. Only then is inclusion truly successful. We believe these positive experiences can help to shape lifelong attitudes within local communities.

To do this, Gateways listens to its grassroots—the people it supports. It is goal- and purpose-focused and uses networking to add value and flexibility to complement other disability services.

Gateways' role in drawing on social capital and renewing it is also intrinsically linked to its ability to put pressure on funders and politicians. Without an active critical advocacy role, Gateways, like other TSOs, risks the prospect of being merely an instrument of the state and business sectors. Gateways' original purpose started from local grassroots action groups that centred on unmet needs of people with a disability. The decision to grow the organisation took place because it was seen that there were more skills required than volunteers—such as parents—were capable of providing. Gateways has since developed into a hybridised organisation, in part modelled on a profit-based organisation; although significantly, through its funding shortfall, it remains structurally and culturally linked to its grassroots origins. Therefore, Gateways provides for the production of social capital by maintaining a partially funded model that still relies on its ability to act as an activist group.

Gateways' grassroots links and its ability to advocate are important to address the weaknesses in the business model identified by Onyx and Dalton (2006). The Gateways experience reveals that small-to-medium organisations make invaluable contributions of social capital that cannot necessarily be measured with business models. Through innovative participatory public communication using a wide range of channels, Gateways focuses on its core values while still trying new things. It balances pragmatism with the critical advocacy of unmet needs in ways that maintain and augment its legitimacy to mandate on behalf of others, often in difficult social conditions where there are competing priorities and scarce resources. Other organisations can learn from the Gateways case study.

Drawing on public communication skills, this organisation has been able to effectively develop a community relations program that meets the economic and social objectives characteristic of an integrated CSR approach. This is especially laudable because for Gateways, the encouragement of participation in the process is made difficult by the complex behaviour of the people it supports. Therefore it should be noted by public communication strategists that corporate approaches to establish accountability with funders can be superficial and risk the TSO's meaningful connection to its grassroots support bases. Furthermore, a focus on big-budget corporate-style communication campaigns that exclude other smaller organisations, such as Gateways, overlooks the important role they have in building social capital, trust, participation, mutuality and reciprocity in local communities.

The role of the third sector—or the diverse community, voluntary organisations and social movements that cannot be classified in government and business sectors—is vital to advocate society's diverse interests and values, often on behalf of those who cannot do it for themselves. However, all community relations programs operate in and are affected by larger social, economic and political contexts. This is especially the case with Gateways, which advocates on behalf of children and adults with disabilities; a group that has been identified as 'in crisis' (*Funding and Operation of the Commonwealth State/Territory Disability Agreement [CSTDA]* 2007, p. 63). Greater community engagement and participation—achieved through CSR-oriented community relations programs that build social capital—lead to the development of better public policy and a democracy that remains true to its ideals. Public communication campaigns are closely aligned to these principles. Gateways' original purpose started at the grassroots level and, in part, remains grassroots-oriented. In keeping this focus, the Gateways 2005–06 community relations campaign meets social, ethical and business ends in complex ways that help redefine the value of TSOs and their contribution to society. So while governments, for logistical purposes, may prefer to deal with a few select large-scale not-for-profit organisations, this may be at a cost to social capital and communities. What does this mean for the role of communication in the not-for-profit sector in society? Public communicators need to urgently investigate these questions in order to build and protect a robust third sector that performs its complex, but undervalued, role in Australian society.

DR KRISTIN DEMETRIOUS

PRACTITIONER PROFILE

Sheila O'Sullivan, veteran of around 300 campaigns, commenced in public relations at Associated Media, South Melbourne, in 1976. She joined Manallacks in 1980, Turnbull Fox Phillips in 1987 and started Socom Public Relations in 1994.

Community relations

This took off in the mid-90s and was the gift that gave birth to Socom. There was a number of colliding events:

➤ *The election of governments with an economic rationalist approach and a strong sense of the primacy of the individual as a focus for decisions; this mirrored the approach of the corporates*

➤ *The consequent sense of disenfranchisement of many people in the community*

➤ *The struggle of many traditional NGOs involved in service delivery that were unable to provide government-funded services at the cost identified by the government*

➤ *The tendency of governments at all levels to pay lip service to their communities; the practice was to appoint (not elect) an advisory council/board/group on a particular subject, or on general topics, and then say that the community had been consulted*

➤ *The spread of technology, with people finding new ways to organise and communicate (as an example, when I started Socom in 1994, there were only two fax machines on the market, both using shiny rolls of paper from which the print would fade quickly).*

Together, these events led to a community backlash against organisations and governments, focusing on their lack of openness and transparency. These events also encouraged organisations to reflect on the communications and consultation practices that had created these poor relationships.

Smarter organisations realised that they could use new strategies and communication technologies to engage their communities, which would result in better decision-making.

The internet was an important development, as organisations could reach a much wider audience and determine if the views of those who claimed to represent the wider community actually did so, or if they in fact only reflected the views of a very small interest group.

The trends in community relations

There has been a complete shift in the past decade to a positive approach among governments to building relationships with communities that reflect:

➤ *The importance of community consultation in allowing decisions to be made that are more aligned with community expectations*
➤ *Greater transparency—the risk to reputation is now the single biggest communication risk to governments and corporations; if you don't tell, then someone else will, and not in a way you would like*
➤ *The emerging trend of governments to talk about the importance of community building and of volunteering.*

In corporations, the agenda of the community relations team is to ensure that the community gives the company a theoretical 'licence to operate'. This is particularly true where the company production is seen to have an environmental disbenefit. The term 'licence to operate' goes beyond the law, to encompass the increasing ability of a community or community group to have an adverse impact on an organisation's performance and reputation.

Community relations and NGOs

Community relations for an NGO that has 88 per cent of its budget from government will inevitably be restricted in what it advocates for. We deal with this issue in our public relations programs for our NGO clients every day.

You can now observe NGOs whose service arms and advocacy arms are separated—notionally or actually—with the spokespeople quite separate, so that each does not compromise the other. For example the Reverend Tim Costello is the advocate to government for World Vision and his funding arm uses celebrities as the advocates. We expect Tim to want to take on a government. We expect his film stars to tug at our individual heart strings.

REFERENCES

Alford J. & O'Neill D. (eds), 1994, *The Contract State Public Management and the Kennett Government*, Deakin University Press, Geelong

Birch D., 2001, 'Corporate Citizenship: Rethinking Business Beyond Corporate Social Responsibility' in Andriof J. & McIntosh M. (eds), 2001, *Perspectives on Corporate Citizenship*, Greenleaf Publishing, UK, pp. 53–65

Butcher J., 2006, 'Government, the Third Sector and the Rise of Social Capital' in *Third Sector Review*, Vol. 12, No. 1, pp. 69–88

Christians C. & Traber M. (eds), 1997, *Communication Ethics and Universal Values*, Sage Publications, London

Corey S., 2004, 'NGOs Watching NGOs' in *Background Briefing Radio National*, www.abc.net.au/rn/talks/bbing/stories/s1078182.htm, accessed 20 March 2007

Demetrious K., 2004, *Public Communication and Citizenship Study Guide*, Deakin University, Geelong

Freeman R. E., 1984, *Strategic Management: A Stakeholder Approach*, Pitman, Boston, MA

Funding and Operation of the Commonwealth State/Territory Disability Agreement (CSTDA), February 2007, The Senate Standing Committee on Community Affairs, Commonwealth of Australia

Gateways Support Services Annual Report 2006, Gateways Support Services, Geelong West

Gateways Support Services Promotional Plan 2004–06 Final Report, Gateways Support Services, Geelong West

Lyons M., 2001, *The Contribution of Nonprofit and Cooperative Enterprises in Australia*, Allen & Unwin, Crows Nest, NSW

Onyx J. & Dalton B., 2006, 'Accountability and Advocacy' in *Third Sector Review*, Vol. 12, No. 1, pp. 7–24

Reserve Bank of Australia, March 2006, *Financial Stability Review*, www.rba.gov.au/PublicationsAndResearch/FinancialStabilityReview/Mar2006/Html/mac_fin_env.html, accessed 20 March 2007

Stevenson N. (ed.), 2001, *Culture and Citizenship*, Sage Publications, London

Zappala G., 2000, 'How Many People Volunteer in Australia and Why Do They Do It?' in *Research and Advocacy Briefing Paper*, No. 4, The Smith Family, pp. 1–4

7 Stakeholder Engagement

The Wivenhoe Dam Upgrade Project

Robina Xavier

AIMS OF THIS CHAPTER

- To demonstrate the importance of public participation in achieving effective outcomes in major infrastructure projects

- To outline the key tactics used in large-scale public participation programs

INTRODUCTION

Much of public relations practice is predicated on the boundary-spanner role (Aldrich & Herker 1977) being the interface between an organisation and its key publics. The boundary-spanner brings key information and views into the organisation for consideration by decision-makers and also communicates the organisational view to external groups to ensure all parties are fully informed.

An extension of this boundary-spanner role is the specialist area of practice in public participation, sometimes known as community consultation and engagement. Public participation practices are used in a variety of public and private projects, and are designed to enhance decision-making by ensuring that a diverse range of stakeholders has input before a final decision is made. Stakeholders can be individuals or groups who 'can affect or [are] affected by the actions, decisions, policies, practices, or goals of the organization' (Freeman 1984, p. 25). It is important to recognise that public participation and consultation are usually about ensuring input into decision-making, not joint decision-making. The decision is still taken by the government body or organisation, however the process helps ensure such a decision is sensitive to the needs and views of relevant stakeholders.

While enshrined in various statutes at state and federal levels, research in some constituencies suggests that legally required participation methods are highly unsuccessful. In the USA, for example, Innes and Booher (2004) suggest such approaches do not meet the most basic goals of public participation and are often counterproductive. Many groups are sceptical of the true intent of public participation programs and whether their opinions have been seriously considered in the final outcome, losing interest in a process that is seen to be done simply to comply with legal provisions. Flawed participation processes impact not just the project under consideration but those that come after, affecting the public's commitment to the overall process.

Public participation processes have existed for as long as there have been publics; however, as a professional field, particular interest in the area grew in the late 1980s in Australia. Professionals in this area are supported by groups such as the International Association of Public Participation (IAP2 website), formed in 1990 to promote the values and best practices associated with involving the public in government and industry decisions that affect their lives. The infrastructure boom in Australia has led to significant growth in this field and the development of best practice examples in strategy. These examples recognise the importance of collaboration, dialogue and interaction (Innes & Booher 2004), which are all critical for effective participation outcomes. Meaningful participation strategies also require organisations to address barriers to participation, building the capacity of stakeholders—particularly disenfranchised ones—to get involved.

Demonstrating these key principles is the public participation and engagement case study on the upgrade to the Wivenhoe Dam in Queensland. Spanning three years, this case outlines the strong commitment by the client, SEQWater, to a process that strengthened relationships in the community and engaged stakeholders in a decision-making process to provide a technical solution to an identified problem. This multiple-award-winning case shows the way parties can work together to achieve a mutual benefit and the value of early relationship building in managing large-scale infrastructure projects.

BACKGROUND

In 2002, new meteorological research on predicted rainfalls in an extreme storm event raised concerns about flood mitigation strategies for the Brisbane region. Central to these strategies is Wivenhoe Dam, built on the Brisbane River near Esk, Fernvale and Lowood, approximately 80 kilometres from Brisbane. One of Australia's largest, the dam serves a dual purpose of water supply storage for the people of Brisbane and adjacent local authorities, and flood mitigation for downstream communities.

The owner-operator of the Dam, SEQWater, realised it needed to upgrade the dam to safely manage any conceivable flood. It formed the Wivenhoe Alliance to manage the $70 million upgrade project over three years. On completion of the project, the dam would be able to safely manage a 1-in-100,000-year flood. The Alliance included SEQWater construction, engineering and project management groups Leighton Contractors, Coffey Geosciences and MWH, and the Department of Commerce (NSW).

The Alliance was tasked with not only delivering a robust physical structure to handle increased water levels, but also to build relationships with the local community to ensure that:

- The most effective building option was selected

- The overall reputation of SEQWater as owner/operator was enhanced.

RESEARCH

The Alliance realised the upgrade project represented a considerable challenge. Major construction projects often have a high risk of causing inconvenience to the local community in terms of traffic, dust and noise, increasing the likelihood of community aggravation and action against the project. Located in a semi-rural environment, this project would impact a community that valued its peaceful surrounds and businesses that benefited from the tourist trade associated with such surrounds.

Making the task even more difficult was extensive media coverage about flood levels in Brisbane which had the potential to heighten community sensitivity to the upgrade project, and raised concerns about the safety of the current dam.

Many members of the community were sceptical about the real outcomes of public participation processes, based on previous experiences, so the Alliance team had to understand these concerns before it could devise an effective program. The team also knew from its experience that different stakeholders would want to be involved at different levels, from being kept informed through to full involvement in the final decision.

The research process started by first drawing on SEQWater's knowledge from its current relationships with stakeholders. The Alliance partners worked closely with key SEQWater staff to identify potential stakeholders and issues they may have. An impact list was developed and updated as new groups or issues emerged. The Alliance also commenced an environmental scan and assessment to study environmental and social impacts for surrounding areas, and compiled data on local wildlife.

Then the direct views of relevant stakeholders were sought. A community reference group was formed, which included local business and community leaders. The group remained active throughout the project and provided an invaluable facility for ongoing community involvement. Specific feedback was sought from representatives of the local Indigenous community. Cultural heritage matters are an important consideration in all infrastructure development programs, and a series of initiatives were implemented to promote strong relationships with the Indigenous community. Recognising the needs of regulatory groups, a government agency reference group with local, state and federal government representatives was formed to discuss regulatory requirements for any upgrade options.

TABLE 7.1: TARGET PUBLICS

Internal stakeholders	As this project was managed through an alliance structure, the client and personnel working through the alliance partners were an important group.
Neighbouring residents and landowners	These parties were in the immediate vicinity of the up-grade activities and were likely to be impacted directly.
Local community	This group included residents and businesses from the surrounding areas, including rural properties and four towns.
Community and interest groups	Including schools, these groups held a social, economic or environmental interest in the project and represented the collective views of their members. Senior officers of these groups were often opinion leaders.
Indigenous groups	These groups had local cultural heritage interests in the region and included the Jagera and Jinibara peoples.

(Continued)

TABLE 7.1: TARGET PUBLICS (continued)

Local councils	The dam is located within Esk Shire and is adjacent to Ipswich and Brisbane City Councils. These councils had an interest in the project on behalf of their constituents.
Government agencies—local, state and federal	A number of agencies had regulatory power over the project and their approval was needed for the project to progress.
State and federal members of parliament	Members whose electorates were in the vicinity of the project were important as they would influence and be influenced by their constituents.

GOALS AND OBJECTIVES

In commissioning the project, SEQWater had two main goals: to identify and gain community acceptance for a physical structure that could manage any conceivable flood, and to enhance its reputation and relationships with the community.

From this, the Alliance developed a series of goals and objectives to direct its program:

- **Goal 1**

  Develop stakeholder acceptance of the project

  - **Objective 1.1**

    Increase stakeholder understanding of the project

- **Goal 2**

  Leave positive community legacies

  - **Objective 2.1**

    Develop and implement projects that provide lasting community benefits

- **Goal 3**

  Improve SEQWater's reputation

  - **Objective 3.1**

    Improve SEQWater's rating in social responsibility, consultation, accessibility and responsiveness through the project

  - **Objective 3.2**

    Ensure no misinformation through the media about dam safety and possibility of an extreme storm event.

COMMUNICATION STRATEGIES AND TACTICS

The project was guided by a comprehensive project management plan, within which a stakeholder and environment plan was developed to ensure high priority for these important areas. From there, a communication plan was developed to guide stakeholder communication and promote effective public participation.

The communication strategy was developed with the understanding that the Alliance needed to build good stakeholder relations for SEQWater to continue after the project was completed. The strategy was based on four key principles:

1   Early, open and honest communication

2   Proactive management of issues

3   Personalised and targeted communication

4   Identified ongoing benefits to the community.

Trust was critical to the project and the Alliance team sought to build trust with stakeholders by providing them with accurate information, timely project updates, and delivering when and how they said they would. The team was also committed to being available to interested stakeholders whenever possible, both through formal and informal processes.

The Alliance recognised that it was working with diverse stakeholder groups and that these groups each had their own information needs. Communication activities were devised to meet the needs of each group, however key messages were also developed to ensure consistency of information provided to all internal and external stakeholders. In addition, the Alliance had the challenge of communicating technically complex processes to stakeholders in an interesting and informative manner.

The project can be divided into three main stages:

• **Stage 1**

Public participation and consultation to select a preferred upgrade option

• **Stage 2**

Public information and liaison during construction

• **Stage 3**

Public participation and consultation to select and implement a signature legacy project.

While there was a different focus in each stage, the relationship principles and communication channels established at the start continued throughout the project, providing consistency of approach for stakeholders.

TABLE 7.2: STAGE 1

DATE	STAGE	MAJOR COMMUNICATION ACTIVITY
February–April 2003	Preliminary planning and design	*Research and planning*: including desk research, key stakeholder briefings/meetings, preparing communication tools, establishing communication channels
May–July 2003	Stakeholder education phase	*Stakeholder communication*: including newsletters, website, project information flyers, community information line, displays, media
July–October 2003	Stakeholder consultation phase to select preferred option	*Stakeholder consultation*: including key stakeholder briefings/meetings, establishing reference groups, displays, community information line, selection workshop of final option
October–November 2003	Stakeholder feedback on preferred option	*Stakeholder feedback*: through briefings/meetings, reference groups, newsletter, media

Stage 1 used a public participation framework to guide relationship building with the community and to achieve the project goals. Various strategies were used in the early stages of the project to ensure interested stakeholders could participate in the decision-making process for the dam upgrade. These included educating stakeholders about the need for the project, providing relevant information to interested stakeholders to inform the decision-making process, and establishing formal and ongoing processes such as workshops and meetings to identify and address stakeholder concerns and preferences.

More than 298 design options had been identified in previous studies and by the Alliance team. These were measured for general design efficiency, with fourteen preferred options selected for further investigation. These options were assessed by the design team against a range of criteria including cost, stakeholder impact and environmental impact. More than 50 per cent of the criteria weighting was related to stakeholder impact factors, leading the assessment team to identify four options for further investigation and assessment. These four options were then presented to the community for stakeholder consideration through the communication activities described above.

Following the extensive consultation process, stakeholder assessments were considered by the Alliance team in reducing the shortlist to the two strongest options, with a formal value management process used to deliver a final option that fully addressed stakeholder considerations. Stakeholder considerations influenced specific design improvements to the preferred option, including the location and orientation of the spillway and the construction methodology used, including traffic flow solutions during the construction period and construction times.

Feedback was provided following the selection process to demonstrate how stakeholder input had been considered and used. A key strategy was to use the same communication methods and intensity as those first used to describe the options being considered. This ensured that all participants who were contacted with information about the options had the same level of opportunity to hear and understand how their input had been a key factor in the selection of the final option and in refining the project itself.

TABLE 7.3: STAGE 2

DATE	STAGE	MAJOR COMMUNICATION ACTIVITY
March 2004– September 2005	Stakeholder information and communication during construction	*Community liaison:* including newsletter distribution, media relations, key stakeholder briefings/meetings, community information line, legacy projects

The construction phase provided a challenge for the Alliance team to deliver on the promises established in Stage 1. The Alliance utilised the same communication channels to ensure the community and relevant stakeholders were fully informed of construction activities. The community information line was monitored to respond to any specific complaints or issues, with benchmarks established to ensure a timely response.

TABLE 7.4: STAGE 3

DATE	STAGE	MAJOR COMMUNICATION ACTIVITY
March–December 2005	Major legacy project design and construction	*Community consultation:* including key stakeholder briefings/meetings, public meetings, media relations

Legacy projects were an important component in the overall strategy of community engagement. Largely funded by the Alliance's project savings, these projects were designed to address the social and economic needs of the community and to provide lasting benefits after the upgrade project was complete.

The public participation process established early in the project was used again to allow the community to identify high-priority activities to be funded from the overall project, which would provide lasting benefits to the community. A range of projects were identified and supported, including contributions to the local kindergartens, greening an old quarry in partnership with a school and TAFE institute, and partnerships with local Indigenous communities to promote their cultural heritage and history.

By far the largest project was Fernvale Futures, which was driven by the Alliance with active support from Esk Shire Council, local business and community representatives, and both the Queensland and federal governments. This $2.1 million project comprised a new master plan for the local town of Fernvale, incorporating an upgrade to the central parkland, extensive street-scaping, and construction of a community facility.

Communication

Numerous communication methods were used during the three-year period to ensure all stakeholders had access to information and could communicate directly with the Alliance using their preferred method.

INTERPERSONAL METHODS

Stakeholder meetings were a key communication method used by the Alliance throughout the project. Meetings ranged from internal briefings for Alliance partners and staff, regular meetings with the community reference group, face-to-face meetings with affected residents, one-on-one presentations with community/interest groups, and presentations to schools and TAFEs.

Public displays were also held to give the community opportunities to review and comment on the project. Alliance personnel at information displays answered queries and monitored community feedback.

Information lines, reply-paid post and fax facilities also gave stakeholders access to further information and the ability provide feedback and discuss issues.

ONLINE METHODS

A project website was established early in the project and regularly updated. This was linked to the Esk Council's community hub. An email feedback mechanism was also established to help stakeholders contact the Alliance with enquiries or complaints.

PRINT METHODS

Flyers, newsletters and advertisements were used to communicate with local stakeholders. A project newsletter was issued quarterly to local communities, advising of project progress, upcoming construction activities, timeframes and potential impacts. These key messages were reinforced by advertisements in the local newspapers. Advertising was also used to promote public display locations, information sessions and open days.

OUTDOOR

Onsite signage was provided to ensure dam users and motorists were aware of the upgrade, and to advise on safety precautions in the area.

MEDIA RELATIONS

To ensure the media had a thorough understanding of the project, briefings were conducted with journalists, media releases were issued regularly and a media kit with background information was developed. Alliance representatives were also made available for media interviews.

EVENTS

Events were used to involve the community and to demonstrate the scope of the project. For example a project launch was held to signify the official commencement of the project and to bring representatives of all the stakeholders together, recognising their interests in the project. Dam open days were held throughout the project to provide the community, media and other stakeholders with an accurate perspective on the project and its progress.

EVALUATION

The Alliance measured its performance throughout the project. Two key community relations review tools were used throughout the three-year period:

1 Surveys to track stakeholder understanding and acceptance of the project

2 Analysis of stakeholder logs and the stakeholder contact database that captured all inquiries, comments and complaints.

In measuring its performance against its objectives, the Alliance used a variety of methods.

OBJECTIVE 1.1

Increase stakeholder understanding of the project: In a survey measuring stakeholder acceptance of the project, approximately 80 per cent of the community reference group 'agreed' and 50 per cent 'strongly agreed'. At least one council also publicly acknowledged that the solution was the best for the area.

OBJECTIVE 2.1

Develop and implement projects that provide lasting community benefits: More than thirty initiatives were completed, including greening an old quarry in partnership with local education providers, partnerships with local Indigenous communities and the Fernvale Futures project.

OBJECTIVE 3.1

Improve SEQWater's rating in social responsibility, consultation, accessibility and responsiveness through the project: Issues raised by the community reference group and the stakeholder reference group during the project were investigated and responded to, with no remaining issues outstanding.

Minimal complaints were raised by stakeholders during the project. These were all responded to and resolved within forty-eight hours.

A survey of the community showed that 94 per cent of respondents believed the Alliance had a 'satisfactory' to 'very high' interest in community views, while 89 per cent felt that the communication had been 'good' or 'very good'.

The project won a number of community participation and engineering awards for its processes. An external audit by the Environmental Protection Agency (EPA) raised no issues or concerns, and the project was used by the EPA as part of its training program for regulatory staff.

OBJECTIVE 3.2

Ensure no misinformation through the media about dam safety and possibility of an extreme storm event: All information reported in the media was accurate and 90 per cent of media coverage was seen as favourable (neutral or positive).

LESSONS LEARNT

The Wivenhoe Dam project was implemented by an experienced Alliance team whose members had worked on many similar projects and had significant collective professional experience.

This project reinforced the importance of full and open public participation from the start, and the establishment of clear principles that would guide the project. The strong commitment to the communication strategy allowed a seamless transition from the consultation and design phase to the construction phase from the stakeholder perspective.

The legacy projects were identified by the Alliance team as critical to its success, and considerable investment was provided to these projects.

The project was deemed highly successful by SEQWater and has won a number of industry awards for its outcomes. A dedicated team of communication and environmental professionals ensured the process was implemented successfully.

PRACTITIONER PROFILE

Lorelei Baum, Stakeholder and Community Relations Manager Northern Region for Leighton Contractors, reflects on the highlights and learnings from the Wivenhoe Dam project and considers the future role that public relations will play in major infrastructure projects.

Every now and then a project comes along that 'gels', where everything comes together exceptionally well, so that even at the start, when it all seems hard, you have a gut feel that it's going to work. Wivenhoe was like that. By the end of the project there were a whole series of fantastic achievements.

My role was most intense towards the end when I came on board full time to build recognition for the project's many outstanding successes. Our strategy was to aggressively target industry awards, and to energise the team towards providing a groundbreaking signature legacy.

Given this focus, I'd say being successful in winning the inaugural Asiapacific IAP2 Award for Decision-Making was a stand-out moment. This was the first award won by the project, and it was particularly important as it comprised a Key Performance Indicator with a financial benefit attached. The fact that the competition included some of Australia's largest companies made it even better!

The other highlight was developing and implementing the Fernvale Futures legacy project. This is truly a stunning outcome, which could never have been achieved without the very strong relationships and trust that had been firmly established between the project and the community and key stakeholders, including the local council, business and community leaders, government representatives and, most importantly, our client, SEQWater. We are still receiving positive recognition for this initiative, which has made a real difference to the local town of Fernvale, with the new community complex providing a vibrant focal point for the town.

There were many learnings from this project. The Wivenhoe Dam Spillway Augmentation was one of the first projects where we used an evaluation process to assess our community relations efforts. We now always evaluate our community relations activities on major projects, and the information we receive is invaluable.

In the last four years I've seen an 'awakening' to the benefits of public relations in the infrastructure sector, with clients and senior management highly cognisant of the contribution good relationships and effective communication can make. A well-run stakeholder and community relations program will always assist the project to move ahead more smoothly. One important reason for this is that issues are identified and addressed before they escalate and become entrenched. I'm certain that more structured issues management will become a standard element of public relations activities on major infrastructure projects in the future.

REFERENCES

Aldrich H. & Herker D., 1977, 'Boundary Spanning Roles and Organization Structure' in *Academy of Management Review*, Vol. 2, pp. 217–30

Freeman R. E., 1984, *Strategic Management: A Stakeholder Approach*, Pitman, Boston, MA

Innes J. & Booher D., 2004, 'Reframing Public Participation: Strategies for the 21st Century' in *Planning Theory and Practice*, Vol. 5, No. 4, pp. 419–36

International Association for Public Participation (IAP2), www.iap2.org

Internal Communication

8

Improving Productivity and Morale at AMP

Donald Alexander

AIMS OF THIS CHAPTER

- To demonstrate that effective internal communication can deliver higher levels of organisational effectiveness

- To understand the core competencies that drive effective internal communication and its rapid growth as a public relations specialisation

- To develop an understanding of effective internal communication practice through analysis of a case study

INTRODUCTION

One of the fastest-growing areas of public relations specialisation is that of internal communications, principally because organisations are becoming increasingly aware that higher levels of employee productivity and commitment make a significant bottom-line contribution:

> The messages that reach (or don't reach) your employees can impact productivity,
> efficiency, and ultimately, employees' loyalty to your organization (Versantworks website).

Internal communication today is not just writing and publishing the staff newsletter or magazine, or managing the intranet. It is a substantive managerial function that means:

- Involvement in the business planning process

- Understanding businesses goals and objectives

- Ensuring managers/supervisors have the requisite skills to be effective prime organisational communicators

- Ensuring the various methods of communication are being used efficiently

- Ensuring that staff are engaged.

In effect, being an internal communicator means being a facilitator.

INTERNAL COMMUNICATIONS VITAL TO THE BOTTOM LINE

In early 2000, Westpac, one of Australia's largest banks, had the highest level of employee turnover of all of its competitors. By 2004, Westpac was reporting savings of more than $1 million a year through substantial reductions in employee recruitment and induction costs, and higher levels of employee commitment. The reason given by the bank's former internal communication manager was a new staff communication program based around changing the organisational culture through rebuilding mutual trust between management and staff, encouraging staff to take responsibility for their own work and senior management's greater awareness of the value of a more open communication style.

The American Productivity & Quality Centre (Powers 1996) completed a comprehensive study to benchmark internal communications in 1996. This study provides valuable evidence as to what fifty organisations identified as being 'best practice' for effective staff communication:

- A key finding was the CEO being accessible and serving as a role model, and also being a strong supporter of internal communication.

- A second finding was that, through involving employees in the planning process, there was a much higher degree of commitment to the organisation's vision (a factor discussed in the case study in this chapter).

- Finally, the use of managers as the primary means of communicating to employees was confirmed.

The best practice organisations also provided managers with information resources and skills training to assist them with this crucial task.

CEOs are increasingly becoming aware of the need to engage employees; they want them to enhance the company's reputation. Stafford (2007) wrote of recent United Kingdom research that CEOs wanted a culture that delivered differentiation, and to that end they had to articulate an exciting vision and minimise the social distance between themselves and their employees.

A US-based remuneration consultancy, Watson Wyatt, released a survey in 2006 that clearly demonstrated a correlation between internal communication and financial performance (Finney 2006). The *Watson Wyatt 2005–06 Communication ROI Study* stated that organisations with high-quality internal communication practices returned a market premium of 19.4 per cent over organisations with poor internal communication, and also delivered 57 per cent higher shareholder returns over five years. In addition, supporting the Westpac evidence, the survey found that companies in this high-performance category had levels of employee engagement four-and-a-half times higher than the competition.

Quinn and Hargie (2004, p. 146) state that the 'value of quality internal communication and its relationship to organisational efficiency has been widely recognised' and quote Stayer (1990), Clampitt and Downs (1993) and Hargie et al. (2003) to support their conclusion. Clampitt and Downs (1993, p. 7) report that the benefits 'obtained from quality internal communications include: improved productivity; reduced absenteeism; high quality (of services and products); increased levels of innovation; fewer strikes; and reduced costs'. Argenti and Forman (2002) have also been quoted by Kalla (2005, p. 302) to the effect that 'companies with effective communication strategies are usually successful'.

This is positive, but there is sufficient evidence in Australia to suggest that organisations still have a long way to go before they can be listed in the best practice category. A 2004 review of over a dozen communication audits of major Australian companies highlighted the fact that employees were not very satisfied with communication within their organisations (Gray 2004). Significant points were that 62 per cent (of a total of more than 100,000 employees) were not satisfied with their organisation's communication with them; that senior management communication was poor (38 per cent); and that upward communication, listening, consultation and involvement were also at low levels (40 per cent). Another poor response was for cross-functional communication and the provision of company information

(38 per cent). One of the few positive responses was that 61 per cent were supportive about communication with their immediate boss.

This clearly demonstrates that while some organisations—such as those described earlier—are doing well, there is still a lot of work to be done by senior management to recognise the impact and effect of internal communication. Gray (2004) believes the answer lies in communicators concentrating their efforts to assist executives and managers in improving their communicating, especially through listening to employees and consulting with them. These findings are supported by Tourish and Hargie (2004, p. 7), who report on a survey of 2600 United Kingdom employees who:

> clearly expressed the view that what was most demotivating of all was lack of
> communication from managers, citing issues such as a complete absence of interaction,
> a general lack of feedback, or meetings taking place behind closed doors.

The authors refer to other research demonstrating a clear linkage between employee satisfaction (driven by communication with their managers) and business performance, and point to a Towers-Perrin (1993, p. 8) study of high-performing US companies, where senior executives had a tendency to seek suggestions from front-line staff, 'delegate, develop two-way communication and seek suggestions'.

In the face of this strong evidence of the link between effective internal communication and organisational success, why do so many organisations not provide more resources towards improving this vital aspect of their organisation's operating effectiveness? What is needed, it is suggested, is for the communication team to provide the evidence from the literature and the case studies to the CEOs and point out the success of a company such as Westpac in directly improving its bottom line.

Another key area, especially for listed organisations, is a growing trend for financial market analysts to place a value on an organisation's non-financial assets (how it manages its people and its reputation). Theaker (2001) quotes Cowlett (1999) to the effect that analysts and portfolio managers base their decision to buy or sell stock on non-financial as well as financial performance. One of the key factors is the ability of an organisation to attract and retain top-quality people, and all the research discussed in this chapter refers to the vital role of effective communication in ensuring committed employees. This is another driver for informing CEOs of the vital link between internal communication and positive reporting to the market.

For examples of winning internal communication award entries, go to:

- The CiB British Association of Communicators in Business Awards (CiB website)

- The United Kingdom Chartered Institute of Public Relations Excellence Awards (a separate category for internal communications) (Chartered Institute of Public Relations website)

- The International Association of Business Communicators Golden Quill Awards (International Association of Business Communicators website)

- The Public Relations Institute of Australia (PRIA) annual awards (the Golden Target Awards) (PRIA website)

- The Public Relations Institute of New Zealand (PRINZ) awards (PRINZ website).

Theoretical platform for internal communication

Miller (1996), quoted by Kalla (2005, p. 302), identified internal communication as the cross-section between communication and 'organisational life, i.e. business, organisational, management, and corporate communication'. For the purposes of this discussion, it is difficult not to agree with Argenti and Forman (2002, p. 128) that internal communication involved creating 'an atmosphere of respect for all employees within the organisation'. Kalla (2005, p. 304) attempts to provide a solution by defining internal communications as integrating all formal and informal communication taking place internally at all levels of an organisation, and where the goal is to include all communication processes simultaneously taking place inside an organisation.

Welch and Jackson (2007) quote Quirke (2000) that internal communication was a core process for organisations, and they reference Yeomans (2006, p. 337): 'Very little attention is paid to internal communication by public relations scholars yet it is viewed as part of an organisation's strategic communication function.' One of the most-published researchers in this field in the region is Dr Colleen Mills from the University of Canterbury in Christchurch, New Zealand, and her list of journal articles and papers is available on the University of Canterbury website.

Measuring internal communication effectiveness

In 1985, Peters articulated what has since become a management mantra: that what gets measured gets managed. More than most other communication specialities, internal communication is highly measurable through instruments such as staff surveys, feedback and market research.

Internal communications managers can assess the extent to which the organisation's goals and objectives are understood, and where changes may be needed. Line manager communication expertise can be tested. Employee feedback on how they feel managers are supporting them and how effectively the organisation informs staff about competitors, customers, products and media are also measurable. Hargie et al. (2002) provide a valuable assessment of the role of communication audits, and conclude that they are under-utilised and should be more widely used as an important research tool.

There is now a wide range of survey methodologies available, and Sampson (1995) has a listing of all the recognised communication audit instruments and their structure, dimensions, administration and reliability factors. This is a very useful starting-off point for anyone considering commissioning or doing an audit. Further support can be found from the 'father' of this aspect of internal communication, Cal Downs, who in 2004 with Allyson Adrian produced an updated version of Downs' original 1987 text, *Assessing Organizational Communication: Strategic Communication Audits*. From a European perspective, Hargie and Tourish (2000) also have a book on communication auditing, while Oliver (2006) sets out a business-critical approach to effective employee communication.

Future directions

In a report by the Melcrum organisation (Melcrum Publishing 2007), the future of internal communications was stated by 1149 respondents as being an increased use of intranets, more communication training for leaders and managers, and a greater use of metrics. Reporting on the research, Dewhurst (2007) said the planned investment in training senior leaders and line managers was indicative of the shift from producing newsletters to taking a more strategic view of the function. Social media and 'Web 2.0' were also raised as future means of communicating internally:

- Only 12 per cent of respondents used blogs, with 23 per cent saying they intended to use this form of communication in the future

- 8 per cent used podcasting

- 6 per cent used Really Simple Syndication (RSS)

- 4 per cent used a wiki.

Commenting on these results, Dewhurst said that, with younger employees who understand and use the new technology, it would only be a matter of time before these new forms of communicating are used more extensively. An Edelman/People Metrics study (Ewing 2006), however, showed that many organisations were hesitant to adopt these new technologies, and that what was needed was an educational program to inform staff about the application of the various new social media channels to all aspects of internal communication. Some major corporations in Australia have started to seek assistance from universities and specialist consultancies with this task.

DRIVING CHANGE AT AMP

Part 1: Initial major change program

BACKGROUND

AMP, a substantial organisation in the financial services sector with more than 4000 employees, was facing a significant challenge. A review by an external consultancy found that the organisation was moribund. There was no focus on customers, senior management

DONALD ALEXANDER

were reclusive, staff morale was low (with little or no communication from management), and the organisation was using its capital reserves as it was no longer profitable. The CEO initiated a major change program to restore profitability, and a central working committee was created that had a specialist communication consultancy as part of the team. The consultancy's view was that at least 15 per cent of jobs were not contributing to the organisation, so it was decided that around 20 per cent of jobs should be cut. A process for managing this approach was agreed by the senior management team, which meant that each job in the organisation (except for two) should be reviewed against certain criteria.

RESEARCH

A network analysis was made to assess who were considered the most effective communicators in each business unit. The role of these communicators was to ensure that all members of their unit were fully aware of the information distributed to staff. A formal communication audit was also made at the start to find the most preferred means of receiving information (face-to-face briefings from the immediate manager came top of the list). The management team was then advised of the outcomes of these two assessments so they could factor them into their own communication planning. Further, regular surveys of staff were made as the program progressed to test if the key messages were being received and understood.

TARGET PUBLICS

The target publics were:

- All staff in the organisation

- External, independent advisors (dependent on AMP products and staff relationships)

- Professional suppliers (lawyers, actuaries, research firms)

- Media (AMP had attracted much negative attention)

- State governments (each state office was likely to be downsized).

GOALS AND OBJECTIVES

AMP's goal was to restore its position as a pre-eminent financial services organisation. To achieve this goal, its objectives were as follows:

- To deliver all planned cost and staff reduction within twelve months with minimum disruption to business and morale (evaluated by regular staff and customer surveys)

- To substantially improve levels of customer service within twelve to eighteen months (tested by quarterly customer quality surveys)

- To improve relationships with the media within twelve to eighteen months

- To change perceptions about AMP from being an 'insurance' company to being a 'financial services' organisation.

COMMUNICATION STRATEGY AND TACTICS

A strategy was agreed to ensure all employees knew what was going to happen, when it would occur and—following Larkin and Larkin's (1994) advice—to communicate some probabilities.

The first step was a presentation to all senior managers by the CEO. The key driver of the program was the need to change to survive as a leading player in the industry. For many, this was the first time they had been faced with such a massive change and, from the questions raised, it was obvious that many thought the CEO would not see the program through to completion. Managers were given a pack of information and instructed to convene a similar meeting with their staff within twenty-four hours. They were asked to advise the steering committee of their meeting arrangements; when some failed to do so, a clear message was sent to those managers from the CEO that, unless they held meetings, the leader of the change program would convene one.

At this stage another process was established—that of a regular mini-questionnaire sent to random staff every two weeks to test their awareness of the program and to seek feedback. All managers were then briefed by the consultants on how to review their staffing and budgets, and meet the targets set. A regular fortnightly email newsletter for all staff was also created to keep them informed of progress, the key timeline dates and any further information that the communication team deemed relevant. This was when matters became very difficult. Very soon after the first newsletter was distributed, two senior managers arrived in the communication manager's office demanding an explanation as to why 'their' staff had received a newsletter from the change management team, and not from them. Their view was that they knew what their staff needed. It took some time for this old culture to be changed.

Part of the review was to enable staff to provide their own input into what they considered should be done in their own area to help achieve the outcomes sought. It was decided (also based on Larkin & Larkin 1994) that managers should be responsible for communicating the outcomes of the review to their groups. A series of workshops was developed by the communication team to ensure every manager was equipped to handle both the good news and the bad news. A script was written by the communication team to ensure consistency across the organisation, and workshops were run as simulations of the staff presentations, with Q&As and human resource support people available to ask and answer difficult questions. Special attention was given on how to handle the 'survivors', as well as those who would be retrenched.

EVALUATION

At the conclusion of the program, a staff-wide survey was made to test levels of feeling about how the program had been handled and the adequacy of communication. The general response was that staff were unhappy about the change program; however they understood and accepted the reasons given to them for the complete upheaval in their work, and also agreed that the organisation had handled departing staff with sensitivity. They further agreed that communication throughout the program had been very good. Before the change program, 45 per cent of staff were satisfied with the communication they received from the organisation; following the program, this rose to 85 per cent.

Finally, staff stated that they were committed to the changed organisation, principally because they had been involved in the review process and therefore understood the rationale behind the program.

LESSONS LEARNT

Key lessons from Part 1 of the process included:

- Some staff—those who managers agreed were vital to the reformed organisation—still participated in the program, but special measures were used, such as putting them into project teams or marking their personnel file.

- Staff should be surveyed at regular intervals.

- Line managers/supervisors should be made responsible for most of the communication, and must be equipped to handle this.

- The senior management team must support the program and actively participate in it.

Part 2: Follow-up change program

BACKGROUND

The second phase was more intense and focused on business planning for the future. The senior management team asked for specialist communication advice right from the start of this process.

COMMUNICATION STRATEGY AND TACTICS

It was agreed that:

- All staff would have the opportunity to participate in planning their own responses to the overall business plan.

- Line managers and supervisors would be the primary means of involving all staff in the planning program.

- Senior management committed themselves to listening and acting on ideas that would contribute to the new direction and desired outcomes.

- Regular surveys of staff would be held during the planning process.

The first step of this phase was taken by senior management who commissioned a series of studies into the industry sector, including for the first time research into competitors and possible new industry entrants. All staff were also encouraged to provide any reports they might have worked on in the past eighteen months as part of their business unit forward planning. From this, the senior management team developed a series of scenarios and each business unit manager was asked to get their team to assess all of them, not just the ones that might impact their own operations.

At this time, the communication team developed a process that was based on line managers and supervisors being at the core of the next stage of the communication plans.

All staff who had supervisory responsibilities, regardless of their location in Australia, were invited to Sydney for a two-day briefing. The session started with the CEO providing an overview and an outline of the company goals, and the objectives he expected the organisation to achieve in the short, medium and long term. Then each business unit manager (a member of the senior management team) gave their overview of what they considered needed to be done to achieve the objectives. Anyone could ask questions of the group that had just presented, and this took some time to complete. In the mid-afternoon of the first day, everyone was organised into cross-functional groups of ten people.

The task of these groups was to go through all the presentations made earlier in the day and discuss how they might impact each business unit, what the collaboration issues might be, and what new ideas might be thrown up as a consequence of the discussion. That evening the groups were asked to commit their discussions to paper and present the highlights to everyone the next day.

The morning of the second day was taken up with presentations from each group, and this created more discussion. The communication team prepared information packs based on the material presented, including areas of discussion for each participant. Each attendee was requested to hold a briefing for their staff within the next forty-eight hours and to report the results to their senior business unit manager. At the conclusion of this process, each business unit then had a few days to write a business plan for the next twelve months.

EVALUATION

The feedback research from a representative sample of all employees was:

- There was a very high level of commitment to the business plan (89 per cent), primarily because everyone felt that they had been engaged in the process.

- Those invited to the briefing had a very high level of engagement (92 per cent). They felt they were trusted, in that they had been asked to attend and participate, and had also been given the responsibility to take the information back to present to their staff.

- Everyone reported favourably on the communication process, especially the face-to-face communication between managers/supervisors and staff, and expressed their hope that this was the way of the future.

Within a year, a further staff study was made with substantially higher-than-average levels of commitment to the organisation's goals and values. The organisation was also exceeding its business targets.

Lessons learnt

For organisational success, internal communications must have a high priority in the strategic planning and implementation process, as without this, employees will not be committed to the values and vision. Unless staff are motivated and feel engaged, most aspects of organisational life will suffer:

- Customers could depart if they deal with an employee with an indifferent attitude.

- Suppliers could switch if they feel they are dealing with a less than enthusiastic staff member.

- New and creative staff might be harder to recruit.

- Staff could depart more frequently, driving up costs.

- Poor internal morale can negatively affect commitment.

The CEO needs to be a core part of the internal communication team. The CEO also needs to be supportive of developing line managers as key communicators, and of implementing regular feedback to test if all the objectives are being met. Tench and Yeomans (2006) refer to a strategic shift in internal communication management toward the co-creation of meaning through employee participation. Building effective two-way communication up and down and across organisational structures can only be for the ultimate benefit of all key stakeholders in the company's successful growth and development.

PRACTITIONER PROFILE

Laurelle McConachy is a Deakin BA (Journalism and Public Relations) graduate working in employee communications. Work experience at Alcoa Australia Rolled Products led Laurelle to the position of Communications Officer with that company during her final year at university, before she moved on to Medibank Private where she is now Internal Communications Advisor.

Why is employee communication important?

Employee communication is vital in ensuring all staff are engaged and informed on what is happening in their workplace, and understanding where they fit in the organisation's plans.

How is it being done?

A number of channels are used to deliver company messages and keep employees 'in the know', including quarterly hard-copy magazines, fortnightly intranet newsletters, breaking news items posted on the intranet, organisation-wide emails, bi-annual staff forums in each state presented by the managing director and deputy managing director, and providing strategic communications advice to business/project leaders when rolling out initiatives and organisational changes.

What role does it play for the organisation?

The Internal Communications Department ensures messages from within the organisation are aligned with external communications messages, creating consistency. Timely delivery of information is essential, in a concise manner that reduces information overload. Rewarding and recognising employee achievements is also a large part of employee communication, increasing engagement.

REFERENCES

Argenti P. A. & Forman J., 2002, *The Power of Corporate Communication: Crafting the Voice and Image of Your Business*, McGraw-Hill, New York

Austin N. & Peters T., 1985, *A Passion for Excellence*, Random House, New York

British Association of Communicators in Business (CiB), www.cib.uk.com/artman/publish/cat_index_26.shtml

Clampitt P. G. & Downs C. W., 1993, 'Employee Perceptions of the Relationship between Communication and Productivity' in *Journal of Business Communication*, Vol. 30, No. 1, pp. 5–28

Cowlett M., 1999, 'Creating a Breed of Company Converts' in *PR Week*, 9 April 1999, pp. 13–14

Dewhurst S., 2007, 'Key Findings from the Pulse Survey' in *SCM*, Vol. 11, Issue 1, pp. 6–7

Downs C. W. & Adrian A. D., 2004, *Assessing Organizational Communication: Strategic Communication Audits*, The Guildford Press, New York and London

Ewing M. E., 2007, 'Changing with the Times: Leveraging the Web to Enhance your Employee Communications Programme' in *Tactics*, March 2007, pp. 12–13

Finney J., 2006, 'A World of Difference' in *Communication World*, July–August 2006

Gray R., 2004, 'Finding the Right Direction' in *Communication World*, November–December 2004, pp. 26–32

Hargie O. & Tourish D., 2000, *Handbook of Communication Audits for Organisations*, Routledge, London

Hargie O., Tourish D. & Wilson N., 2002, 'Communication Audits and the Effects of Increased Information: A Follow-up Study' in *The Journal of Business Communication*, Vol. 39, No. 4, pp. 414–36

Hargie O., Rainey S. & Dickson D., 2003, 'Working Together, Living Apart: Inter-group Communication within Organizations in Northern Ireland', in Schorr A., Campbell W. & Schenk M. (eds), *Communication Research and Media Science in Europe*, Mouton de Gruyter, Berlin

Institute of Healthcare Management, http://ihmpapers.co.uk/professional-development/professional-development/implementing-an-effective-employee-communications-strategy.html

International Association of Business Communicators, www.iabc.com/awards/gq

Kalla H. K., 2005, 'Integrated Internal Communications: A Multidisciplinary Perspective' in *Corporate Communications: An International Journal*, Vol. 10, No. 4, pp. 302–14

Larkin T. J. & Larkin S., 1994, *Communicating Change: How to Win Employee Support for New Business Directions*, McGraw-Hill Inc., New York

Melcrum Publishing, 2007, *Delivering Successful Change Communication*, www.melcrum.com/store

Oliver D., 2006, http://ihmpapers.co.uk/professional-development/professional-development/implementing-an-effective-employee-communications-strategy.html, accessed December 2007

Peters T. J., 1985, *A Passion for Excellence: The Leadership Difference*, Random House, New York

Powers V. J., 1996, 'Benchmarking Study Illustrates how Best-in-class Achieve Alignment, Communicate Change—Includes Profiles of Participating Companies' in *Communication World*, December 1996

Public Relations Institute of Australia (PRIA), www.pria.com.au/aboutus/cid/126/parent/0/t/aboutus

Public Relations Institute of New Zealand (PRINZ), www.prinz.org.nz

Quinn D. & Hargie O., 2004, 'Internal Communication Audits: A Case Study' in *Corporate Communications: An International Journal*, Vol. 9, No. 2, pp. 146–58

Sampson W. R., *Communication Satisfaction Audits*, www.uwec.edu/Sampsow/Measures/CSQ.htm, accessed 5 February 2008

Stafford M., 2007, 'The Rules are Changing—Are We?' in *SCM*, Vol. 11, Issue 1, p. 5

Stayer R., 1990, 'How I Learned to let my Workers Lead' in *Harvard Business Review*, Vol. 68, pp. 66–83

Tench R. & Yeomans L., 2006, *Exploring Public Relations*, Pearson Education Limited, Essex

Theaker A., 2001, *The Public Relations Handbook*, 2nd edn, Routledge, London

Tourish D. & Hargie O. (eds), 2004, *Key Issues in Organizational Communication*, Routledge, Abingdon, Oxon

Towers-Perrin, 1993, *Improving Business Performance Through Your People*, Towers-Perrin, San Franciso, CA

United Kingdom Chartered Institute of Public Relations, www.cipr.co.uk/excellence/

University of Canterbury, www.mang.canterbury.ac.nz/people/mills_pub.shtml

Versantworks, www.versantworks.com, accessed 1 January 2007

Watson Wyatt Worldwide, www.watsonwyatt.com/research/resrender.asp?id=2006-US-0039&page=1

Welch M. & Jackson P. R., 2007, 'Rethinking Internal Communication: A Stakeholder Approach' in *Corporate Communication: An International Journal*, Vol. 12, No. 2, pp. 177–98

Financial Public Relations

Domino's Pizza and Elders Rural Bank

Dr Joy Chia and Robina Xavier

9

AIMS OF THIS CHAPTER

- To understand the broad field of financial public relations and how it is practised

- To understand the specialist investor relations role and its challenges

- To develop an understanding of financial public relations and investor relations in practice through an analysis of two case studies

INTRODUCTION

A sector of public relations that has received little attention, because it is still in the early stages of development, is financial public relations. Financial public relations encompasses communication management with financial communities about an organisation's position and future strategy (Tench & Yeomans 2006), with the overall aim of increasing the organisation's financial performance. This can include communication with a range of stakeholders—including shareholders, financial analysts, stockbrokers, employees, financial, media, and potential and existing customers—to promote investment opportunities as well as investment products that customers can purchase to enhance their wealth. It can also involve raising the profile of companies that operate primarily in financial markets, such as banks, insurance companies, superannuation funds, private equity groups and funds managers. Financial public relations is undertaken for all types of organisations including companies that are privately owned, government-sponsored organisations and those that are listed on the stock exchange.

Within this broad field is the more focused area of investor relations, or shareholder relations as it is sometimes known, which focuses primarily on communicating with investors or shareholders of companies that trade their shares on a stock exchange. This is a specialist public relations role where practitioners develop relationships with potential investors, the financial media and financial analysts, and 'advise companies engaged in transactions such as mergers and acquisitions and initial public offerings' (Burgess 2007, p. 43).

Financial public relations practitioners need to be conversant with the regulatory framework of stock exchanges and financial institutions such as the Australian Stock Exchange, and the Australian Securities and Investment Commission. Communication management always takes place within these corporate regulatory frameworks, so practitioners require precise understanding of relevant laws and regulations to communicate appropriately. Building relationships with the financial community also requires particular skills, knowledge and understanding of 'investment markets, an understanding of investors' information needs and financial knowledge' (Burgess 2007, p. 45). To achieve this understanding, market research is important to identify the needs specific to various investor groups.

Public relations educators prepare students for this growing sector of professional practice by building their skills in specialist financial public relations management. In these specialist roles, public relations practitioners build relationships with journalists responsible for market analysis and investor relations reporting. As Guth and Marsh (2005, p. 289) put it: 'investment analysts, mutual fund managers, and financial journalists don't like to be surprised. They require current information on a company and immediate updates about any events that might affect the company's financial performance', and these events might change several times in a day as the share market changes, take-over bids are challenged, and international market fluctuations impact local markets negatively or positively.

Communication management in financial public relations involves much more than two-way symmetric communication and exchange (Grunig 2001), as practitioners need to communicate with diverse audiences, communicate through a variety of media with a view to increasing transparency, inform potential investors, and provide multi-discussion channels for exchange and relationship-building with organisations. The authors of this chapter emphasise the need to improve and manage relationships effectively as a core component of public relations practice (Chia 2005; 2006). In financial public relations, this means that loyalty, trust and confidence are developed in corporations' shareholder relationships because of the emphasis on valuing the potential investor or shareholder, and understanding the importance of simultaneously developing a relationship and conducting a transaction. This also means that care needs to be taken not to create an environment of over-confidence in the market, as some scholars (Lattimore et al. 2004) indicate that this can result in panic buying (and inflating the market price above its real value) or selling (as shareholders might think that shares are being talked-up). In this environment financial public relations could be viewed as spin or hype attempting to protect an organisation's reputation.

The sophistication of shareholders and potential investors is such that not only is communication more complex, it is also more intense because of constant online exchange about the value of shares as these shares adjust to market fluctuations. Gregory (2004) contends that this results in groups dissolving and reforming, and constantly challenging organisations' communication with them. In this complex business environment, closed systems—such as those evident in the Enron collapse (Cutlip et al. 2006)—indicate that the role of financial public relations is also to develop dialogue and consultation internally with employees and management so that changes in an organisation's financial position are understood and managed from within.

Financial public relations is used by companies in good times and bad. Mention Enron and you move into world of greed where 'dirty works inside a company can cut a stock in half in just a few stock-market minutes' (Cruver 2002, p. 346). Internal and external communication in the Enron saga and collapse was selective, with shareholders and potential investors given only one form of communication—that Enron is a great company and it is great to invest in this company. Some scholars (Lattimore et al. 2004, p. 281) point out that one of the problems with the collapse of Enron was caused by shareholders being unaware of the bad news about the company; Enron investors were not treated equally or even recognised. There was a need to know when communication was misleading. There was also a lack of empowerment of employees' decision-making, as employees—including the public relations team—were shut out, leaving questions unanswered about the organisation's demise. Corporations such as Enron may have been tempted to promote themselves in a positive way, with a view to developing their brand and reputation, but this was deceptive. The Enron saga and the saga of other international corporate collapses left shareholders angry, stranded, and demanding accountability and sound governance.

Australian investors and shareholders have also experienced corporate collapses (Burgess 2007), crushing public confidence and resulting in investors demanding greater transparency about company transactions. Shareholders have voting rights and they want to know about issues that may affect them (Baines et al. 2004). Changing circumstances and considerable market activity involved in acquisitions and mergers have increased the opportunity for more Australian financial public relations positions in organisations such as Telstra and Woolworths, which hired specialist financial public relations consultants (Burgess 2007). Even so, compared to the United Kingdom, where 90 per cent of listed companies employ investor relations or financial public relations personnel, only about a quarter of listed Australian companies have hired specialist financial public relations staff.

Although financial public relations practice is emerging, it is sometimes affected by:

- A poor understanding of the possible role that public relations could play

- Doubt about public relations practitioners having the skill to manage financial strategy

- Doubt about the difference communication management could and would make to potential investors or shareholders.

As such, part of the challenge to the profession will be to promote the wider and specialist skills of its professional practitioners, and to spell out the difference that effective communication management can make. The position and responsibilities of financial public relations need to be made clear to the business and financial community (Chambers 1999). Articles in prominent Australian media such as the *Australian Business Review Weekly* (Burgess 2007) increase public awareness and provide a pathway for potential investor advice, especially as many investors may be confused by the complexity of communication about financial markets and the possibilities these markets present. Increasingly investors receive their information about diverse stocks and shares online, and they are gradually managing more complex investment portfolios. It is therefore important that they are fully conversant with the communication about their investment, and its meaning to their financial engagement with banks, credit agencies and financial markets.

Haywood (2002) suggests that corporate candour is essential as financial news is making international media headlines. New companies emerge when others are closing their doors, resulting in redundancies, and shareholders and potential investors demanding up-to-date information. More importantly, consistency of message management about organisations' corporate value must be supported by management, as investors may also be nervous about a company's environmental policies or how it is managing its resources (Haywood 2002).

As confidence in the corporate sector is low, scholars (Cutlip et al. 2006; Collis 2003) point to the importance of developing loyalty through open, consistent messages to diverse investor audiences.

In the Australian business environment 'with 181 floats on the Australian Stock Exchange last year, all competing for shareholder attention, companies are maintaining competitiveness by increasing their marketing to investors, often using investor relations consultants' (Burgess 2007, p. 43) to provide targeted professional advice. The need for financial public relations seems evident, but the Australian public relations profession is still coming to terms with the extent and potential of this role and the skill required to manage it.

The following cases demonstrate the breadth of financial public relations practice, from the specialist investor relations required to raise money and list a company on the stock exchange, to broader financial profiling to help a financial institution attract depositors.

DOMINO'S PIZZA LISTS ON THE ASX

Background

Domino's Pizza has operated in Australia for more than twenty years, expanding to all states and becoming Australia's largest pizza maker. While well known for its quality pizzas, it was also a highly successful business, recording annual profits in excess of $9 million. But the owners of the Domino's Pizza master franchise in Australia had bigger plans for the business and needed further capital injections to fulfil these plans. Their challenge was to take Domino's, the household name with strong consumer support, and make it into an attractive investment choice for institutional and individual shareholders in Australia.

An initial public offering (IPO) and listing on the Australian Stock Exchange (ASX) was planned for May 2005. This would involve the company, Domino's Pizza Australia New Zealand Limited, producing a prospectus that outlined the investment opportunity for potential shareholders and provided a mechanism through which people could apply to buy shares in the company. When this process was finished, the company could join the official list of the ASX, which would allow all interested parties to trade in the company's shares.

Research

Extensive internal and external research was required to prepare the Domino's media and investor relations program. Media interest in earlier IPOs was tracked to identify relevant issues and their cycles, and the positions of relevant journalists were determined. Detailed media lists of financial journalists around Australia were prepared to support the communication program as it unfolded.

Research within Domino's focused on identifying areas that would help promote the company to investors, as well as identify any areas where issues might arise that would need further explanation for interested publics.

Research was also undertaken with the various parties that would be involved in the float of the company, including the company's investment bankers, to confirm their needs and identify any relevant issues that they believed might affect the process.

Target publics

The target publics for the IPO and the listing were quite specific:

- Potential investors (institutional and individual)
- Advisers to potential investors (including stockbrokers)
- Financial media
- Regulatory bodies that would be involved during the process (such as the ASX).

Goals and objectives

The goals for the program were devised around six key stages in the float process. The overall goal was to maximise awareness among key audiences during the entire process, which would assist the company in raising its A$75 million target. A secondary goal was to use the IPO process to build further consumer awareness of Domino's Pizza and its products.

Specific objectives were to:

- Educate the investment community about Domino's Pizza
- Ensure the credibility of the company's management team
- Achieve media coverage at critical times throughout the process to support the stockbroker sales program
- Neutralise any negative commentary that might affect the float process.

Communication strategy and tactics

The communication program was adapted to suit each stage of the IPO and listing process. The first four stages related to establishing the primary market for the company; that is, those investors who buy their shares directly from the company through the prospectus. The last two stages related to establishing the secondary market, when the company's shares are listed on the ASX and can be bought and sold through the exchange.

The six stages and the key activities for each are described below.

STAGE 1: INVESTOR MARKETING

This stage of the investor relations process is often called market conditioning; that is, preparing the stock market and its participants for something to come. Prior to the company's prospectus being lodged, Domino's undertook profile-raising activities to ensure that potential investors were aware of its operations and its value as a business. These involved media announcements of store expansions and entry to new markets, demonstrating the company's strong growth potential, and general business stories in key magazines such as *Business Review Weekly* and *Franchising Magazine*. The company also realised the power of their employees in selling a positive message, so it undertook a national employee communication campaign through emails and teleconferences to ensure that employees knew the company's plans.

As the financial media would be an important channel through which to reach potential investors, it was important to ensure that the journalists knew as much about Domino's as possible. Background briefings were held with key journalists to ensure that they had an accurate understanding of the company's business and to build personal relations between the company's personnel and the journalists.

STAGE 2: PROSPECTUS LODGMENT

Companies can only formally discuss the details of their proposed capital-raising once their prospectus is lodged. A legal document, the prospectus outlines all the benefits and risks for potential investors and is designed to help them make a decision about investing in the company. The lodgment of a prospectus is a major news item for most companies, so a full media program—including briefings with key financial journalists and media releases to the financial and general media—is undertaken. Domino's also took this opportunity to brief financial analysts on their plans. Analysts are an important public as they undertake research on companies and make recommendations as to whether companies and individuals should invest.

It is clear that Domino's was under particular scrutiny when it released its prospectus to the market, as the document provides significant detail about the company. Therefore, management was well briefed before the event on questions the media may have, and responses were prepared to potential issues that may arise.

STAGE 3: RETAIL OFFER PERIOD

Domino's wanted to attract a large percentage of individual shareholders to invest in the company. These shareholders make up what is called the 'retail' market. The company devised a communication plan, using the media to get individual shareholders interested in the capital-raising and to support the activities of the stockbrokers, who were also trying to sell shares to their clients. The media schedule included placing stories on profiles of key managers, features on the company's activities, and ongoing interviews with key journalists to ensure Domino's featured regularly in the mass media. This involved significant creativity by the communication specialists to ensure a range of news angles were devised and targeted at the appropriate media outlet.

STAGE 4: OFFER CLOSES

In a little under three weeks, the offer to the public closed and it was then time for the company to determine if it had met its target of raising A$75 million. Business journalists were interested in this stage, as a company that attracts subscriptions for more than its target is seen as highly attractive, whereas one that attracts less than its target is often the focus of a negative news story.

Potential shareholders in Domino's wanted to buy more shares in the company than were available, so Domino's was able to release a positive statement outlining its success.

STAGE 5: LISTING

Once the applications for shares were sorted and the shares allocated to the company's new shareholders, the company was ready to list on the ASX. This is a once-in-a-lifetime opportunity for any public company, and is always a time for strong media interest. Domino's management participated in a range of interviews and photo opportunities on its listing day and its shareholders were rewarded with an immediate profit. Shareholders who bought the shares for A$2.20 from the company could have sold them on listing day for A$2.35, despite an overall drop in the stock market on the day.

STAGE 6: ONGOING INVESTOR RELATIONS

While the float period was one of intense activity over three months, the ongoing investor relations program also mounts considerable challenges for companies. It is important that, immediately post-float, the company has well-entrenched policies and procedures to support its communication with shareholders and support groups in line with regulatory requirements and the goals of the company. For Domino's, this meant establishing protocols and procedures to maintain positive communication with key audiences, to ensure the ongoing fair valuation of the company's share price and the establishment of internal systems to ensure a consistent communication message to all publics. The company also had to develop a financial calendar of key communication milestones.

Evaluation

The Domino's public offering was heavily oversubscribed and the listing price on the first day of trade represented a premium on the purchase price.

Media monitoring and analysis techniques were used to map the significant media coverage gained throughout the listing period of March to May. Coverage was achieved in a range of high-profile media outlets, including the *Australian Financial Review*, *Sydney Morning Herald*, *BRW* and *Sky Business News*.

Lessons learnt

One of the key lessons learnt from the Domino's float was the need to have a well-planned media approach to ensure coverage throughout a period of interest. While an individual news item can be generated from many events, maintaining media coverage for three months on a self-generated issue requires significant planning and creativity. This was mapped out in advance and took advantage of a broad consideration of the news relevance of company activities. Specific targeting of the media with stories of interest also ensured higher coverage.

Domino's has used its successful communication strategy to support its ongoing growth with a well-planned investor relations schedule, including twice-yearly results announcements, an annual report, an AGM for shareholders, media and analyst briefings, and a specialist investor section on its website for easy access to current and archived information. From humble beginnings, Domino's now operates more than 600 stores, sells 35 million pizzas each year and is owned by more than 1800 shareholders, who all get to share in its success.

ELDERS RURAL BANK LAUNCH

An example of effective and mutually beneficial financial public relations was the launch of Elders Rural Bank, 'Banking on the Bush', in June 2000. This case study was reported in Kellaway et al. (2003), but in the context of this chapter and the changing environment of financial public relations, the authors include commentary within the current context of the case study.

The successful development of a relationship between the public relations consultancy Porter Novelli and its client, Elders Rural Bank, points to the importance of financial public relations in effective communication management of Australian financial institutions. However, the case study is one that represents management by a public relations consultancy, rather than a specialist financial public relations consultancy.

Background

'Elders Rural Bank was the first bank granted a licence following a 1997 Commonwealth Government inquiry into the Australian financial system that opened the way for increased competition in the financial sector' (Kellaway et al. 2003, p. 58).

Elders Bank is a joint venture between Elders Limited, which is owned by Futuris Corporation Limited, and the Bendigo Bank Limited. The regulatory body responsible for recommending that Elders Bank be given a licence was Australian Prudential Regulations Authority, and the licence was approved and granted by the Federal Financial Services and Regulation Federal Minister at the time of the launch.

The public relations consultancy Porter Novelli was hired by Elders Limited to manage the launch of Elders Rural Bank. This consultancy was hired because of its niche rural client base, rural expertise and rural knowledge. This expertise was important to its understanding of a financial institution with a particular clientele—the rural community—with reach to metropolitan communities that would be important to the success of a new bank.

Research and understanding the market

Launching a bank requires extensive research to understand what consumers want and need. At the time of the launch, when many rural and city bank branches were closing, attempting to launch a new bank was a public relations opportunity but also risky business. Consumer trust had been tested as many banking customers had become disillusioned with the entire banking sector, because that sector seemed disinterested in the banking needs of regional Australia. Within this environment of distrust, trust of Elders was most important to strategic public relations planning. The Elders name was part of the rural community and had developed consumer confidence in the management of many products, such as farm merchandise and real estate.

Porter Novelli found that:

- It could build on the relationships that Elders had established in other areas of its 180-year-old business.

- The public relations role was not well understood by Elders, so part of the success of a new bank launch involved Porter Novelli educating its client about public relations.

- The challenge was to successfully launch Elders Rural Bank in 150 branches across Australia on launch day, and to work with the regional managers and staff in making this possible.

The primary research was qualitative, as this allows the practitioner to uncover meanings and understandings with a view to grasping regional customers' needs. Qualitative research is especially important in the early stages of public relations planning as the practitioner needs to unravel the understandings and interpretations of publics important to the success of a public relations plan (Sarantakos 1998; Grunig & Huang 2000). In the case of Elders Rural Bank, this included:

- Briefing sessions with Elders and with Elders Rural Bank marketing and brand managers; these sessions provided opportunity for dialogue, testing of ideas and reframing of these ideas

- Desktop research of the processes and information generated to secure a licence

- Government and private sector research on the preferred information sources in regional communities and rural industries

- Review of existing internal communication practices and issues.

The preliminary research developed a framework for public relations planning and put into place an understanding of the specific banking needs of regional and rural Australia. The success of financial public relations is in targeting publics in line with their identified needs. In the process of the research, Porter Novelli established a relationship with Elders, so that Elders and Elders Rural Bank began to understand the possibilities of public relations intervention and management within a relational context. One of the strengths of the Elders Rural Bank launch is that Porter Novelli became part of Elders' organisational culture and planning, a relationship that continues through the demands of droughts and the challenges of the rural sector (Booth 2007).

Target publics

Preliminary research by Elders and Porter Novelli identified the following target publics, their attitudes and understandings, and the possible role they might play in achieving the objectives of the Elder Rural Bank launch:

- Rural/regional investors (did not perceive Elders as a fully licensed bank)

- Metropolitan investors (low awareness of Elders)

- Existing Elders customers (considerable loyalty to the Elders brand)

- Specialist rural sector media (aware of Elders but not of its finance services)

- Metropolitan finance editors (low awareness of Elders, but high awareness of Elders Rural Bank)

- Regionally based print, radio and television media (reasonable awareness of Elders and high awareness of banking service issues)

- Elders staff (limited knowledge of bank and public relations activities).

Preliminary research uncovered gaps in the perception of Elders' customers and in the potential of Elders to manage a bank. A loyal customer base wanted to continue their relationships with Elders, and these customers needed precise, engaging communication to build on this loyalty and gain customer trust. Simultaneously, ensuring that Elders staff understood and supported public relations initiatives, and ensuring that relevant media were fully aware of the key role of Elders Rural Bank for metropolitan and rural customers, was integral to the success of the bank. Internal communication was open and inclusive, and employees took a key role in external communications, targeting media to promote the new bank—the employees were Elders Rural Bank ambassadors.

Goals and objectives

The overall goal was to launch Elders Rural Bank to metropolitan and regional Australia and secure A$150 million in deposits within the first twelve months.

Specific objectives were:

- To inform Elders staff Australia-wide about the new bank prior to the launch

- To inform seventy district finance managers, and motivate 25 per cent of them to actively participate in public relations activities to promote a planned 150 branches

- To achieve media coverage reaching finance and agribusiness sectors, and metropolitan investors

- To attract deposits from both regional and metropolitan Australia.

Communication strategy and tactics

The key to the success of the launch of Elders Rural Bank was the multi-layered or multi-faceted approach. This aimed to maximise credibility and also to appeal to the target publics by recognising their different needs and the different levels of engagement of customers, media and staff with Elders and the new bank.

LEVEL 1

Preliminary research indicated that Elders was trusted by its customers, and that customers were more likely to listen to those with whom they were familiar. Launching a bank was a new experience for many of Elders staff. Focus on local delivery by local staff who understood their customers was integral to Porter Novelli's strategy, and the public relations tool kit developed for district finance managers and branch managers was a key supportive tactic. Once the managers gained skill and confidence, they trained other staff. Staff were:

- Assisted in managing media releases tailored to the local media

- Provided with tips on working with the media (for those who may not previously have done so)

- Offered suggestions for local advertising, and ideas for events, stories and photos, as well as being given Elders Rural Bank media guidelines.

The kits were well prepared, but staff needed to be encouraged to take ownership of these kits and take an active role in promoting their new bank.

LEVEL 2

To make the public relations tool kit successful, Porter Novelli conducted training at manager level in five states over a period of six days, by:

- Briefing managers on their role, what was involved in promoting Elders Rural Bank and what the bank was offering to customers

- Briefing managers about the public relations and marketing strategies, and the tactics to achieve these strategies

- Workshopping ideas for local events to promote the bank.

The authors emphasise that building relationships and having one-to-one discussion with the bank's staff were most important to the success of the launch (Chia 2006). This personalised approach—where staff were given the opportunity to practise and take part in impromptu interviews—also skilled the staff for the future management of other aspects of Elders Rural Bank's development. From a public relations perspective, this approach showcased partnership and collaborative public relations relationship management that were personal and strategic.

LEVEL 3

At the same time as the 150 branches were prepared for the launch, Porter Novelli linked major regional media to state and district finance managers; local newspapers were linked to branch managers; and metropolitan finance media and the Canberra Press were linked to the chairman of the board.

The following media materials were developed to appeal to various media sectors:

- A media alert for metropolitan-based finance and rural editors, and Canberra press gallery boxes and journalists—sent immediately after official clearance was given, and giving media less than an hour to arrive at Parliament House for a media conference

- Three different media releases—a national version for metropolitan audiences, a version for specialist rural media, and a local community version for regional media

- Two videotaped news releases—one for all regional television newsrooms, and a South Australia-specific version featuring endorsement from the South Australian Premier.

For the success of this part of the plan, Porter Novelli briefed and informed its client, organised media interviews, set up a system to manage media calls, staggered distribution to the media in line with deadlines and priorities, and organised relevant spokespersons for respective media. Media training of local staff, guided by the public relations tool kit, made it possible for the public relations consultants to manage such diverse publics with their diverse range of needs, interests and knowledge of Elders.

LEVEL 4

Porter Novelli developed a database so that:

- Tailored media programs could be developed

- Media materials could be automatically tailored

- The client's marketing team could be networked/linked to specific media

- Local relevance and appeal could be highlighted.

Through automatic electronic tailoring, Porter Novelli used technology for effective short- and long-term management of targeted media programs. This initiative is one that scholars such as Baines et al. (2004) support—online management of aspects of financial public relations is essential so that clients benefit from the most efficient public relations intervention to increase market share and opportunity.

LEVEL 5

The launch—the event that put Elders Rural Bank on the Australian financial landscape— began with an announcement by the Federal Minister for Financial Services at a media conference at Parliament House, Canberra, that Elders Bank's licence was approved and that the announcement had gone to the Australian Stock Exchange.

As Elders Bank became a reality, a helpline service was set up for Elders staff, by means of which Porter Novelli personnel offered advice and support, dealt with media requests, and provided assistance with launch events. This public relations relationship management role continued, as the launch of Elders Rural Bank was as much about new relationships and marketing opportunities as it was about a new product.

Evaluation

The launch was very successful with objectives achieved and exceeded:

- **Objective 1**

  To inform Elders staff Australia-wide about the new bank prior to the launch

  All staff Australia-wide received information and key staff received copies of media releases and a document on questions and answers for the media as part of their media training program.

- **Objective 2**

  To inform seventy of the district finance managers, and motivate 25 per cent of them to actively participate in public relations activities to promote a planned 150 branches

In fact, 95 per cent of the district finance managers attended preliminary training. A survey of these managers indicated that the public relations kit and the helpline encouraged them to generate local publicity for seventy branches. In a later survey of the same managers, all of them reported that targeting local media had raised the bank's profile.

- **Objective 3**

  To achieve media coverage reaching finance and agribusiness sectors, and metropolitan investors

  Over 100 interviews were requested nationally in the first two days after the launch, and extensive media coverage was generated through print, radio and television. More than thirty people, including three television networks, attended the Canberra Parliament House launch.

- **Objective 4**

  To attract deposits from both regional and metropolitan Australia

  Over A$120 million deposits were made in five weeks and in one year the bank achieved over A$1 billion in assets, exceeding all expectations. The reach to the Australian audience was considerable, and a survey by the Elders customer service centre showed that 87 per cent of the people who contacted Elders did so because of an article they had read in regional or national media.

This is a public relations success story that resulted in an additional outcome—Porter Novelli was recognised for its excellent work and won a Golden Target Public Relations Institute of Australia (PRIA) national award.

Lessons learnt

The Elders Rural Bank launch was successful for many reasons. From managers, to board members, to staff in direct contact with customers—each was prepared for the launch, understood the product, was trained in managing media, and was supported in the process of carrying out their respective role and duties to manage the new product. Personal relationships were developed within teams, and a partnership approach underpinned all public relations intervention. This made the launch an Australia-wide success. If Porter Novelli had attempted to manage the media from its end alone, the engagement of local customers and the regional media would not have been as successful.

Knowledge of media important to financial markets was critical to the success of the bank, and is a vital component of successful financial public relations in general. Managing the launch at different levels and linking the bank to relevant media was a strategic success, resulting in long-term benefits to Elders and Elders Rural Bank. Promoting a new brand was managed through the inner knowledge and training of staff, making them ambassadors for Elders Rural Bank. These ambassadors knew their brand, they believed in their new product, and they were empowered by being involved in the promotion of the bank at a local level. By working with staff as partners, the launch was also cost-effective as local resources were utilised.

In this case study, the public relations consultancy developed a strong client relationship that has continued through the challenges of drought and the rural downturn, where all rural businesses have been tested. A relationship has been built between the customers and the bank, and confidence in the bank continues. The public relations role in facilitating open, transparent communication to the public in an organisation that also values its employees has been most important to the continued employee ambassador role. The bank's CEO is looking for new business developments for the bank with greater metropolitan input, but with a continued commitment to regional Australia (Booth 2007).

If this launch was planned in 2007–08 the internet would be an important tool in the bank's promotion, making the bank visible to an even wider media and public audience. Online banking is popular, so the banking community expects up-to-date online communication about what is happening and new directions. As online interactivity brings the needs of the banking community to the 'desk top' of city managers, Elders Rural Bank customers have a greater opportunity to have a say about what they want from the bank. Email communication is now paramount to all business management (Cutlip et al. 2006; Seitel 2007) and is the primary communication tool. However, financial public relations management includes meeting face-to-face with sectors of the bank to maintain personal interest and develop strong relationships.

The future of financial public relations in Australia is most promising as the demands of shareholders, investors and the wider financial community indicate that strategic corporate communication management can make a difference to corporations' success at all levels. The case studies discussed in this chapter demonstrate the effectiveness of professional financial public relations practice in Australian business management.

PRACTITIONER PROFILE

Matthew Hart, Director of BBS, reflects on the float of Domino's Pizza and the future of investor relations.

It was really interesting being involved in this major milestone for the company. We had been working for Domino's for some time and had seen it grow store numbers and reach a stage in its evaluation where it could list. It was also the first pizza maker to list on the Australian Stock Exchange and this meant that the communications needed to switch to the financial/investor focus, rather than the previous focus of having fun with pizza. For me, it was good to apply communications skills to a different context.

Every company's IPO is different but there are common phases that need to be addressed properly if it is to be successful. This form of communication is also different because all communication needs to adhere to regulatory guidelines and rules. There's certainly no room for 'spin' or 'making things up' when people are investing millions of dollars in a company!

I think financial and investor relations is a growing market because the financial community (even mum and dad investors) requires a more sophisticated level of communication. In the past, people might have bought shares and sat on them. With internet trading etc, people are more involved in their investments and want up-to-date information on the company's performance. For the public relations industry, financial and investor relations helps to showcase the professionalism of our industry and helps to remove the stereotype that public relations people spend lots of time at champagne lunches.

REFERENCES

Baines P., Egan J. & Jefkins F., 2004, *Public Relations, Contemporary Issues and Technique*, Elsevier, Butterworth Heinemann, UK

Booth M., 2007, 'Agribank Sets its Sights Beyond the Farm Gate' in *The Advertiser*, 3 March 2007, p. 78

Burgess K., 2007, 'Public Relations' New Horizons' in *Business Review Weekly*, 15–21 February 2007, pp. 43–5

Chambers L., 1999, *The Guide to Financial Public Relations: How to Stand Out in the Midst of Competitive Clutter*, St Lucie Press, Boca Raton, FL

Chia J., 2005, *Relationship Management: Developing Relationship Management Parameters Critical to the Effective Management of Relationships between Public Relations Consultants and their Clients*, PhD thesis, University of South Australia

Chia J., 2006, 'Measuring the Immeasurable' in *PRism Online Journal*, Vol. 4, No. 2, http://praxis.massey.ac.nz/evaluation.html, for PRism Special Edition on Measurement and Evaluation

Collis T., 2003, 'Financial Public Relations' in Gregory A., *Public Relations in Practice*, Kogan Page, US Institute of Public Relations

Cruver B., 2002, *Enron, Anatomy of Greed: The Unshredded Truth from an Enron Insider*, Arrow Books, University of Texas

Cutlip S., Center A. & Broom G., 2006, *Effective Public Relations*, 9th edn, Prentice Hall, Englewood Cliffs, NJ

Gregory A., 2004, 'Public Relations and Management' in Theaker A., *The Public Relations Handbook*, 2nd edn, Routledge, Oxfordshire

Grunig J. & Huang Y.-H., 2000, 'From Organisational Effectiveness to Relationship Indicators: Antecedents of Relationships, Public Relations Strategies, and Relationship Outcomes' in Ledingham J. & Bruning S. (eds), *Public Relations as Relationship Management: A Relational Approach to the Study and Practice of Public Relations*, Lawrence Erlbaum Associates, Mahwah, NJ, pp. 23–53

Grunig J., 2001, 'Two-way Symmetrical Public Relations, Past, Present and Future' in Heath R., *Handbook of Public Relations*, Sage, Thousand Oaks, CA, pp. 11–30

Guth D. & Marsh C., 2005, *Public Relations: A Values-driven Approach*, 3rd edn, Allyn and Bacon, USA

Haywood R., 2002, *Corporate Reputation: The Brand and the Bottom Line*, 3rd edn, Kogan Page, London

Johnston J. & Zawawi C., 2004, *Public Relations: Theory and Practice*, 2nd edn, Allen and Unwin, NSW

Kellaway L., Fewster R. & Macleod-Smith B., 2003, 'Banking on the Bush: The Launch of Elders Rural Bank' in *Asia Pacific Public Relations Journal*, Vol. 4, No. 2

Lattimore D., Baskin O., Heiman S., Toth E. & Van Leuven J., 2004, *Public Relations: The Profession and the Practice*, McGraw-Hill, Boston, MA

Lerbinger O., 2006, *Corporate Public Affairs: Interacting with Interest Groups, Media and Government*, Lawrence Erlbaum, Mahwah, NJ

Newsom, D., Vanslyke Turk J. & Krukeberg D., 2007, *This is PR: The Realities of Public Relations*, 9th edn, Thomson Wadsworth, Belmont, CA

Pelsmacker P., Geuens M. & Van den Bergh J., 2007, *Marketing Communications: A European Perspective*, 3rd edn, Prentice Hall, Pearson Education, London

Sarantakos S., 1998, *Social Research*, Macmillan Education Australia, Melbourne

Seitel F., 2007, *The Practice of Public Relations*, 10th edn, Prentice Hall, Upper Saddle River, NJ

Tench R. & Yeomans L., 2006, *Exploring Public Relations*, Prentice Hall/Pearson Education, London

Tymson C., Lazar P. & Lazar R., 2002, *The New Australian and New Zealand Public Relations Manual*, Tymson Communications, Chatswood

10

Marketing Public Relations

Launching FUndies

Dr Gwyneth V. J. Howell and
Dr Katherine Mizerski

AIMS OF THIS CHAPTER

- To understand how marketing, advertising and public relations work together in an Australian and online context

- To better understand the emerging role of marketing public relations

- To develop an understanding of marketing public relations in practice through case study analysis

INTRODUCTION

Due to the heavy proliferation of media, consumers are now inundated with messages to persuade them to purchase a particular product or service. As a result, marketers are finding it increasingly difficult to ensure their messages have the desired impact on consumers.

Academics and practitioners suggest that advertising, marketing's prime communication tool, has lost its effectiveness due to message saturation and increased cynicism among consumers. Today, advertising no longer produces the results marketers require. Although exaggerated claims and excessive volumes are contributing to the decline in advertising's effectiveness, credibility is the fundamental issue (Ries & Ries 2002).

As advertising struggles to regain its credibility and audience loyalty, public relations has evolved to be one of the most persuasive tools in the marketing mix. Marketers are increasing their budget allocations to public relations, as its techniques are more effective in reaching consumers and encouraging action, especially in terms of brand building. Public relations is capable of strategically enhancing both relationships with stakeholders and the organisation's image, thereby leading to a successful attainment of marketing objectives.

MARKETING PUBLIC RELATIONS

In essence, marketing public relations involves public relations being used to support marketing functions and objectives. While these functions differ, their integration forms a synergistic relationship that benefits those who utilise it. A recent review of the current role of public relations identified that 'marketing and public relations are viewed as complementary functions' (Wu & Taylor 2003, p. 474).

Henry Jr (1995, p. 3) suggests that marketing public relations 'is the successful combination of a variety of communication techniques, which, when skilfully and professionally used, will help a company achieve its sales and marketing objectives'. Harris (1991, p. 12) defines marketing public relations as 'the process of planning, executing and evaluating programs that encourage purchase and consumer satisfaction through credible communication of information and impressions that identify companies and their products with the needs, wants, concerns and interests of consumers'. Marketing public relations is essentially used to support the sales of goods and/or services.

The marketing landscape continues to evolve and experience significant change, including product proliferation, decreasing brand loyalty, increasing consumer demand and message clutter. There is also increased fragmentation among audiences and increased levels of consumer apathy and cynicism. Weiner (2005) suggests that salient benefits of marketing public relations include:

- Increased brand message credibility

- Improved media involvement among consumers

- Increased ability to deliver targeted messages

- And, most importantly, increased capacity to break through message clutter to connect with consumers and stakeholders.

Marketing public relations in action

There are three main steps in implementing a marketing public relations campaign. First, research of the current market and the identification and analysis of key publics is essential. These enable marketers and public relations practitioners to measure key public attitudes to issues or products, and identify key approaches that will significantly enhance how the organisation's communication message will be received, heard and understood.

Second, key decisions are made on how resources should be allocated in terms of public relations tactics that will focus on specific target publics, such as the selection of the most effective media. Identified media may include traditional media such as newspapers, magazines and television, and online media such as blogs, websites, chat rooms and MySpace™. Using an array of media directories and reference publications, marketers and public relations practitioners can compile lists of media to send media releases to or information regarding their product or service. This is considered one of the main channels of communication in marketing public relations. Therefore it is vital that the correct media to achieve the best outcomes for the campaign are selected, thereby reducing wastage in terms of budget and staff.

Third, the overall results of a marketing public relations campaign need to be measured and evaluated. Research in the field should measure the perceptions, opinions and beliefs of the key target publics. Cutlip et al. (2006) suggest that one measure of the media effect is in terms of exposure; that is, the coverage and retention of specific key messages by target publics. While coverage and retention are important, change of behaviour to product purchase is the crux of a marketing public relations campaign. Finally, it is imperative that the financial implications of the campaign are analysed to determine whether an increase in sales or consumption of services has occurred.

Marketing public relations on the web

Corporate websites are used by organisations to build relationships with stakeholders (Aikat 2000) and to provide a variety of organisational information and services, as well as to engage in commercial activities with the stakeholders who seek to use this medium to communicate with an organisation (Liu et al. 1997). Further, websites allow organisations to communicate with the media in a more efficient and effective manner (Kimmel 2004). This communication medium creates a range of marketing public relations opportunities and challenges for any organisation (Jo 2002).

The web presents marketers with a powerful tool that may be used in a variety of ways including education, the collection and retrieval of information, and the rapid and automated distribution of information to various stakeholders (Shin & Cameron 2003). With an increasingly integrated global economy, the web ensures that time and space are no longer barriers to commerce. Not only does the web improve interactivity, evaluation and information delivery services, it also increases the size of the audience with which organisations can communicate (Ihator 2001). The web has changed the model of communication between organisations and their key publics, as information can appear in various electronic forms, including on major news sites, niche sites, complaint sites, blogs, discussion boards, and message groups (Neil 2000). Furthermore, the new economics of the web, driven by the global trend of e-commerce, has basically changed traditional business operations and the business landscape (Rossiter & Bellman 2005).

FUNDIES

The FUndies company successfully used public relations in one of Australia's most recent and highly successful product launches; however, as this case study will show, its rollout was not without setbacks, and required ongoing monitoring, research and innovation to achieve the company's effective business model.

Background

The concept for FUndies, a web-based business providing women's intimate wear, began in Western Australia in 2002. As a stay-at-home mum, Jo Walters, the founder of FUndies, was looking for a home-based business venture. With a background in public relations and an MBA from a top-level university, Walters undertook a thorough analysis to identify existing opportunities. While several possible options were identified, none seemed to suit Walters' criteria of home-based, positive-revenue-generating businesses that fulfilled a niche market.

It was at a party that the idea presented itself. One of the women expressed frustration with her current undergarments and lamented the fact that, with young children at home, she did not have time go out and purchase such 'luxuries'. Hence, the idea of FUndies was born.

Research

Research indicated that there was an untapped market for a shop-at-home lingerie business that provided 'luxury intimate apparel'. With backing from her family, Walters developed a small range of feminine undergarments and 'tested' them on her friends. The lingerie was designed not to compete with large manufacturers, but to provide an affordable range of comfortable, yet stylish, underwear.

Initially set up in her home—with sales being made via a 'party' arrangement, where a host would invite their friends to a party to view and purchase the product—Walters quickly realised that she was on to something. The question then became: How can we grow this market and expand beyond the traditional (and sometimes poorly regarded) party approach? It was time for further market analysis to identify growth opportunities and the most appropriate target market/key publics.

Target publics

Research undertaken identified two primary target groups:

1   The first group consisted of stay-at-home mothers who found it difficult to manoeuvre around the shops—particularly in often-crowded lingerie departments—with prams or toddlers and to shop within time constraints.

2   The second target group was working women who found it difficult to find time to shop for lingerie.

While distinctly different in terms of life stage, the two markets had several things in common: (a) time-poor, (b) moderate-to-high levels of disposable income, and (c) the desire for feminine, sexy, undergarments. These two markets became the focus for the FUndies strategy.

Goals and objectives

Walters realised that in order to be successful, she needed to set realistic goals and objectives. This would allow her to evaluate whether or not the strategies employed were effective. Based on her original need to have a home-based, positive-revenue-generating business, Walters set her primary goal to become one of, if not the leading, shop-at-home lingerie business within five years. A series of objectives was developed to help Walters obtain this goal. The objectives, designed to be measurable, were as follows:

• To expand beyond the original geographical market (Perth) to reach a larger national target audience

• To have 70 per cent of original contacts sign up to receive future emails

• To obtain repeat customer business from 50 per cent of the target by aiming for 100 per cent customer satisfaction

• To generate positive word of mouth about the brand.

Communication strategy and tactics

The main limitation of the initial venture was that lingerie parties had a limited reach, and, as a one-person business, it was not possible for Walters to hold more than four parties a week. However even booking four parties a week was proving to be a challenge, as people were wary of buying lingerie in this setting. Using her background in public relations and e-marketing, Walters set about designing a website that could be used to complement the parties. Initially, the web address was provided to party attendees so that they could order at a later date if they wished. However this strategy did not increase sales and the business continued to experience the issue of limited exposure.

A further problem was the location of the business. To make the business a success, FUndies had to expand beyond its current limited geographical area and look for a means to promote the product outside the party structure. As a website was already established, FUndies sought to employ marketing public relations tactics to cost-effectively reach a broader market. The challenge now was how?

STAGING THE LAUNCH

Events management skills are a useful part of the public relations practitioner's tool kit. Events represent a unique form of service product development to satisfy diverse publics including consumers (residents and/or tourists), government, community and cultural groups, media and business sponsors, and financiers (Van Der Wagen 2005).

FUndies staged an event in Perth to launch the website for the product range. This event was designed to attract the key media and opinion leaders who communicated with the two target publics. It was essential to attract opinion leaders as, while they were not the primary target market, their attendance ensured maximum coverage for the launch.

The launch provided a platform to showcase the product, and also allowed FUndies the opportunity to personally promote various options available in the range and information about the website. To further increase recognition of the brand and to encourage guests to 'experience' the product, each guest received a FUndies lingerie bag that could later be used to protect the lingerie in the washing machine. Included in the bag was a sample of the lingerie, various cross-promotional items, and a full-colour brochure that included information on the range, prominently featuring the web address. The bags were handed out by a trained person to ensure that the proper size of lingerie was given to the attendees (except in the case of men who were given a standard-size item that would fit most women, so they could pass that part of the gift along). This tactic ensured that opinion leaders and media would be exposed to the product and brand name on an ongoing basis, and had been used before in the successful launch of Peter Alexander Sleepwear in 1999 (now a highly successful online and retail brand with a multimillion dollar annual turnover). The FUndies launch received extensive state-wide and local media coverage, and improved the awareness of the brand within Western Australia.

AFTER THE LAUNCH: NEW TACTICS

Unfortunately, using tactics that had been successful elsewhere did not translate into increased sales for FUndies and the website received very few visits. Again using research, FUndies determined that brand loyalty could be achieved once consumers used the product. The review of the campaign to date identified that the biggest issue was changing consumer behaviour and attracting the key publics to purchase and experience the product.

FUndies was also limited in terms of market due to the lack of knowledge of the brand outside Western Australia. While successful, the launch had only reached a narrow geographical market. Budgetary constraints meant that it was not possible to hold launches in all major cities, so another strategy had to be developed to communicate key messages to the target publics. Using direct mail, a FUndies bag along with a personalised letter was distributed nationwide to a number of opinion leaders and key media. This tactic was successful as the product and website received coverage in all the major dailies, as well as in traditional magazine media.

While awareness of FUndies brand increased throughout Australia, and sales and webpage hits increased, these still were below expectations. Research indicated that women were reluctant to buy lingerie from a web-based business because they could not try it on and, unlike many other products, they were unable to return the lingerie if it did not fit. To overcome this problem, FUndies instituted a scheme whereby if the shopper returned to the website for a future purchase, after having bought lingerie from FUndies that did not fit, they would receive a 50 per cent discount on the purchase price of the second item. This message was featured prominently on the webpage to encourage people to explore the site.

This guarantee of satisfaction was successful, and sales began to increase. However many of these sales were being made using the half-off guarantee, resulting in decreased profits. After a period of six months, the guarantee message was moved to small print at the bottom of the webpage and restrictions on the number of times it could be used by an individual were introduced. The effect of this was to decrease sales—the company had to find another way to reach out to its customers.

In 2006, FUndies was approached to make a donation to an event to raise money for breast cancer research. The event was being hosted by a local health club and involved a fashion show and an auction. Drawing on the public relations tactic of sponsorship, FUndies became a major sponsor for the event. This involved the models wearing FUndies, and FUndies lingerie bags (similar to those used at the launch) being given to people who attended.

Although it did not receive national press exposure, the event was covered by local print and television media. In addition, as part of the sponsorship deal, FUndies obtained the email addresses of all attendees. FUndies sent a direct email piece inviting people to join the FUndies mailing list and achieved a 90 per cent response to this request.

In order to build on this initial success, FUndies undertook an annual sponsorship of the breast cancer event. Further, in 2007, FUndies used a marketing public relations tactic to support cancer research—for every purple bra sold during Breast Cancer Awareness month, FUndies agreed to donate A$1 to breast cancer research. Information on this promotion was sent to local papers and received widespread coverage. Following the success of this, FUndies ran a similar campaign in the lead-up to Father's Day. Focusing on their new men's line, they agreed to donate A$1 from the sale of every men's item to cancer research.

Since FUndies began donating to cancer research, registered web-users have increased by 240 per cent. Sales have also increased and are now triple what they were in the previous twelve months. FUndies attributes this success to the right mix of product, marketing public relations, and cause-related marketing tactics. Plans to continue sponsoring cancer research have already been written into the 2008 plan, and FUndies hopes to sponsor local events in all major cities.

Evaluation

This case illustrates that a good business idea requires careful thought and consideration before any individual launches their own business. Marketing public relations offers small companies the opportunity to establish awareness about their products and services in a cost-effective manner. The advent and high adoption of the World Wide Web has changed the marketing and sales landscape. No longer are companies required to establish a physical sales presence in terms of a shopfront; today multimillion-dollar sales businesses operate in the online environment. However, as this case illustrates, just creating a website does not guarantee sales.

Using a mix of marketing public relations tactics enabled FUndies to establish a business, and then increase sales and grow the online business through an innovative strategy that employed both traditional and non-traditional public relations strategies. Traditional public relations—such as media relations, cause sponsorship and awareness events—supported the online e-public relations and sales promotion to enable this company to expand its current market share, and establish a successful online lingerie business in Australia.

Developing the website was just one stage in the business's development. Without the traditional public relations activities, FUndies would not have been able to attract and maintain its loyal market share. These tactics ensured that communication with the key publics was achieved, thus ensuring the business's ongoing success and growth.

Careful and continuous review of the strategy being employed ensured that FUndies was not relying on ineffective tactics. The twelve-month growth figures indicated that the current strategy was effective in reaching and communicating the brand's features to the key stakeholders. The inclusion of the current strategy in the subsequent strategic plan recognised that once a successful strategy is identified, it should be built upon to encourage repeat patronage of the current target market.

LESSONS LEARNT

This case illustrates that public relations is marketing's best solution in communicating with a message-saturated society. While public relations lacks control over message content, timing, delivery and visual appearance of the message, people are more likely to believe its messages than those of advertising, as information gathered from a television program or newspaper article appears more trustworthy and reliable.

Looking at opportunities to create awareness about the product was critical to the success of this online sales venture. The use of traditional public relations—such as the launch events and media relations activities with traditional media—enhanced the message about the product and drew people to the online shopfront; while the online activities—such as emailing customers information about new products, and a well-designed and easily navigated website—were essential in developing customer loyalty and sales.

Many public relations theorists tout the two-way symmetrical communication model as 'best practice' in public relations. This case illustrates that by listening and responding to the publics' concerns—such as allowing discounts on future sales if the sizing was incorrect—enabled FUndies to increase customer loyalty and develop a larger market share for their products.

The combination of traditional and new marketing public relations was very effective in building brand awareness and knowledge, increasing category usage and brand sales, cutting through message clutter, and increasing the credibility of messages. Interestingly, this was once the dominant area of advertising in terms of sales of goods and services. 'A well-planned public relations assault can secure businesses with a level of credibility and establish and preserve a formidable market share long after the print ads yellow and the billboards weather and peel' (Elliott 1996, p. 15). Exposure on the web, television, radio programs or in newspapers, awards marketers a credibility that is capable of changing attitudes and influencing behaviours (Strenski 1991). FUndies has successfully employed marketing public relations to establish credibility for its product and has also been successful in influencing behaviours with the key publics.

DR GWYNETH V. J. HOWELL AND DR KATHERINE MIZERSKI

CONCLUSION

Due to the heavy proliferation of messages that each individual is exposed to daily, advertising has lost its effectiveness and can no longer produce the results marketers seek. The web has diffused the effects of advertising further, exponentially increasing the individual's exposure to a range of messages. Realising this, marketers have begun to employ public relations as a major tool of their marketing plans as, philosophically speaking, public relations messages have greater effect on consumers and audiences than demanding them to buy or use a particular product or service.

Consumers are becoming more cynical and distrusting of traditional advertising's messages and, as a result, are becoming increasingly harder to reach. 'Consumers look to trusted and independent sources for advice on what to do and confirmation they are doing the right thing. Often they do not accept the advertising message as they used to' (Common 2005, p. 15). The strength of public relations within marketing lies in its ability to strategically reach these hard-to-get audiences by nurturing the organisation's relationships with them. Weiner (2005, p. 22) asserts that 'public relations can begin to supplant "paid media" because it offers so much of what advertisers envy—involvement, credibility and value'.

Niederquell (1991, p. 23) suggests that 'marketers must learn to trust the ability of public relations to cut through message clutter and to create new channels of communication that reach opinion makers and thought leaders'. Moreover, marketers must trust that public relations offers more credible sources and techniques for delivering messages than advertising, and is thus a power that any marketer would be foolish to reject.

Public relations is more effective and credible than advertising in conveying messages to audiences and consumers in a cost-effective way, and is driving marketing plans to achieve far greater results. The use of the web—for a start-up company with a virtual shopfront and therefore much lower costs—illustrates the powerful influence of marketing public relations on the success of a small manufacturing company.

REFERENCES

Aikat D., 2000, 'A New Medium for Organizational Communication: Analyzing Web Content Characteristics of Fortune 500 Companies' in *The Electronic Journal of Communication*, Vol. 10, No. 1/2, www.cios.org, accessed 7 December 2005

Arndt J., 1967, 'The Role of Product-related Conversations in the Diffusion of a New Product' in *Journal of Marketing Research*, Vol. 4, pp. 291–5

Barr T., 2000, *newmedia.com.au: The Changing Face of Australia's Media and Communications*, Allen and Unwin, St Leonards, NSW

Bezjian-Avery A., Calder B. & Iacobucci D., 1998, 'New Media Interactive Advertising vs. Traditional Advertising' in *Journal of Advertising Research*, July/August, pp. 23–32

Bourland-Davis P. G., Graham B. L. & Fulmer H. W., 1997, 'Defining a Public Relations Internship through Feedback from the Field' in *Journalism and Mass Communication Educator*, Vol. 52, No. 1, pp. 26–33

Brignall III T. W. & Van Valey T., 2005, 'The Impact of Internet Communications on Social Interaction' in *Sociological Spectrum*, Vol. 25, pp. 335–48

Common G., 2005, 'The Importance of Influencers Elevates PR Role' in *PR Influences*, July–August 2005, www.prinfluences.com, accessed 3 July 2007

Common G., 2007, 'The Importance of Influencers Elevates PR Role' in *PR Influences*, www.prinfluences.com, accessed 3 July 2007

Cutlip S., Center A. & Broom G., 2006, *Effective Public Relations*, 9th edn, Pearson, Upper Saddle River, NJ

Elliott J., 1996, 'Sales are Proof PR Works' in *Public Relations Tactics*, Vol. 3, No. 5, p. 15

Enright A., 2006, 'Front, Center: From his Position, Ries Looks at Marketing Then, Now' in *Marketing News*, 1 March, pp. 11–13

Grunig J. E. & Grunig L. A., 1998, 'The Relationship between Public Relations and Marketing in Excellent Organisations: Evidence from the IABC Study' in *Journal of Marketing Communication*, Vol. 4, pp. 141–62

Harris T. L., 1991, *The Marketer's Guide to Public Relations: How Today's Top Companies are Using the New PR to Gain a Competitive Edge*, John Wiley & Sons Inc., New York

Harris T. L., 1993, 'How MPR adds Value to Integrated Marketing Communications' in *Public Relations Quarterly*, Vol. 38, No. 2, pp. 13–18

Harris T. L., 1998, *Value-added Public Relations: The Secret Weapon of Integrated Marketing*, NTC/Contemporary Publishing Group, IL

Henry Jr. R. A., 1995, *Marketing Public Relations: The Hows that Make it Work*, Iowa State University Press

Ihator A., 2001, 'Corporate Communication: Challenges and Opportunities in a Digital World' in *Public Relations Quarterly*, Vol. 46, No. 4, pp. 15–19

Jo D.-G., 2002, 'Diffusion of Rumours on the Internet' in *The Information Society Review*, pp. 77–95

Kimmel A. J., 2004, *Rumors and Rumor Control: A Manager's Guide to Understanding and Combatting Rumors*, Lawrence Erlbaum Associates, Mahwah, NJ

Kollock P. & Smith, M. A., 1999, 'The Economies of Online Cooperation: Gifts and Public Goods in Cyberspace' in Smith M. A. & Kollock P. (eds), *Communities in Cyberspace*, Routledge, London, pp. 200–69

Liu C., Arnett K., Capella L. & Beatty R., 1997, 'Web Sites of the Fortune 500 Companies: Facing Customers through Home Pages' in *Information & Management*, Vol. 31, pp. 335–45

Marken G. A., 2002, 'The Challenges of International Relations in an Internet World' in *Public Relations Quarterly*, Vol. 47, No. 3, Fall, pp. 28–30

Marken G. A., 2004, 'CEO Still Sets the Tone, Agenda of Public Relations' in *Public Relations Quarterly*, Vol. 49, No. 1, pp. 16–17

Neil B., 2000, 'Crisis Management and the Internet' in *Ivey Business Journal*, Vol. 64, No. 3, p. 13

Niederquell M., 1991, 'Integrating the Strategic Benefits of Public Relations into the Marketing Mix' in *Public Relations Quarterly*, Vol. 36, No. 1, pp. 23–4

Ries A. & Ries L., 2002, *The Fall of Advertising and the Rise of PR*, Harper Collins Publishers, USA

Rossiter J. A. & Bellman S., 2005, *Marketing Communication: Theory and Applications*, Pearson Education, Malaysia

Shin J-H. & Cameron G. T., 2003, 'Informal Relations: A Look at Personal Influence in Media Relations' in *Journal of Communication Management*, Vol. 7, No. 3, pp. 239–53

Strenski J., 1991, 'Marketing Public Relations Sells: Case Studies Prove It' in *Public Relations Quarterly*, Vol. 36, No. 1, pp. 25–6

Taylor M., Kent M. L. & White W. J., 2001, 'How Activist Organizations are Using the Internet to Build Relationships' in *Public Relations Review*, Vol. 27, No. 3, pp. 263–84

Van der Merwe R., Pitt L. F. & Abratt R., 2005, 'Stakeholder Strength: PR Survival Strategies in the Internet Age' in *Public Relations Quarterly*, Spring, Vol. 50, No. 1, pp. 39–49

Van Der Wagen L. & Carlos B., 2005, *Event Management for Tourism, Cultural, Business and Sporting Events*, Pearson Prentice Hall, Upper Saddle River, NJ

Weiner M., 2005, 'Marketing PR Revolution' in *Communication World*, Vol. 22, No. 1, pp. 20–5

Wu M. Y. & Taylor M., 2003, 'Public Relations in Taiwan: Roles, Professionalism, and Relationship to Marketing' in *Public Relations Review*, Vol. 29, No. 4, pp. 473–83

Strategic Events 11

New Zealand's Bid to Host the Rugby World Cup 2011

Joseph Peart

AIMS OF THIS CHAPTER

- To understand the managing of events on an international scale

- To understand the role of the public relations practitioner in event management

- To develop understanding of event management through a case study approach

- To develop an understanding of the pre-event and lead-up stages of the event management process

INTRODUCTION

One night in mid-November 2005, every news channel in New Zealand carried a moment that prompted viewers to rise to their feet and celebrate in accord with the scene on their television sets, which showed rugby officials standing and hugging each other.

It was, for the New Zealand Rugby Union, a historic moment when the Chairman of the International Rugby Board, flanked by his selection panel, announced: 'The 2011 Rugby World Cup will be held in [pause for effect] New Zealand!'

What follows is an account of the campaign by the New Zealand Rugby Union to win the rights to stage the Rugby World Cup in 2011. The case study is based on comment and analysis from the perspective of public relations best practice. At the conclusion of the case study, the analysis shifts to a closer look at the politics of sport and how the patriotic agenda of sporting countries adds complexity to sports communication campaigns in a global arena.

BACKGROUND

According to many, New Zealand was the outsider when the International Rugby Board met in Dublin on 17 November 2005 to select the host union for the Rugby World Cup 2011. Pitted against heavyweights South Africa and Japan, the New Zealand bid—mounted jointly by the New Zealand Rugby Union (NZRU) and the New Zealand Government— was picked by one English newspaper to come 'a distant third'. Instead, New Zealand will host the world's third-largest sporting event. The 'rugby-mad nation' celebrated.

Despite low public expectations, the New Zealand bid team always believed their well-targeted and carefully paced campaign had them well in the running. They were right, and the record kept by NZRU Public Relations Manager Brian Finn of his work in relationship-building, political lobbying, media liaison, and club and player communication won the Special Event Category and Supreme Award in the Public Relations Institute of New Zealand's (PRINZ) 2006 national awards.

New Zealand has been involved in the Rugby World Cup since its creation, having taken a lead role in envisaging and hosting the first tournament in 1987. It then dramatically lost the sub-hosting rights to the 2003 tournament to Australia. Publicity surrounding this loss concentrated on the unwillingness of sponsors and long-term ticket holders to forego their privileges. However the loss was keenly felt, as New Zealand's friendly rivalry with its larger, high-performance neighbour drives many of its sporting successes.

In 2004, the NZRU began discussing a bid to host the 2011 tournament and established a Bid Advisory Group to consider the feasibility. In January 2005, the group advised that a case could be mounted for New Zealand to bid for the Rugby World Cup, but only with the comprehensive support of the New Zealand Government. The NZRU and the New Zealand Government then established a Joint Bid Office to investigate further, and in May 2005 a formal bid was lodged with the International Rugby Board (IRB) for New Zealand to host the 2011 tournament.

THE CAMPAIGN
Research

New Zealand's bid had a number of hurdles to clear, including the perceived fallout from the 2003 tournament decision, doubts about the NZRU's capabilities, and a view that the country did not have the infrastructure required to host a major global event. Research into other bids—such as the selection of France as the host union for the 2007 Rugby World Cup and London's successful 2012 Olympic bid— demonstrated a need for sporting tactics. A contender did not need to have the highest public profile or be the front runner to succeed, as long as it had the momentum at the finish line.

Target publics

The primary audience was the twenty-two IRB Council members who would cast a vote. Secondary audiences included the boards of the national and regional rugby unions, which the delegates represented, and key influencers within international rugby.

Goals and objectives

The New Zealand bid had to change perceptions around New Zealand's abilities to host the tournament and convince the IRB Council members that New Zealand would be the best country to host the Rugby World Cup in 2011. This objective defines the desired outcome of a singular decision from a comparatively small number of highly placed officials. There are also some qualitative overtones and strategic aspects in the wording of the objective. Strategically, the bid team members believed they had to 'change perceptions', perhaps from those they felt had formed around New Zealand's previous unsuccessful bid to host the tournament.

In this situation, the blending of strategic and specific intentions was highly appropriate, raising the question whether textbook definitions can be too rigid. For instance, Austin and Pinkleton (2001) and Cutlip, Center and Broom (2006), like many others, differentiate between 'goals' and 'objectives'; and Tymson et al. (2002) are even more prescriptive about 'SMART' objectives, where the mnemonic stands for 'specific, measurable, achievable, relevant and time-based'.

Communication strategy and tactics

The strategy for this campaign rested on the interaction between influencers, decision-makers and grassroots supporters. The strategy also made sure that its prime target audiences understood the connection between their rugby constituencies and their decision-making power. The NZRU was able to demonstrate that the 'rugby culture' in New Zealand would be a key element in ensuring the success of this country as the venue for the games.

The interplay between opinion leaders and grassroots is examined in the next section. Here the key point of interest is the NZRU's realisation that its primary and secondary audiences were numerically small, but crucial. It was this concentration of the communication effort on 'the few' that inspired variations in persuasion strategy from some of the more recognised theory.

If the NZRU's situation is compared with mass-media-dependent campaigns, these differences will become apparent. For instance in *Strategic Public Relations Management*, Austin and Pinkleton (2001) remind readers of several 'classical' models of persuasion that can be used to assist in the creation of effective message strategies. They look at Mendlesohn's Three Assumptions for Success:

1   Message targeting

2   Assuming the target public is uninterested

3   Setting mid-range goals (Austin & Pinkleton 2001, p. 291).

In the NZRU's case, message targeting was really the only one of these assumptions that applied, and Finn and his team made particularly effective use of well-framed messages.

TARGETING 'PROMINENT PERSONS'

Of equal interest to Austin and Pinkleton would have been the NZRU's focus on compact, politically-sensitive audiences. The authors could well choose to re-examine their approach to McGuire's 1989 Domino Model, which is clearly intended to include the influence of mass media. McGuire's model (as quoted by Austin & Pinkleton 2001, p. 291) starts with the audience in a state of ignorance. McGuire moves through a hierarchy of twelve levels, and it is the last five of these levels that reflect the situation in which the NZRU bid team found itself:

8   Information search and retrieval

9   Decision motivation

10 Behaviour

11 Reinforcement

12 Post-behavioural consolidation.

The NZRU ensured that its information was valid, well-researched and backed up: it managed the motivation of the IRB Council through its well-stage-managed 'prominent persons' visits and presentations. The council's 'behaviour' was, of course, its voting. The delicate step from the early votes to the final decision moved the entire management of the persuasion onto an interpersonal level. In this regard, Austin and Pinkleton note that among the 'benefits of adding interpersonal communication' this process is 'more likely to change a strongly held attitude' (2001, p. 293).

Put crudely, it would not have helped to have aired too many arguments in public. So the NZRU kept a relatively low profile during the preliminary negotiations. Perhaps, according to Austin and Pinkleton's views, even the New Zealanders' acceptance of their position of 'underdog' (or third choice) helped their case.

While the NZRU's bid team concentrated on their primary and secondary audiences, they no doubt recognised that their 'prominent persons' group (see 'Implementation: 17 November' on p. 168) would be influenced by a groundswell of public support within New Zealand. To this end, they kept up a steady flow of news stories about the progress of the bid and the coordinated effort that was being made.

GRASSROOTS UNDERWRITING

There is little doubt that New Zealand's hosting of the British and Irish Lions supporters in 2005, and the successful staging of big games during that visit, helped convince the IRB that this country was ready for the World Cup. In that success, the 'grassroots' rugby players and supporters played a major part.

Hospitality was offered generously by provincial towns and the general welcome by the Kiwis was expressed through city council preparations and tourism operations, including accommodation providers. New Zealand may not have shone so brightly among such large numbers of rugby followers had it not been for the 'people power' that was ignited.

The stage was set, then, for the NZRU to choose its communication campaign messages with the certainty that the bulk of the country's population was behind them. The bid team also knew that the rest of the rugby world had seen that Kiwis could and would rise to the occasion.

This concept of grassroots underwriting of big decision-making is a reversal of some of the more traditional models of opinion leadership, such as Lazarsfeld's 'two-step model' (Bobbitt & Sullivan 2005). Bobbitt and Sullivan noted that Lazarsfeld applied the concept of opinion leaders influencing others' views about issues; whereas the US 'father of public relations', Edward Bernays, observed as early as 1923 that many opinion leaders are not even aware of their role and the amount of power that they have.

Turning Lazarsfeld's model upside down, the NZRU was persuasive in its argument that the opinion leaders had the backing of the grassroots, and that this support would translate itself into the kind of hospitality accorded to the British and Irish Lions in 2005. Furthermore, the NZRU managed its media relations proactively—keeping the 'rugby public' and the electorate throughout New Zealand informed every step of the way to its successful tender for the 2011 tournament.

The term 'grassroots' has become associated in the literature with community activism and protest movements—such as Beck's theories of a risk society (quoted by Demetrious 2002)—whereas in the sporting world it usually refers to the junior and provincial levels of the game. In the case of New Zealand rugby, the clubs and associations were kept informed through the mass media of the World Cup bid. They continued to support it in the knowledge that money coming into the game at an elite level would filter down to a grassroots level.

This apparent inversion of Lazarsfeld's two-step flow is commonly used by practitioners of political lobbying, which is why it is a suitable metaphor for the NZRU's approach in this case. After all, it was primarily a lobbying campaign, albeit a multi-faceted one.

Messages written for the campaign

New Zealand's key message to the global rugby community was that a tournament in New Zealand would be an 'all rugby' experience for fans, players, officials and sponsors. New Zealand also promised 'a stadium of 4 million', which emphasised the breadth of interest in rugby but also mitigated the possible issue of New Zealand's small stadiums. Finally, New Zealand's bid highlighted the legacy that New Zealand rugby had already created for the global game through historic tours and matches, and exporting rugby talent in the form of players, coaches and administrators around the world.

Supporting messages also highlighted that New Zealand would provide:

- An environment where players could perform at their best

- Excellent rugby facilities and venues

- A tournament based on traditional rugby values

- A welcoming and safe country

- Superb broadcasting coverage

- A media-friendly tournament

- A unique partnership between rugby and the government

- A guaranteed tournament fee

- A conservative budget with potential upside underpinning the most commercially successful Rugby World Cup ever

- A tournament that would run smoothly and seamlessly.

Planning

The communication strategy was to create momentum for New Zealand's bid at key stages in the campaign, and this also allowed New Zealand to maximise its unique opportunities during 2005.

This started with lodging the bid. The positioning and themes of the bid documents highlighted New Zealand's strengths and key points of difference, and set the tone for the campaign. The 'all rugby' brand, on a black jersey with a silver fern, gave immediate recognition and rugby credibility to all materials and communication.

A number of strategic opportunities were identified during 2005 through which New Zealand could win support:

1 New Zealand's hosting of the DHL New Zealand Lions Series, which included hosting the IRB's Executive Committee and a visit by the Rugby World Cup technical evaluation team

2 The release of the IRB's technical evaluation report to the three bidding countries

3 The lead-in to and the final presentation on 17 November 2005.

The Lions Series (1) gave New Zealand a unique opportunity to demonstrate its capabilities to host a major rugby event, while emphasising the ability of New Zealand's tourism and sporting infrastructure to accommodate large numbers of sporting visitors.

The IRB's technical evaluation report (2) would be critical in determining what the IRB technical review team believed to be the strengths and weaknesses of the three bidders. For this reason, it was decided that the New Zealand bid team would not engage the voters around the world in person—as others had done—until after this report was released, giving them an opportunity to emphasise any of the noted strengths and mitigate any weaknesses.

In the run-up to the 17 November vote (3), New Zealand had an opportunity to further press its claims, given the fact the All Blacks would be playing in Wales and Ireland in the period leading up to the vote. The NZRU also made a strategic decision that, while opportunities would be created to inform the media about New Zealand's bid, the campaign to influence international voters would not be conducted through the media. The feedback was that this approach did not sit comfortably with many international rugby administrators. It was also felt that personal and direct communication to the delegates and their key influencers would be more effective. This was in strong contrast to the efforts of the other two bidding countries.

Implementation

LODGING THE BID

The implementation of the 'campaign' phase began with the lodging of the bid. NZRU Chief Executive Chris Moller delivered the bid in person to the IRB, along with a short presentation highlighting New Zealand's bid messages.

Prior to the bid team's departure, a press conference was held to formally announce New Zealand's bid and its key themes, and a photo opportunity was staged on the tarmac at Wellington Airport as the crates containing the twenty-four bid books, each weighing 45 kilograms, were loaded on to the plane.

DHL NEW ZEALAND LIONS SERIES

The DHL New Zealand Lions Series, staged from May to July 2005, was a critical platform to showcase New Zealand's bid credentials. The NZRU—working with government agencies, provincial rugby unions, local authorities and stadiums—had taken every step to make the series the most successful rugby event staged in New Zealand, but also to ensure that key stakeholders left with the right impressions of New Zealand and its Rugby World Cup credentials. These stakeholders included the British Lions touring party, their officials, media and supporters.

The NZRU hosted a meeting of the IRB Executive Committee in Wellington which allowed for a special presentation to these key members of the IRB Council. The New Zealand Government also demonstrated its support for the bid, with the Prime Minister hosting a private dinner for the committee members at Premier House. These functions, coupled with the spectacle of the second test between the All Blacks and the Lions, added to the impression made.

The NZRU then hosted members of the IRB's technical evaluation team during the final stages of the Lions series, and were able to demonstrate New Zealand's venue and match-hosting capabilities in a 'live' situation. Special presentations were also made to visiting media during the series, with the key take-out being the demonstrated capacity of New Zealand to cope with and satisfy the needs of 25,000 overseas rugby visitors.

WORLD TOUR

Following receipt of the IRB's technical evaluation report, the NZRU dispatched an information pack and DVD to each of the IRB's member unions, highlighting

New Zealand's bid themes and showing the colour and excitement generated during the Lions series. The report had already emphasised that New Zealand's bid was credible and 'low risk'.

Additionally, NZRU Chairman Jock Hobbs and Chief Executive Chris Moller embarked on a thirteen-country tour in October 2005 to each of the voting delegates and their rugby unions. The focus of this visit was to address New Zealand's strengths and weaknesses, and to highlight the relationship links between their union or region and New Zealand, and the benefits that a Rugby World Cup in New Zealand would offer to them and their stakeholders.

17 NOVEMBER

The make-up of the final presentation team allowed New Zealand to emphasise the relative strengths of its bid. Jock Hobbs, a respected member of international council and former All Blacks captain, would open and close the presentation. Prime Minister Helen Clark, the only national leader to accompany a bid team, would emphasise the government's commitment. Colin Meads, one of the world's greatest rugby players, would talk about the rugby experience in New Zealand. NZRU Chief Executive Chris Moller would highlight the operational and commercial capabilities, and current All Blacks Captain Tana Umaga would provide a player's perspective. The five presenters were supported by a video package that pressed home New Zealand's key themes.

'A STADIUM OF 4 MILLION'

The issues of New Zealand's small population and relatively modest stadiums were identified as potential concerns. However, leveraging New Zealand's national interest in rugby, the 'stadium of 4 million' theme was developed to highlight the intense focus and attention that a Rugby World Cup in New Zealand would create. This theme was brought to life in the video sequence that opened the final presentation.

'DOLLARS AND SETS'

Commercial issues were perceived to be a weakness for New Zealand. However, under the current structure for the Rugby World Cup, the key revenue stream to the IRB from the tournament is from television rights. New Zealand's strength and experience in rugby broadcasting was a key point of difference—a Rugby World Cup in New Zealand would deliver an unparalleled broadcast product that would be attractive to fans and sponsors around the world. Similarly, New Zealand was able to highlight the success of the Lions series telecasts into the United Kingdom. The fact that the IRB's decision on 17 November was being beamed live into New Zealand via the world's only dedicated rugby channel on Sky Television was also noted by IRB Council members.

As evidenced throughout the mass-media literature, the impact of television on sport has been one of the tectonic shifts in the political economy of the media. It has reached a point where: 'The maintenance of television and sponsorship revenues requires a successful, well-resourced All Black team' (Hope 2002, p. 249).

For the NZRU it was more than a matter of simple economics. Television rights had to be a pivotal argument in persuading the IRB that the host for this large tournament could be a small country, with limited resources but unlimited enthusiasm for rugby. The combination of a historic, almost religious fervour for the game, arguably the biggest brand in world rugby (the All Blacks) and friendly hospitable natives, only needed television support to tilt the IRB pragmatists in New Zealand's favour.

'A FAMILIAR LOOK'

New Zealand's bid branding featuring the 'all rugby' mark on a black jersey with a silver fern emphasised the iconic status of New Zealand rugby in international sport, and was a distinctive and unifying image that connected all of the bid communications and material.

'LOCAL TOUCHES'

The letter that was delivered to each voting delegate only hours before the final vote not only emphasised the key messages and benefits of a Rugby World Cup in New Zealand, but also called on local Irish influences, even quoting from Oscar Wilde in exhorting IRB delegates to consider New Zealand's bid.

'They're drinking our beer here'

The NZRU arranged for the main bar in the IRB hotel in Dublin to stock New Zealand beer Steinlager® in the days leading to the vote and, on the night before the IRB Council meeting, All Blacks legends Sir Brian Lochore and Colin Meads were present, hosting some of those who were due to vote on New Zealand's bid the next day.

'Persuasive people'

The impact of New Zealand's presenting line-up was immediate:

- It included the first-ever visit by a current head of government to the IRB offices
- It was the only line-up to include the current national team captain, who was preparing to play a critical test match just over forty-eight hours later.

'Closing it out'

Each of New Zealand's speakers addressed the IRB directly, personally and powerfully. To hit home the message that it was not just New Zealanders who aspired to see a tournament held in New Zealand, the final message was a video, filmed in all parts of the world and featuring young school or club players, expressing—in their own language—that they too hoped they could play in a Rugby World Cup in New Zealand in 2011.

Evaluation and lessons learnt

On the afternoon of 17 November 2005, the IRB Council selected New Zealand as the host for the 2011 Rugby World Cup.

A number of critical factors for New Zealand's success were identified, including:

- The focus on the voters and their objectives

- The partnership with the government

- The standing of New Zealand's IRB representatives, and the combined impact of the team that delivered the final presentation.

New Zealand's win highlighted the need to have a concerted and coordinated message, and to ensure that message is delivered to the right people, at the right time, in the right way. It also demonstrated the power of passion and simple personal persuasion in achieving a successful communications outcome.

CONCLUSION

It must have come as no surprise to IRB delegates when New Zealand's Prime Minister, Helen Clark, and senior All Blacks turned up in Ireland to support the bid to host the Rugby World Cup.

On the surface, this could be seen as simply 'good PR'. But Mike Green of Loughborough University sees more at stake in such political patronage than the good graces of a few elite sportspeople and their supporters:

> There can be little argument that the significance of sport as a politically salient cultural institution has increased over the past 40 years or so. Sport is now a particularly malleable and high-profile instrument for countries as diverse as China, Singapore, Belgium, Australia, Canada and the United Kingdom (Green 2007, p. 921).

When choosing between bids for the Olympics or the Rugby World Cup, sports decision-makers expect to see tangible government support. This can be a financial commitment to underwrite the event and/or the building of infrastructure. However, the visible presence of a country's leader underscores a political and patriotic commitment, linked to the nation's culture. So the willingness of the New Zealand Government to help fund the expansion of Eden Park (venue for the Rugby World Cup) to accommodate the expected crowd for the tournament final was also evidence that would help ensure every chance for the NZRU's bid.

The message of 'excellent rugby facilities and venues' was substantiated, along with that of a 'welcoming and safe country'. This was closely detailed and underscored in the content and mood of information and activities delivered by the NZRU during the New Zealand leg of the 'world tour' by the IRB's technical evaluation team. It was backed up by the first-ever visit by a current head of government to the IRB offices.

The NZRU clearly accepted and exploited the crucial role of television as a means of overcoming some of their country's disadvantages. Their message 'superb broadcasting coverage' was backed up by New Zealand's strength and experience in rugby broadcasting. This was highlighted by the success of the Lions series telecasts in the United Kingdom.

It is also worth noting that the IRB's decision on 17 November was being beamed live into New Zealand via the world's only dedicated rugby channel, a point that was noted by IRB Council members. Superb lobbying, and the whole philosophy of 'patriots at play' while their nations watched and applauded, seems to have won the hearts and minds of the council.

REFERENCES

Austin E. W. & Pinkleton B. E., 2001, *Strategic Public Relations Management*, Lawrence Erlbaum, Mahwah, NJ

Bernays E. L., 1923, *Crystallizing Public Opinion*, Boni and Liveright, New York

Bobbitt R. & Sullivan R., 2005, *Developing the Public Relations Campaign—A Team-based Approach*, Pearson Education, Boston, MA

Cutlip S. M., Center A. H. & Broom G. M., 1994, *Effective Public Relations*, 7th edn, Prentice Hall, Englewood Cliffs, NJ

Demetrious K., 2002, 'Grassroots Energy: A Case Study of Active Citizenship and Public Communication in Risk Society', in *Journal of Communication Management*, Vol. 7, No. 2, pp. 148–55

Green M., 2007, 'Olympic Glory or Grassroots Development?' in *International Journal of the History of Sport*, Vol. 24, No. 7, pp. 921–53

Grunig J. (ed.), 1992, *Excellence in Public Relations and Communication Management*, Lawrence Erlbaum, NJ

Hope W., 2002, 'Whose All Blacks?' in *Media, Culture & Society*, Sage, London

Lewin K., 1951, *Field Theory in Social Science*, Harper & Row, New York

Maguire J. & Poulton E. K., 1997, 'European Identity Politics in Euro 96', paper presented at the International Sociology of Sport Association Symposium, Oslo

Smith R. D., 2002, *Strategic Planning for Public Relations*, Lawrence Erlbaum, Mahwah, NJ

The New Zealand Herald, Editorial, 5 July 2007, p. A18

Tuck J. & Maguire J., 1999, 'Making Sense of Global Patriot Games' in *Football Studies*, Vol. 2, No. 1, pp. 26–54

Tuck J., 2003, 'Making Sense of Emerald Commotion: Rugby Union, National Identity and Ireland' in *Identities: Global Studies in Culture and Power*, Routledge, London

Tymson C., Lazar P. & Lazar R., 2002, *The New Australian and New Zealand Public Relations Manual*, Tymson Communications, Chatswood, NSW

12 Risk Communication

The Toowoomba Water Fight

Chris Galloway

AIMS OF THIS CHAPTER

- To outline the key components for practitioners to consider in risk communication campaigns

- To illustrate different approaches to risk communication campaigns through a case study

INTRODUCTION

Today's 'risk society' (Beck 1992) seems focused on the 'risk management of everything' (Power 2004). The concerns behind this focus prompt considerable communication activity, as risk is 'a condition in which there is a possibility that people or property could experience adverse consequences' (Lindell & Perry 2004, p. 1). Some risk-related communication comes from organisations that want to 'tame fears' (Beck 1992, p. 75) about technologies that publics see as risky in some way. Campaigns of this type typically involve large organisations (Palenchar 2005, p. 753). Some communication is driven by governments or government agencies responsible for managing various kinds of risk on behalf of the community. Other communication is generated by 'outrage' (Sandman 1993) felt by worried and therefore active publics who oppose the interpretations of risk presented to them. The result can be vigorous debates about how to manage the risk, with—as in the case study in this chapter—both sides claiming their views have a scientific basis.

Risk communication is considered to be a public relations sub-discipline. (One definition of risk communication is 'communication intended to supply laypeople with the information they need to make independent judgment about risks to health, safety and the environment'—Morgan et al. 2002, p. 4). It

> provides the opportunity to understand and appreciate stakeholders' concerns related to
> risks generated by organisations, engage in dialogue to address differences and concerns,
> carry out appropriate actions that can reduce perceived risks, and create a climate
> of participatory and effective discourse to reduce friction and increase harmony and
> mutuality (Palenchar 2005, p. 753).

This case study involves both a local government body and a grouping of activists. It shows that people may use factors other than scientific data to make up their minds on risk questions (Palenchar 2005, p. 754) and suggests that this fact should be taken into account in planning public relations risk communication campaigns.

BACKGROUND

On 29 July 2006, the people of Toowoomba—a parched Queensland city 140 kilometres inland from the state capital, Brisbane—voted on a proposal to include recycled and treated sewage effluent in their drinking water. The water supply crisis that prompted the proposal was presented as a risk to the community's future viability. Not to act on the proposal would imperil Toowoomba's prosperity, it was suggested. However opponents had a different view of the possible economic costs to the city if the plan went ahead. They claimed that it could result in risks to individuals' health, saying there was enough uncertainty about the effects of the change for the idea to be voted down. In the end, after what one observer called a 'savagely fought referendum' (Devine 2007), a clear majority of voters said 'No'.

However the debate did not end there. Politicians at both local and state level continued to argue over water issues (in Australia, constitutional authority for water management, including recycling, belongs to the states—Radcliffe 2006), and a leading Toowoomba anti-recycling councillor carried the fight to other parts of the state. It is possible that, in future, citizens of Toowoomba may not only face continuing water supply difficulties, but also pay much more for the water they do obtain. The Toowoomba case showed that social concerns can overwhelm a professional information campaign, as Mackey (2006) demonstrates in his study of a proposal to site a biosolids production plant near a Victorian township. In that situation, concerned citizens forced a small water authority to drop its initial plan. The authority eventually succeeded in building a biosolids facility—but in a different location, and after it adopted a different communications approach from the one it used at first.

Toowoomba is Australia's second largest inland city (the federal capital, Canberra, is bigger). It has long faced water supply problems. Since 1998, as the city has grown, demand for water has outstripped the available resource. In 2006, a Queensland Government review found that the amount of water the city could safely take from its dams each year was about 28 per cent less than it had been using. This finding highlighted the extent to which Toowoomba had been overdrawing supplies and made it 'critical that we find and develop alternative sources of water', according to the Toowoomba City Council ('Demand Management Going Well ...' 2006, p. 1). Because Toowoomba is so far from the sea, possible solutions open to cities closer to oceans, such as desalination, are not feasible. Accordingly, the Toowoomba City Council developed a Water Futures demand management strategy that included a range of actions, including education and advertising, designed to promote water conservation and to ensure adequate continuing supply. In addition to a set of initiatives designed to encourage citizens to use water wisely, the council undertook a 'water wise makeover' of its own buildings to reduce water use. Controversy arose around another part of the strategy: a scheme for a water treatment plant to treat and recycle sewage effluent, so water from this source could be added to the city's drinking supply.

The council sought federal funding for the $23 million cost. It was told that central government support was conditional on taking the issue to local voters in a plebiscite, as provided for in the *Local Government Act*. The plebiscite question was: 'Do you support the addition of purified recycled water to Toowoomba's water supply via Cooby Dam as proposed by the Water Futures Toowoomba Project?' The poll was held after the council ran 160 public forums, an advertising and information campaign, and offered 'taste tests' of water produced by the treatment process proposed for Toowoomba.

The council's proposal was opposed by Citizens Against Drinking Sewage (CADS), backed by high-profile developer and former mayor Clive Berghofer, in a campaign some commentators thought was characterised by 'scaremongering'. It was certainly memorable: the 'No' camp argued that if the recycling proposal was accepted, the city would become known as 'Poowoomba' and could incur economic losses as people would no longer wish to move there. Both sides used the internet to promote their views. The debate prompted considerable discussion in web-logs from both pro- and anti-recycling advocates. Berghofer himself denied that the campaign he led was based on a fear appeal. He told an interviewer:

> I haven't run any scare campaign whatsoever. All I have put in is cold hard facts. It's like smoking, you don't ever smoke and you die tomorrow, it might take 10, 20, 40 years before you die. Same as asbestos. Same as this water. We don't know ('From the Toilet to the Tap' 2006).

The Toowoomba vote was held against a background of ever-intensifying debate and public concern about the parlous state of water supplies to Australian communities throughout much of the country. Such concern is not new and, according to Radcliffe (2006), detailed consideration of the potential for recycled water use in Australia was given as far back as 1977 and 1978. Fresh impetus arose in the early 1990s—the emphasis, however, being on the use of recycled water 'for purposes for which drinking water standards were unnecessary' (Radcliffe 2006, p. 78). More recently, as Australia has grappled with the effects of abnormally prolonged drought, water has become a much more significant issue in state and federal politics as well as in local government. Water supply is now recognised as one of the most critical challenges facing the country, and water management as one of its most important policy issues.

Inevitably, there has been some finger-pointing: suggestions that if dam-building or other water plans had been set in motion earlier, the crisis would have been less acute. At the time of the Toowoomba vote and subsequently, the political contests mostly centred on claims-making about whose water plan was best. The point-scoring continued as water authorities tightened water use restrictions and maintained or stepped up water conservation social marketing campaigns (social marketing is the use of marketing techniques to persuade people to adjust their behaviour to help achieve an outcome thought beneficial to society).

Market research surveys have produced mixed messages about the acceptability of recycling effluent, related perhaps to the way the question was asked. For example a 2007 *Sydney Morning Herald*/AC Nielsen survey showed that 78 per cent of Australians would support the introduction of recycled water (Metherell 2007). In this survey, the respondents were told that one option to increase water supplies would be 'to treat sewage and other waste water', and that the water would be 'safe for drinking and other household purposes'. They were then asked whether they would support or oppose recycled water being used to augment supplies. However two years earlier, a UMR Research poll had shown that 68 per cent of people were uncomfortable about such an idea. The question they were asked was whether they were 'very comfortable, mildly comfortable, mildly uncomfortable or very uncomfortable with drinking recycled sewage, including toilet water, that is treated to drinking-water quality' (Metherell 2007).

COMMUNICATION STRATEGIES AND TACTICS

Both the Toowoomba City Council and its opponents sought to sway opinions among eligible voters. However their approaches to doing so were different. The next section discusses the council's campaign, then that of the 'No' group.

Toowoomba City Council

The council's campaign took an evidence-based line, founded on what it called 'the facts' ('The "Yes" Case' 2006), with at least four key themes:

1   The recycling and treating of effluent is the best choice.

2   It will be safe.

3   Not doing this will cost you more.

4   The future of the city demands this.

The 'Yes' case, posted on the council website, positioned the plebiscite as 'a vote for Toowoomba's future. Our city has no future without clean drinking water.' The proposal was, in part, cast as necessary because of local impacts of global climate change: 'Our growth, together with a long drought and the reality of climate change, has made it clear we cannot solely rely on rain filling our dams. There is a solution that will provide safe, clean drinking water and is also the best option for protecting our natural environment'— although the council's 'facts' did not spell out why it thought treating effluent was better for the environment.

The council was at pains to point out that seven treatment and disinfection barriers would intervene in the process between wastewater entering the local 'water reclamation' plant and its provision to citizens as drinking water. 'This process will be world's best practice!' it claimed, adding that 'If Water Futures—Toowoomba does not go ahead, the cost to Toowoomba ratepayers will be much higher! Other options cost far more to build and Federal Government funding ... would be lost' ('The "Yes" Case' 2006).

In discussing alternatives to recycling and treating sewage effluent, the council noted that four other water supply proposals had been made:

1   To build a pipeline from the main dam that services the Brisbane area (a plan rejected by the Queensland State Government)

2   To build a new dam to service the city

3   To use water produced in the process of coal mining

4   To swap bore water from farming areas to the west of Toowoomba for recycled water.

'Each of these options were [sic] analysed and found not to be able to reliably supply the amount of water Toowoomba needs for the future or were too expensive to build and operate, or both' ('The "Yes" Case' 2006, p. 2).

Opposing positions were not forgotten: 'Opponents have claimed that these alternatives have not been properly considered. This is not true' ('The "Yes" Case' 2006, p. 2). The council also took a swipe at other claims from opponents:

> The Water Futures project will not cause the real estate market to collapse or stop business coming to Toowoomba. Residents and businesses are attracted by a safe and reliable water supply. In Orange County, California, house prices have doubled in the 7 years since the upgrading of their recycling scheme was announced ('The "Yes" Case' 2006, p. 3).

Water Futures opponents

'The "No" Case' (2006) criticised both the council's deliberative processes and the water reclamation project itself, the latter targeted especially because of uncertainty over the safety of the proposed sewage treatment and also on grounds of cost. On process, the nay-sayers claimed that:

> Council hasn't allowed public debate but has held closed, one-sided information sessions for selected groups. Without full information you would be wise to vote 'NO'. The Water Futures project was developed in secrecy. Trust is now missing ('The "No" Case' 2006, p. 3).

The opponents also asked, 'Why has Council voted itself $460,000 of your money to advertise their case only?' They alleged that the council had been 'influenced by a large multinational corporation, CH2M Hill, to adopt Water Futures. CH2HM has already been paid over $140,000 for "community education" as well as consultancy fees. They stand to gain from the construction of the project' ('The "No" Case' 2006, p. 3). Describing the recycling plan as 'a risky water supply option' ('The "No" Case' 2006, p. 3), the opponents attacked it on the grounds that not enough was known about the technology and the possible effects of adopting it. They noted that the council's plan called for 25 per cent of water supplied to residents to come from sewage reclamation: a high ratio by international standards and one, they argued, that would require 'detailed review and further studies'. The technology was 'new and requires more testing' ('The "No" Case' 2006, p. 1). Turning some council language back at it, the opponents noted that the council had designated Cooby Dam, through which the treated water would be supplied, as a 'living laboratory'. In an apparently contradictory statement, they pointed out that 'there are no guidelines for drinking recycled water' and, in the same statement, cited the 'Queensland Water Recycling

Guidelines' as saying that 'there are many man-made chemicals that may potentially be found in sewage and it is not possible at this time to set safe concentrations for all of these chemicals' ('The "No" Case' 2006, p. 1). The opponents recalled that 'the tragedies of thalidomide, asbestos and mad cow disease were caused by the ignorance of the long-term effects of new science' ('The "No" Case' 2006, p. 3). They added: 'Toowoomba shouldn't have a water supply process that still needs testing. Any water supply for over 100,000 people should use tried and proven methods. We are not guinea pigs' ('The "No" Case' 2006, p. 2).

The opponents also mounted an economic argument, claiming that: 'Final building costs of Water Futures are not definite. The ongoing operating costs of the plant have not been properly calculated. The $68 million costing will blow-out.' They claimed not only that 'businesses, industry, families, retirees and travellers will be discouraged from visiting, investing or living in the "Garden City"', but also that 'Food processors in Toowoomba will find their products unmarketable to the wider population. Some may leave, causing unemployment' ('The "No" Case' 2006, p. 2). Contending that 'Drinking recycled water is not a generally acceptable thing to do', the opponents suggested that Toowoomba would be perceived as having 'an inferior water supply by modern standards' and that this perception would destroy the city's 'clean and green image', making it unattractive ('The "No" Case' 2006, p. 2).

AFTER THE VOTE

After 61.8 per cent of Toowoomba voters rejected the effluent plan, the Queensland State Premier, Peter Beattie, promised a referendum on recycled water in the south-east corner of the state. However, in January 2007, an apologetic Beattie scrapped the idea of a poll, saying the state government had no choice but to add treated waste water to the drinking supply. It also announced plans to launch an 'extensive' education plan to sell the idea of drinking recycled sewage. Beattie said the campaign would be:

> not so much about swaying opinion, although I wouldn't mind if that happened. It's more about ... explaining exactly what we're doing, explaining this is about water security, this is about drought-proofing the south-east corner as much as is humanly possible ('Qld Govt to Sell ...' 2007).

EVALUATION

Commentary in both online and other media gives a flavour of the debate.

The 'Yes' case was buttressed by sound science arguments, affirmed by Councillor Michelle Alroe, who stated on a city website: 'I have looked at the research and I thoroughly trust the science, which is the foundation of our Water Futures Toowoomba

project' ('Why We're Voting YES' 2006). On the same website, Councillor Michelle
Schneider commented:

> Opponent's [sic] claims regarding the health implications of water recycling is [sic] just
> scaremongering. Wherever recycled water is used, strict Health Department guidelines for
> water quality and management must be met. It is highly treated recycled water that has
> been strongly endorsed as a safe source of water.
>
> I am appalled by the conspiracy theories, the political agendas and the misinformation
> surrounding the issue. The issue is water, and our lack of it. Are the people who are against
> Water Futures able to give the community a viable option? ('Why We're Voting YES' 2006).

The face-off was encapsulated in a radio interview on the day of the poll with Malcolm
Turnbull, then the Prime Minister's Parliamentary Secretary for Water:

> LISA MILLAR: What have you thought about the quality of the debate going on in
> Toowoomba over the last few weeks?
>
> MALCOLM TURNBULL: I think the no case has obviously been a scare campaign. It's
> been based more on emotion rather than science.
>
> LISA MILLAR: And the people who say 'Poowoomba'—they're drinking sewage—what
> do you say to them?
>
> MALCOLM TURNBULL: Well nobody's drinking sewage. The water that will be
> produced from this process, as I said, will be purer than the water in Toowoomba's dams
> today. So drinking sewage is nonsense, that's ridiculous.
>
> I mean, this Poowoomba thing is ludicrous, it's childish. And it's only being promoted by
> those people on the 'No' side.
>
> ('Poowoomba: Turnbull Supports Treated Sewage Water' 2006)

In earlier statements, reported in January 2006, Turnbull was reported as telling the local
Toowoomba paper, *The Chronicle*, that he was satisfied with the scientific and media
evidence supporting the purity of recycled water. He realised that communities had
a psychological concern: the so-called 'yuk factor' ('Turnbull Does an About Face ...'
2006). However it is interesting that, in an online forum posting, one 'No' voter did not
include this element in an explanation of the major drivers of the opposition campaign.
A correspondent known as 'amber4350' commented:

> As a NO voter, I can assure you that the major contributing factors were:
>
> 1   The lack of better management and adequate investment in water infrastructure
>
> 2   The lack of community consultation

3   A view that Council was either not capable or not willing to examine practical alternatives

4   No long-term studies on safety to health and the environment

All of which caused the community to lose faith in its Council.

(The Forum website 2006)

In another online posting at a different website, a Toowoomba resident identifying himself as a 'Yes' voter named 'Ross' commented that:

> the No campaigners ran a shrewd campaign. The more rabid nay-sayers called themselves CADS. Citizens Against Drinking Sewage ... really rational people! Also, the clever slogans 'It's OK to say No' and 'a No vote puts ALL options on the table including recycling' not necessarily for drinking, and the support of Clive Berghofer, a local folk-hero, were master strokes ... Add the Yuk factor ... anti-science technophobia, enough vague conspiracy theories and a sense of victimisation, and some lame TCC [Toowoomba City Council] stunts like water tasting of Singapore recycled water, and the No vote was a shoo-in (Larvatus Prodeo website 2006).

Even though the Toowoomba debate was suffused with political argumentation, the decision to put the recycling question to the vote aligns with European perspectives on this issue. The European Communities' view, cited by Schäfer and Beder (2006, p. 248) is that although the evaluation of likely harm requires scientific assessment, the desired level of protection of citizens from that harm is a political decision. Making that decision requires public participation, ideally at the earliest possible point. In Toowoomba, faced with a binary 'Yes–No' decision, voters confronted not only opportunities to attend 'for' or 'against' meetings and the activities of elected representatives who were split on the issue; they were also required to evaluate both a council-run information campaign that claimed to be objective and an opposition effort that did not hold back from making attention-getting statements to spearhead a persuasive communication campaign. The latter relied heavily on stimulating emotional responses. As Schäfer and Beder (2006, p. 248) point out, fear is an important factor in motivating public response: 'issues related to water recycling can be highly emotional, in particular when male sperm counts, extinction of threatened species or images of drinking excrement come into play'.

The council's campaign sought to reassure citizens on safety concerns by spelling out the detail of the planned treatment process. In effect, it ran a 'technical' communication campaign that asked voters to trust a multi-stage technology implementation. It was asking citizens to decide with their heads, with the application of their logical faculties. This is what Petty and Cacioppo (1986, cited in Benjamin 1997) call the central route to persuasion—when people are cognitively involved in assessing messages and are highly motivated to do so, they can be persuaded by the quality of the arguments presented to them. But Petty and Cacioppo also describe a 'peripheral' route to persuasion. They say that many of us use mental shortcuts in confronting messages and that we rely on cues, slogans and other factors—such as the credibility of a spokesperson or an incentive—in deciding whether we will allow ourselves to be persuaded.

In Toowoomba, the use of shortcuts such as 'It's OK to say No' seems to have been one factor in the opposition campaign's success, along with a psychological revulsion to the idea of drinking recycled sewage. As Queensland Opposition Leader Jeff Seeney commented:

> It's more than just about science. Some people can rationalise this, some people can't. You're talking about using human waste as a source of water for human sustenance and that invokes a whole lot of emotive responses, almost instinctive responses, in people that need to be respected ('Recycled Water Inevitable in NSW, says PM' 2007).

This might have been what Councillor Snow Manners of the 'No' campaign had in mind when an interviewer asked him whether he was confident that the community knew enough about the science of water. Speaking in the immediate aftermath of his campaign's success, he replied: 'The community does not need to know anything about the science' ('From the Toilet to the Tap' 2006, p. 5). Later, however, he was reported as saying that the booklet his group was distributing sought to 'generate a proper scientific debate on the subject by presenting opposing scientific views. The Government is using emotion and fear, not information, to sell the concept of sourcing city water from sewage treatment plants' (Water Futures 2007).

But there is more to the outcome of the debate than this. Another factor in people's thinking may have been what the environmental and risk communication literatures call the 'precautionary principle'. The principle is controversial and articulated in various ways. Cooney (2004) gives one explanation of it:

> Precaution has emerged as a broad principle weighing in favor of environmental protection in the case of uncertainty. The core of the principle can be understood as *countering the presumption in favor of development*. Where there is uncertainty concerning the impacts of an activity, rather than assuming human economic activities will proceed until and unless there is clear evidence that they are harmful, the precautionary principle supports action to anticipate and avert environmental harm in advance of, or without, a clear demonstration that such action is necessary. Precaution shifts the balance in decision-making toward 'prudent foresight', in favor of monitoring, preventing or mitigating uncertain potential threats. This is a broad notion susceptible of supporting a very wide range of operational measures (Cooney 2004, p. 5).

The principle goes beyond deciding to 'do no harm' if an outcome is unknown in a climate of scientific uncertainty. Supporters see it as a moral standard, a 'decision-making and action tool with ethical power and scientific rigor' (Tickner et al. 1999, p. 2). In Toowoomba, in the face of conflicting claims, people may have decided that they did not know enough to make a sound decision and opted for the path of precaution. They may have done so even if it meant ruling out one possible solution to the city's water woes.

LESSONS LEARNT

The risk communication literature has lessons for professional communicators faced with situations such as the one that confronted the Toowoomba City Council. Krimsky and Plough (1988, p. 302) say that, according to their analysis of five case studies, 'the clarity of risk information, selecting the proper channel, or ensuring adequate public education does not fully address the divergence of technical and popular attitudes toward risk'. Here they are making two key points:

1   Attitudes toward risk questions held by technical experts may differ from those held by laypeople.

2   When this is the case, it is not sufficient to follow the textbook approach to communication campaigns, such as ensuring that relevant information is clearly communicated.

Why is this so? When people consider risk questions—such as the risk to the future of a city (in this case, Toowoomba) if it does not follow a proposed path of action, or the risk (if any) of drinking treated recycled sewage effluent—they often use a different set of criteria from those followed by experts. Popular criteria such as 'Is it fair?' may differ from technical ones such as 'Can we prove this scientifically?' This is not to say that the popular view is wrong, although some communication about risk questions is best summed up as an expert position that 'If you knew what I know (or could understand what I understand) then you would think the same way.'

Krimsky and Plough (1988) say that there are two competing models available to interpret risk information. One of them they call the 'technical' model, the other, the 'cultural' or 'popular' model. 'Our analysis suggests that effective risk communication does not treat the cultural model as an error to be corrected. Indeed, the successful risk communicator must act as a translator between the two models' (Krimsky & Plough 1988, p. 302). To extend their argument, public relations people dealing with risk debates need to recognise that laypeople will not necessarily share expert assessments, no matter how sound the science on which they are based. Science-based reports 'proving' that a technology is safe or that an end product such as recycled effluent may be drunk with equanimity may have a multitude of 'facts' behind them. But, some laypeople may reason, 'experts' have been wrong before. Technologies once thought to be safe have later been found to be dangerous. In the light of that history, other considerations may weigh more heavily than technical views about the acceptability or otherwise of a risk. These considerations may include a 'yuk factor', but also include calculations as to the credibility of the message sources available on the topic in question, influences from one's social networks and attitudes to activist groups seeking to effect change. Schäfer and Beder (2006) sum up the issue so well that they are worth quoting in detail:

> The uncertainties involved in water recycling are often of a technical nature and concerned with questions of contamination, adequate treatment and usage of recycled water. They provide the incentive to do more research, more thoroughly monitor quality and to more tightly control recycling processes. However the issue of recycling is not merely a technological one. The concept of 'toilet to tap' is somewhat emotionally charged; a response that is understandable given the breadth of human experience with disease resulting from drinking water contaminated with sewage (Schäfer & Beder 2006, p. 241).

Attwater and Derry (2005, p. 194, referring to Al-Zubari 1998) agree: 'To effectively transform "wastewater" into a valued resource, underlying transformations in organisation, information, and informed behavior are essential. Acceptability involves not only overcoming technical challenges, but [also] social differences in psychology and cultural values as they relate to water.' Addressing water professionals, Davis (2006) comments that:

> We may be naïve to imagine that the factors which are ultimately decisive in public decision-making are the facts, figures and analytical tools which are dear to the hearts of the managers, engineers, scientists and consultants of the water industry. We may be able to work more effectively with the public if we take cultural and aesthetic values into account, rather than assuming they are extraneous to water resource planning (Davis 2006, p. 8).

Davis' view may yet be a minority one: according to Russell et al. (2006, p. 2), there is a 'prevalent view in the [water] sector that people simply need technical information to correct misperceptions and overcome emotional responses'.

The Toowoomba City Council's communication campaign appears to have followed a textbook, largely technical approach to 'educating' a lay public on a risk issue. Yet arguably this is not enough when the issue is controversial (as recycling was in Toowoomba), and when the stakes are high (as they were claimed to be in Toowomba: nothing less, it was said, than the future prosperity of the city was on the line). When a community faces an extraordinary situation, such as prolonged drought and over-reliance on limited water supplies, it has moved beyond 'business as normal' to a 'post-normal' situation. For many affected citizens, normal approaches simply do not go far enough to meet their concerns and address the crisis. Their interest is not only in dealing with the present threat, but also staving off potential ones—of becoming better able to deal with major risks in the future.

Schäfer and Beder (2006) emphasise that it is

> not enough merely to offer the public a choice of a limited range of 'solutions' at the end of
> the decision-making process. Innovative approaches in water recycling involve the public
> from an early stage so people can take part in developing suitable options. Such processes
> can indeed be observed in a limited number of successful recycling strategies (2006, p. 248).

While laypeople may lack the technical qualifications of, say, a scientist specialising in water
recycling, many citizens have significant expertise that can be brought to bear on issues such
as the one facing Toowoomba. Recruiting this expertise to the challenge of confronting
a significant threat to a community not only recognises this fact but also, implicitly,
acknowledges that science—appealed to by both sides in Toowoomba—has its own
limitations, its own politics. Further, professional communicators dealing with issues such
as the Toowoomba one could consider forming partnerships with community development
professionals with the aim of jointly working to strengthen the community's resilience in
the face of risks that might arise in the future.

Davis (2006, p. 4) comments that 'Water professionals often believe that they have
already defined both the right questions and their answers'. He goes on to offer a list of
problems that can undermine effective communication. Without suggesting that they
necessarily apply to the Toowoomba case, his compilation is instructive:

- Providing data that is incomprehensible to the public

- Superficial communication that does not address valid concerns

- Inadequate listening skills

- Questionable timing (a matter of the stage at which people's views are being sought:
  when questions are being defined or when proposed solutions are being advanced)

- Unwillingness to acknowledge or express values (here Davis has in mind a reluctance by
  'resource professionals' to acknowledge their own values in policy discussions with the
  public)

- Limiting avenues for input to those that are easily provided but are not easily accessible
  by a wide range of stakeholders.

Davis concedes that 'communication about the treatment and quality of recycled water is
particularly challenging' (2006, p. 5) and that in some cases, public concerns about water
quality seem to show a kind of 'water innocence' (2006, p. 6), given that many existing water
supplies rely on treatment of water from sources that may already contain some wastewater.
However, when public relations people are working on a risk communication campaign—
whether it be for an established body such as the council, or an activist group such as the 'No'
public in Toowoomba—they can play an important role in helping to enrich the quality of
public debate by challenging such 'innocence', and working to ensure that risk decisions are
based on the fullest possible citizen participation, taking into account both fears and 'facts'.

CHRIS GALLOWAY

REFERENCES

Attwater R. & Derry C., 2005, 'Engaging Communities of Practice for Risk Communication in the Hawkesbury Water Recycling Scheme' in *Action Research*, Vol. 3, No. 2, pp. 193–209

Beck U. (tr. Ritter M.), 1992, *Risk Society: Towards a New Modernity*, Sage, London

Benjamin J., 1997, *Principles, Elements and Types of Persuasion*, Thomson Wadsworth, Belmont, CA

Cooney R., 2004, 'The Precautionary Principle in Biodiversity Conservation and Natural Resource Management: An Issues Paper for Policy-makers, Researchers and Practitioners', International Union for Conservation of Nature and Natural Resources, Cambridge, UK, www.pprinciple.net/publications/PrecautionaryPrincipleissuespaper.pdf, accessed 14 March 2008

Davis C. K., 2006, 'Ethical Dilemmas in Water Recycling', www.emwis.org/documents/pdf/200609_BeijingManuscriptSubmitted.pdf, accessed 1 April 2007

'Demand Management Going Well But It's Not Enough', 8 December 2006, www.toowoomba.qld.gov.au/index.php?option=com_content&task=view&id=15, accessed 6 February 2007

Devine M., 2007, 'Debnam Punt Has a Bit of a Stink', in *Sydney Morning Herald*, 18 February 2007, www.smh.com.au/news/miranda-devine/debnam-punt-has-a-bit-of-a-stink/2007/02/17/1171405496136.html, accessed 1 April 2007

Forum, The, 7 August 2006, http://forum.onlineopinion.com.au/thread.asp?article=4742&page=0, accessed 14 March 2008

'From the Toilet to the Tap', 2006, reported by Horstman M., *ABC: Catalyst*, 9 November 2006, www.abc.net.au/catalyst/stories/sll1785041.htm, accessed 21 March 2007

Griffith C., 2007, 'Recycled Water Fight Begins' in *Courier Mail*, 20 March 2007, www.news.com.au/couriermail/comments/0,23836,21414489-3102,00.html, accessed 21 March 2007

Krimsky S. & Plough A., 1988, *Environmental Hazards: Communicating Risks as a Social Process*, Auburn House, Westport, CT; London

Larvatus Prodeo, 1 August 2006, http://larvatusprodeo.net/2006/07/31/crikey-story-toowoomba-votes-on-recycled-water/, accessed 14 March 2008

Lindell M. K. & Perry R. W., 2004, *Communicating Environmental Risk in Multiethnic Communities*, Sage, Thousand Oaks, CA

Mackey S., 2006, 'Competing Community Relations Campaigns in Australia: Public Relations Efforts For and Against a Biosolids Production Facility' in Parkinson M. G. & Ekachai D. (eds), 2006, *International and Intercultural Public Relations. A Campaign Case Approach*, Pearson Education, Boston, MA

Meade K., 2007, 'Water Campaign Hits Below the Belt' in *The Australian*, 21 March 2007, p. 5

Metherell M., 2007, 'We'll Drink Recycled Sewage', in *Sydney Morning Herald*, 12 February 2007, www.smh.com.au/news/national/well-drink-recycled-sewage/2007/02/11/1171128816473. html, accessed 7 January 2008

Morgan M. G., Fischoff B., Bostrom A. & Atman C. J., 2002, *Risk Communication: A Mental Models Approach*, Cambridge University Press, Cambridge

Palenchar M. J., 2005, 'Risk Communication' in Heath R. L. (ed.), 2005, *Encyclopaedia of Public Relations*, Sage, Thousand Oaks, CA; London; New Delhi, pp. 752–5

'Poowoomba: Turnbull Supports Treated Sewage Water', 2006, reported by Millar L., www.abc. net.au/am/content/2006/s1700353.htm, accessed 5 March 2007

Power M., 2004, *The Risk Management of Everything*, Demos, London, www.demos.co.uk/ catalogue/riskmanagemenhjtofeverythingcatalogue, accessed 20 February 2006

'Qld Govt to Sell Recycled Water Idea', 2007, (no author cited), in *The Age*, www.theage.com.au/ news/National/Qld-govt-to-sell-recycled-water-idea/2007/, accessed 30 January 2007

Radcliffe J. C., 2006, 'Future Directions for Water Recycling in Australia' in *Desalination* 187, 2006, pp. 77–87

'Recycled Water Inevitable in NSW, says PM', 2007, reported by McCutcheon P., 29 January 2007, www.abc.net.au/7.30/content/s1835830.htm, accessed 7 February 2007

Russell S., Lux C. & Hampton G. (n.d.), 'Opportunities for Deliberation and Understanding: Engaging with Citizens about Water Recycling Technologies', http://ts6.cgpublisher.com/ proposals/115/index_html, accessed 26 March 2007

Sandman P. M., 1993, *Responding to Community Outrage: Strategies for Effective Risk Communication*, American Industrial Hygiene Association, Fairfax, VA

Schäfer A. I. & Beder S., 2006, 'Role of the Precautionary Principle in Water Recycling' in *Desalination* 187, Nos 1–3, pp. 241–52

'The "No" Case', 2006, www.toowoomba.qld.gov.au/index.php?option=com_ content&task=view&id=78, accessed 6 February 2007

'The "Yes" Case', 2006, www.toowoomba.qld.gov.au/index.php?option=com_ content&task=view&id=78, accessed 6 February 2007

Tickner J., Raffensperger C. & Myers N., 1999, *The Precautionary Principle in Action: A Handbook*, Science and Environmental Health Network, www.biotech-info.net/handbook.pdf

'Turnbull Does an About Face on Water', 2006, (no author cited), in *The Chronicle,* Toowoomba, 31 January 2006, www.thechronicle.com.au/storyprint.cfm?storyID=3670669, accessed 14 March 2008

Wardill S., 2007, 'Campaign Countered' in *Courier Mail*, 20 March 2007, www.news.com.au/couriermail/story/0,23739,21418529-5005340,00.html, accessed 21 March 2007

Water Futures, 20 March, 2007, http://waterfutures.blogspot.com/2007_03_01_archive.html, accessed 14 March 2008

'Why We're Voting YES', 2006, www.toowoombawater.com.au/general/why-were-voting-yes.html, accessed 6 March 2006

13

Issues and Crisis Management

James Hardie Industries

Dr Gwyneth V. J. Howell

AIMS OF THIS CHAPTER

- To introduce the key considerations in determining a crisis response strategy

- To demonstrate the different outcomes achieved from proactive and reactive strategies

- To consider the effects of selected issues management and crisis communication strategies in a complex case

INTRODUCTION

Crises are unpredictable events that can impact an organisation's viability, credibility and reputation (Mitroff et al. 1987; Baker 2001). The size of the organisation is irrelevant; crises can and will happen (Barry 2002; Barton 1993; Mitroff 2005; Oliver 2004). Recent research indicates that even though 27 per cent of organisations will fail to exist after the onslaught of a crisis, the majority remain unprepared (Farmer & Tvedt 2005; Fearn-Banks 2002).

Few topics have generated greater interest in public relations for the past fifteen years. It has been clearly demonstrated that proactive strategies can better manage crises; that is, effective monitoring and management of the crisis in the initial or warning stage of a crisis can reduce the consequences of a crisis on an organisation. Yet most organisations still do not employ proactive crisis communication programs.

Both researchers and public relations practitioners have struggled to operationalise the specific role of public relations in crisis situations (Coombs 2002). The result is public relations strategies that generally are defined either by lists of quantitative variables that are expensive to measure and difficult to integrate; or qualitative models, often restricted to procedural devices and context-specific applications (Cornelissen 2000). These reactive crisis public relations strategies are the least effective, yet the most common crisis strategies used (Marra 1998).

Being able to identify and manage issues is a vital function of the proactive stage of the crisis management lifecycle (Wilcox et al. 2005). Issues management focuses on a systematic approach where practitioners aim to predict potential threats and problems with the aim of resolving these issues before they mature into full-blown crises (Tench & Yeomans 2006). Using proactive strategies, practitioners are able to better manage ongoing issues. While not all issues can be resolved prior to the onset of a crisis situation, an issue ignored is a crisis ensured. Currently, crisis management continues to be identified as a tactical response to a situation, while issues management is based on a strategic response.

This chapter examines how in 2001 James Hardie Industries (JHI), Australia's dominant asbestos producer, used proactive issues management to limit media coverage and influence government policy related to its asbestos liabilities. The chapter then traces the company's failures to manage the resulting crisis using reactive public relations when its external publics and the intervening public (media interests) became alerted to the corporation's agenda in 2004. A comparison of the tactics employed in these two campaigns is described.

This case presents compelling lessons for all public relations practitioners and academics in terms of using proactive rather than reactive public relations during a crisis. In the case examined, public relations practitioners framed a matter of potentially great public interest (i.e. asbestos-related health issues for people exposed to this material) as being under the level of public interest. This chapter then examines the public fallout when primary publics and the intervening public (media interests) became alerted to the corporation's agenda. Publicly available documents and media reports are reviewed to examine the corporation's communication strategy and the tactics it used to manage the media and various publics. A full timeline of events is provided at the end of the chapter.

BACKGROUND

JHI's core business is the production of fibre cement and other building materials. Between 1917 and 1987 the organisation manufactured asbestos-related products (Noonan 2004) and dominated the Australian market for asbestos cement products, with market share approximating 90 per cent (Jones 2004). As a building product, asbestos has the desirable attributes of being light, portable, long lasting and cheap. However the inhalation of asbestos fibres can cause a number of painful and lethal conditions, including asbestosis (a form of lung fibrosis), mesothelioma, and lung and asbestos-related Pleural disease (Tossavainen & Takahashi 2000). An estimated 7000 Australians have already died from asbestos-related cancers, and this is predicted to rise to 18,000 deaths by 2020 (Prince et al. 2004). In addition, other asbestos-related illnesses are predicted to be responsible for up to 40,000 deaths in the same time frame (Prince et al. 2004). The financial estimates of Australia's total liability for future asbestos claims is about $6 billion (Quinlaven 2004).

STAGE 1: PROJECT GREEN, 2001

In December 2001 JHI restructured with the ostensible purpose of expanding its international operations from its bases in the USA, Australia, New Zealand, the Philippines and Chile (James Hardie website). As a result of the restructuring, JHI became listed on the Dutch Stock Exchange as James Hardie Industries NV (JHINV). A consequence of this move was the switch of jurisdictions and legal obligations from Australian laws to Dutch.

To facilitate relocating to the Netherlands, JHI explored avenues to remove an area of business that was 'detract[ing] from value creation' and could prevent the company from growing in the lucrative US market (Macdonald, cited in New South Wales Government 2004a, p. 129). This part of the business was the company's subsidiaries which had manufactured and sold asbestos-related products for the past eighty years. In 1998 JHI began to explore ways of managing the asbestos business, and particularly the separation from any legacy issues that may be associated with asbestos from the new Dutch-based entity. This project was instigated in 2001 and featured a communication plan that became known as the 'Project Green Board Paper Communication Strategy'. Internal documentation illustrates that JHI was aware of ongoing negative coverage of the asbestos issue and that it sought to manage the media coverage of the issue through building better networks with key media personnel. However, JHI was wary of the tone of media coverage, outlining that:

> Journalists [can] freely adopt the roles of crusader, critic and ombudsman ... journalists will be receptive to criticism of us ... we are the 'lightning rod' for [negative] public opinion ... and they will seek unions, lawyers, victims and others to provide 'good copy' (New South Wales Government 2004a, p. 146).

Further, JHI elected to establish a Medical Research and Compensation Foundation (MRCF), which would provide funds for those seeking compensation for asbestos-related diseases.

Key publics

JHI's communication priority has always been to three primary publics: shareholders, customers and suppliers. However to be successful, the Project Green Board Paper Communication Strategy identified a range of additional primary publics. These are depicted in Figure 13.1.

Figure 13.1: JHI primary publics: 2001

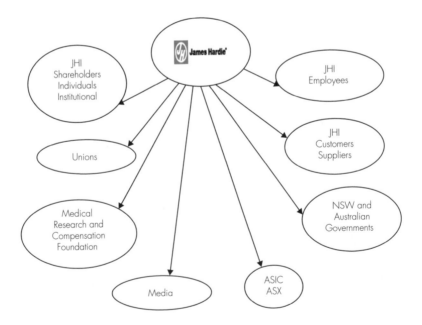

Goals and objectives

Five key issues were identified:

1 Attract as little public attention as possible beyond the financial markets

2 Optimise support for the move from shareholders and the investment community

3 Position the initiative as a business news story, not a general news issue

4 Neutralise opposition from hostile stakeholders

5 Minimise the potential for government intervention (New South Wales Government 2004a, p. 152).

In the communication strategy, JHI's Public Affairs Vice President Greg Baxter described the rationale to support the public relations strategy:

> We believe that our communication strategy will deal effectively with the numerous risks involved in executing the separation proposal and that therefore the separation proposal can be implemented as recommended (New South Wales Government 2004a, p. 141).

Communication strategy and tactics

The public relations strategy focused on the financial press, as JHI was more concerned with business than social issues. JHI developed a range of tactics that used established relationships with journalists, civil activists and other identified parties, and tailored its communication messages to a specific business and finance media context. The then CEO and Chairman of JHI, Peter Macdonald and Peter McGregor, were available for interviews at the JHI briefing. Leading civil lawyer Armando Gardiman—who JHI regarded as a potential adversary if victims decided to retain him to act on their behalf to access compensation from the MRCF—explains:

> I can remember putting the phone down [after speaking with Peter Macdonald] and the first thought was 'that [the amount of money in the MRCF] just can't be enough money' ... I didn't appreciate at all why they were ringing until I read the communication and risk strategies that were in the Board papers of 15 February, 2001, and now I appreciate that I wasn't special at all. I was just one of a whole lot of people they rang up in an effort to ensure that any critical comment might be neutralised (Ferguson 2004, p. 38).

The announcement of the establishment of the MRCF and the separation of JHI's asbestos-related companies was made on Friday, 16 February 2001. The announcement strategy framed the MRCF as a business story by timing it to be announced with the third quarter company results that were made to analysts and business media only. The main reason was to 'spin' the message to the financial media and announce separation in a 'pure business context [to] focus on the financial outcomes' for JHI (New South Wales Government 2004a, p. 153).

To ensure the message of separate entities was enforced from the announcement, the MRCF staged a separate (JHI-organised) press conference and media briefing with only the MRCF Chair, Sir Llew Edwards, available for interviews. The challenge for JHI was to ensure that the key messages for both JHI and the MRCF were complementary, but also appeared to be 'independent of each other' (New South Wales Government 2004a, p. 155). This was achieved by JHI staff producing all the documentation for both briefings. JHI undertook 'pre-announcement consultation' with senior advisers in the Carr government to ensure 'we are forewarned ... should the government's response be negative' (New South Wales Government 2004a, p. 156).

An additional tactic used was to limit the time between the announcement and the business presentation to selected business and finance journalists to one hour (a reduction of two-and-a-half hours from the JHI norm), in order to minimise the risk that the general media would have the opportunity to address or 'hijack' the separation issue in a public forum. Further, Baxter intended that JHI would not web-cast the briefing 'live', as was usually done, which would be explained as being 'due to technical difficulties' (New South Wales Government 2004a, p. 153). As outlined in the strategy document, 'if there are any legal issues, we would simply not make it available or edit it as required' (New South Wales Government 2004a, p. 153). During cross-examination at the Special Commission of Inquiry, JHI Chief Financial Officer Peter Shafron attempted to downplay the announcement's timing as 'simply convenience'. However Shafron did ultimately concede that a very significant reason it was so timed was to reduce media scrutiny as to why the MRCF had been established (New South Wales Government 2004b, p. 358).

Evaluation

The media coverage in 2001 supported the separation and 'much of the reporting by the financial press at the time about this offshore move was positive, along the lines of this is JHI shedding its asbestos liabilities, which the finance reporting concluded would be a drag on their future profits' (Jones 2004, p. 9). The communication strategy had been successful, and the key publics identified by JHI were supportive of the business separation. The other affected publics were unaware of the potential (and eventual) effect these business changes would bring.

In 2003 JHI cancelled $1.9 billion partly paid shares in its Australian company, without disclosure to the Australian Stock Exchange, the New South Wales Supreme Court, the

MRCF, or any other interested party (Higgins & Manning 2004). The implication of these shares being cancelled was that JHI 'would not have to provide more funds to the MRCF to handle asbestos compensation' (New South Wales Government 2004a, p.142). The cancellation of the partly paid shares resulted in a critical shortfall of funds for anticipated victims of asbestos.

STAGE 2: REACTIVE PUBLIC RELATIONS CRISIS, 2004

In 2001, JHI's carefully crafted communication strategy achieved its primary objective of very limited media coverage related to the company's separation of its asbestos liabilities from the organisation. However, in 2004, a Special Commission of Inquiry into the MRCF was convened by the New South Wales Government to investigate JHI's conduct in the separation of its asbestos-producing companies from its new Dutch-based entity, JHINV. The Commission reviewed the actions of the company in the funding of compensation for its asbestos victims, and examined the communication strategy devised to support the separation of the asbestos liabilities. The media and the court of public opinion described the communication strategy as 'PR spin' (Combet, cited in Jones 2004, p. 11).

JHI's 2004 public relations strategy was reactive, failing to respond and manage publics that had been specifically targeted and neutralised during the 2001 separation.

Key publics

Mitroff (1994) suggests that companies that do not properly identify key publics and monitor their concerns will experience corporate identity problems. In 2004 it was apparent from the media coverage that other primary publics—victims, unions, and state and federal governments—were not a focus of JHI's public relations campaign. JHI Chairman Meredith Hellicar asserted that JHI would not respond to media coverage, electing to only respond to matters before the commission.

Her public comments came as the media presented details of why JHI has long been referred to as a company that has 'routinely placed PR spin above substance' (Long 2004, p. 9). Yet, during this period, JHI was closed to the media—an 'intervening public' (Cutlip et al. 2000) that had been the driving force in publicly debating the issues relating to the separation of JHI's business operations and the under-funding of the compensation fund. This is depicted in Figure 13.2, which illustrates the importance of the media in shaping the opinions of primary publics.

Figure 13.2: The impact of the media

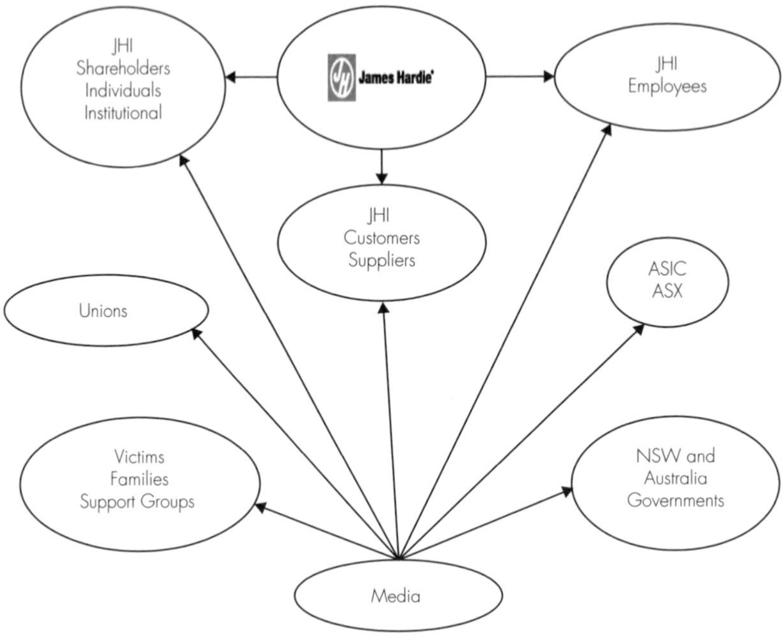

Communication strategy and tactics

In 2004, after the projected MRCF shortfall was revealed, JHI initially tried to deny responsibility for the MRCF's crisis and played down its role in Australia's asbestos industry (Buffini & Priest 2004a). JHI's public relations strategy in 2004 was in complete contrast to its 2001 strategy, where the organisation sought to convey 'openness, transparency and conviction' to its key publics (New South Wales Government 2004a, p. 167).

In defensive mode, JHI's strategy and tactics were starkly different from those of 2001. The 2004 program was deficient in the most basic of crisis communication tactics: disseminating information quickly, accurately and in a candid manner (c.f. Fearn-Banks 2002). After first denying responsibility, JHI indirectly blamed its actuary, Trowbridge Deloitte (Sexton 2004), instead of proactively addressing the problems of its own management and accountability (Higgins & Manning 2004). JHI's actions run counter to issues management theory that 'blame cannot be shifted if the crisis is caused by managerial factors' (Sen & Egelhoff 1991, cited in Seeger et al. 2001, p. 162).

Without a sympathetic mass media through which to communicate its message to various publics, JHI resorted to communicating with its key primary publics (including shareholders and customers) directly. This correspondence was reported as 'understating the company's involvement in manufacturing asbestos products' during the time of the Special Commission of Inquiry (Buffini 2004a, p. 4) and denying the alleged use of public relations for manipulation (Priest 2004a; Priest 2004b; Walter, cited in Buffini 2004b, p. 5). The JHI letter maintained the company was liable for 'around 15 per cent of future claims' (ACTU 2004, p. 4). Although JHI withdrew the letter from circulation, General Manager James Chilcoff insisted it was 'not misleading' (Buffini 2004a, p. 4).

Evaluation

On 21 December 2004—after the Special Commission of Inquiry and its findings against JHI were made public and with extensive media and public pressure—JHI agreed to a deal negotiated by Greg Combet, ACTU Secretary, on behalf of all present and future asbestos disease claims. The company agreed to make up the $1.5 billion shortfall in the MRCF's funding. This marks the largest financial settlement in Australian history (Mills 2005). In reaching this agreement, Combet made the following observation:

> Companies like this put a lot of money, millions of dollars, really, into PR spin, and bring in professionals to spin this sort of rather deceptive web to try and con people into believing that, in this particular case, that the setting up of a trust with $293 million was some act of benevolence (cited in Jones 2004, p. 47).

The matter was finally resolved in 2007, and JHI has now made provision in its ongoing operations to allocate $4 billion to assist the victims and their families.

Lessons learnt

Mass media are highly influential stakeholders during crises, filtering and framing perspectives, and with a tendency to reinforce current public biases (Nelkin 1987). In 2001 JHI was well aware of the media being a key stakeholder and implemented strategies accordingly; yet in 2004 JHI made a series of errors in its media strategy.

Public opinion about the organisation directly affected the impact of coverage (Barton 1993). While existing public opinion towards both JHI and the industry in which it operates has increased bias in mass media, JHI has not sought to manage these attitudes (Douglas & Wildervsky 1982; Nelkin 1987). Dutton and Duncan (1987) assert that the public's attention to an issue or crisis tends to affect organisational response to that issue or crisis. This holds true for JHI. JHI chose not to respond to the initial media coverage in 2004 and, as a consequence, previous asbestos coverage and other information provided to the mass media was used, increasing the impact of the threat (Susskind & Field 1996).

This chapter explored that while JHI was prepared to rely on public relations in 2001, in 2004 the company chose to disregard the true value of public relations when attempting to manage the unfolding crisis. Carney and Jorden (1993) and Fearn-Banks (2002) maintain that a communication strategy is essential in preparing for a crisis. While JHI undertook extensive preparation to avert a crisis in 2001, it failed to do so in 2004. Further, an effective crisis public relations program would have had a profound effect on the short- and long-term results for JHI (Marken 1998). JHI's share price was adversely affected by this crisis in 2004; however, since mid-2005, the company has made strong gains in its share price and continued to post strong annual profits.

There are several key areas where JHI could have better managed the 2004 crisis, drawing on its own framework utilised in 2001:

- In 2004, JHI did not undertake a communication audit to examine the areas in which it was susceptible to adverse publicity, and then craft strategies to manage these issues (Carney & Jorden 1993; Marken 1998).

- JHI failed to identify all the publics involved with and affected by the crisis (Hendrix 1995; Pinsdorf 1999). As a result, key publics acted outside the communication channels JHI had established and managed.

- The company did not develop key messages for each target public (Pinsdorf 1999). This ensured that key publics and the media gained control of the message and drove the agenda for coverage in 2004. This behaviour is in direct contrast to exhaustive public relations activities of 2001.

- While academics and practitioners agree that the channels of communication used during crises are vital (Grunig & Grunig 1992), JHI was closed to the media and sought to correspond directly with shareholders, making claims that offended other key publics.

In public relations, diligence is an essential aspect of the role, and, regardless of the preparation, communications strategies will only be successful if all avenues are explored and public relations practitioners are prepared for the unexpected (Fearn-Banks 2002). Public relations professionals face the same issues—and as a result the communication challenges are similar—as the principles of the strategies in normal business operations (Mitroff 1996). The most important issue faced by public relations professionals in dealing with a crisis is maintaining control of the message.

TABLE 13.1: TIMELINE OF EVENTS

DATE	ACTION
1917	JHI commences operations
1935	First case of asbestos-related disease in a JHI factory in Australia is reported

(Continued)

TABLE 13.1: TIMELINE OF EVENTS (continued)

DATE	ACTION
Mid-1940s	JHI becomes aware of the suggestion that the inhalation of asbestos fibres could cause asbestosis, but only in circumstances involving inhalation over a sufficiently lengthy period of time
Late 1950s	JHI becomes aware of the suggestion that the inhalation of asbestos fibres could cause lung cancer
Mid-1960s	JHI becomes aware of the suggestion that the inhalation of asbestos fibres could cause mesothelioma
February 1998	JHI explores ways to remove the asbestos area of the business during a board meeting
March 1998	Review of other organisations' management of 'difficult' issues by board subcommittee
2000	JHI suffers from extensive negative media coverage relating to asbestos issues
July 2000	JHI retains Jack Forrest QC
August 2000	JHI retains Hawker Britton and Gavin Anderson & Co. to develop a formal stakeholder management strategy
December 2000	JHI insists the Trowbridge Deloitte seminar paper about funding for the MRCF is removed from its website
8 January 2001	Project Green Board Paper Communication Strategy is presented to management
Mid-January 2001	Discussion with management team relating to the amount of funding for medical research; decision of $3 million is made by CEO Peter Macdonald
17 January 2001	Detail of advice for Carr government management of issue is tabled at JHI board meeting
17 January 2001	Board papers note the uncertainty of funding for the MRCF
25 January 2001	Detailed Q&A drafted and presented to management
February 2001	Project Green Board Paper Communication Strategy is fine tuned
11 February 2001	Federal Parliament closes session
15 February 2001	Board papers claim MRCF is fully funded

(Continued)

TABLE 13.1: TIMELINE OF EVENTS (continued)

DATE	ACTION
16 February 2001	Third quarter results are announced; the establishment of the MRCF
16 February 2001	Media interviews with CEO and chairman after announcement with financial media only
September 2001	JHI announces that 98 per cent of shareholders had voted to support a proposed corporate restructure, which transformed JHI into JHINV, a Netherlands-headquartered company
October 2001	JHI changes its ASX code from HAH to JHX
December 2001	Company restructure and move to Netherlands
2003	JHI cancels the $1.9 billion partly paid shares into the MRCF
2003	Hawker Britton withdraws from association over JHI's cancellation of shares
2003	JHI retains Caliburn Partnership to assist internal public relations team
December 2003	Use of asbestos in Australia is finally banned
January 2004	JHI's Public Affairs Vice President Greg Baxter resigns to work for News Limited
February 2004	Julie Sheather is promoted to Vice President Corporate Affairs
13 August 2004	Special Commission of Inquiry final day of hearing
13 August 2004	JHI proposes a statutory scheme that would strip victims of their right to sue the company for compensation
21 September 2004	Special Commission of Inquiry report presented and recommends ASIC investigate possible criminal charges for Macdonald
28 September 2004	Macdonald stands aside as CEO and Shafron stands aside as Chief Financial Officer; Macdonald agrees to be responsible for the business operations of JHI and will remain based in the USA
23 October 2004	Macdonald and Shafron resign from JHI
24 October 2004	Macdonald is retained as a consultant to JHI, with a US$60,000 per month retainer
21 December 2004	JHI agrees to pay $1.5 billion shortfall into the MRCF
26 January 2006	JHI is yet to pay the $1.5 billion shortfall into the MRCF

(Source: New South Wales 2004a, 2004b, 2004e, 2004f, 2004g, 2004h)

PRACTITIONER PROFILE

Tony Jacques is Issues Manager, Asia-Pacific, Dow Chemicals.

Through countless textbooks, seminars and conferences, 'issue and crisis management' has become almost a compound noun. In fact, I have described them as the 'Siamese twins of public relations'.

For the practitioner, the line between the two can easily become blurred in overlapping daily tasks. But properly understanding the differences is very important in going forward.

While issue management has remained fairly consistent since the early 1980s, formal crisis management has developed beyond a mechanistic response process, which focused primarily on what to do and say when it hits the fan, and how to explain afterwards. This early approach involved communications mainly as media and community relations in support of those actually managing the crisis event.

Over recent times, crisis management has begun to develop as a much more integrated continuum of established management activities, from crisis preparedness and prevention through to post-crisis recovery. This has brought the need for a broader range of skills—especially in issue management—to help identify and respond to issues before they become crises, and to manage the issues that can develop after the crisis.

As changing technology and societal expectation increase the speed, scale and potential impact of issues and crises, I believe communications practitioners need to accelerate the move beyond the reactive role to implement issue and crisis management at a truly strategic level.

REFERENCES

ACTU, 2004, 'ACTU Pushes James Hardie to Withdraw Asbestos Letter', 24 August 2004, www.actu.asn.au/public/news/1093319267_17307.html, accessed 16 September 2004

Baker G. F., 2001, 'Race and Reputation: Restoring Image Beyond the Crisis' in Heath R. L. (ed.), *Handbook of Public Relations*, Sage Publications, Thousand Oaks, CA

Barry A., 2002, *PR Power: Inside Secrets from the World of Spin*, Virgin Books Ltd, London

Barton L., 1993, *Crisis in Organisations: Managing and Communicating in the Heat of Chaos*, South-Western Publishing Company, Cincinnati, OH

Buffini F. & Priest M., 2004, 'James Hardie Asbestos Woes Hit $2.2bn' in *The Australian Financial Review*, 29 July 2004, p. 1

Buffini F., 2004a, 'Unions Force Hardie to Withdraw Asbestos Letter' in *The Australian Financial Review*, 25 August 2004, p. 4

Buffini F., 2004b, 'Directors Sell Out to Spin Doctors: Walter' in *The Australian Financial Review*, 1 September 2004, p. 5

Carney A. & Jorden A., 1993, 'Prepare for Business-related Crises' in *Journal of Integrated Communication*, Vol. 49, No. 9, pp. 34–5

Coombs W. T., 2002, *Ongoing Crisis Communication: Planning, Managing, and Responding*, 2nd edn, Sage Publications, Thousand Oaks, CA

Cornelissen J. P., 2000, 'Toward an Understanding of the use of Academic Theories in Public Relations Practice' in *Public Relations Review*, Vol. 26, No. 3, pp. 315–26

Cutlip S. M., Center A. H. & Broom G. M., 2000, *Effective Public Relations*, 8th edn, Prentice Hall, Upper Saddle River, NJ

Douglas M. & Wildavsky A., 1982, *Risk and Culture: An Essay on the Selection of Technological and Environmental Dangers*, University of California Press, London

Dutton J. & Duncan R., 1987, 'The Creation of Momentum for Change through the Process of Strategic Issue Diagnosis' in *Strategic Management Journal*, Vol. 8, pp. 279–95

Farmer B. & Tvedt L., 2005, 'Top Management Communication During Crises: Guidelines and a "Perfect Example" of a Crisis Leader' in *Public Relations Quarterly*, Vol. 50, No. 2, pp. 27–31

Fearn-Banks K., 2002, *Communications: A Casebook Approach*, 2nd edn, Lawrence Erlbaum, NJ

Ferguson S., 2004, 'James Hardie: The Great Escape' in *Sunday*, Nine Network Transcripts, http://sunday.ninemsn.com.au/sunday/cover_stories/article_1638.asp, accessed 15 September 2004

Grunig J. E. & Grunig L. A., 1992, 'Models of Public Relations and Communication' in Grunig J. E. (ed.), *Excellence in Public Relations and Communication Management*, Lawrence Erlbaum Associates, Hillsdale, NJ

Hendrix J. A., 1995, *Public Relation Cases*, Wadsworth, Belmont, CA

Higgins E., 2004, 'Spinning their Way to a Disaster' in *The Australian*, 14 October 2004, p. 5

Higgins E. & Manning P., 2004, 'Asbestos Giant Acted Illegally' in *The Australian*, 29 July 2004, p. 1

Howell G. V. J. & Miller R., 2006, 'Setting the Public Agenda using Public Relations: James Hardie Industries' Management of Legacy Issues associated with Asbestos Products' in *Public Relations Review*, Vol. 35, No. 6

James Hardie, 2004, *Address by Meredith Hellicar: Chairman James Hardie Industries: To the Company's Annual Information Meeting*, 15 September 2004, www.ir.jameshardie.com.au/repositories/files/2004.AIM.ChairmansAddress.pdf, accessed 23 September 2004

James Hardie website, www.jameshardie.com.au/AboutUs/

Johnston J. (n.d.), 'Critical Perspectives on Current Structures Governing Internet Plagiarism: Challenges to Public Relations and Journalism Education' in *Australian and New Zealand Communication Association Conference Proceedings*, www.bond.edu.au/hss/communication/ANZCA/papers/JJohnstonPaper.pdf, accessed 29 July 2005

Johnston J. & Zawawi C., 2004, 'What Is Public Relations?' in Johnston J. & Zawawi C. (eds), *Public Relations: Theory and Practice*, 2nd edn, Allen & Unwin, Crows Nest, NSW

Jones T., 2004, 'James Hardie Shirking Moral Obligations: Combet' in *LateLine*, 21 July 2004, ABC Television transcript, www.abc.net.au/lateline/content/2004/s1159074.htm, accessed 22 July 2004

Law Link, New South Wales Attorney General's Department (n.d.), *Counsel Assisting Submissions Special Commission of Inquiry into the Medical Research and Compensation Foundation Section 2*, www.lawlink.nsw.gov.au/Lawlink/Corporate/ll_corporate.nsf/0/c3379fb7c0ca448cca256ede0031c444?OpenDocument, accessed 18 December 2004

Long S., 2004, 'Commission finds James Hardie had a "Culture of Deceit"' in *AM*, 22 September 2004, Australian Broadcasting Corporation, www.abc.net.au/am/content/2004/s1204351.htm, accessed 23 September 2004

Marken G. A., 1998, 'On-line Public Relations' in *Public Relations Quarterly*, Vol. 43, pp. 26–8

Marra F., 1998, 'Crisis Communication Plans: Poor Predictors of Excellent Crisis Public Relations' in *Public Relations Review*, Vol. 24, No. 4, pp. 461–75

Mills K., 2005, 'Combet Proved Himself a Hardie Battler' in *The Australian*, 4 January 2005, p. 2

Mitroff I. I., 2005, *Why Some Companies Emerge Stronger and Better from a Crisis: 7 Essential Lessons for Surviving Disaster*, AMACOM, NY

Mitroff I. I., Shrivastava P. & Udwadia W. A., 1987, 'Effective Crisis Management' in *The Academy of Management Executive*, Vol. 1, No. 3, pp. 283–92

Nelkin D., 1987, *Selling Science: How the Press Covers Science and Technology*, Freeman, NY

New South Wales Government, 2004a, 'Report of the Special Commission of Inquiry into the Medical Research and Compensation Foundation: Project Green Board Paper for 15 February 2001: James Hardie Industries Limited Meeting of Board of Directors', www.cabinet.nsw.gov. au/hardie/K.pdf, accessed 18 December 2004

New South Wales Government, 2004b, 'Report of the Special Commission of Inquiry into the Medical Research and Compensation Foundation: Asbestos and James Hardie', www.cabinet. nsw.gov.au/hardie/J.pdf, accessed 18 December 2004

New South Wales Government, 2004c, 'Report of the Special Commission of Inquiry into the Medical Research and Compensation Foundation: Media Releases', www.cabinet.nsw.gov.au/ hardie/R.pdf, accessed 18 December 2004

New South Wales Government, 2004d, 'Report of the Special Commission of Inquiry into the Medical Research and Compensation Foundation: Counsel Assisting's Issues Paper', www.cabinet.nsw.gov.au/hardie/H.pdf, accessed 18 December 2004

New South Wales Government, 2004e, 'Report of the Special Commission of Inquiry into the Medical Research and Compensation Foundation: Vol. 1, Part C', www.cabinet.nsw.gov.au/ hardie/PartC.pdf, accessed 18 December 2004

New South Wales Government, 2004f, 'Report of the Special Commission of Inquiry into the Medical Research and Compensation Foundation: Asbestos and James Hardie', www.cabinet. nsw.gov.au/publications.html, accessed 18 December 2004

New South Wales Government, 2004g, 'Report of the Special Commission of Inquiry into the Medical Research and Compensation Foundation: Project Green Board Paper for 15 February 2001: James Hardie Industries Limited Meeting of Board of Directors', www.cabinet.nsw.gov. au/publications.html, accessed 18 December 2004

New South Wales Government, 2004h, 'Report of the Special Commission of Inquiry into the Medical Research and Compensation Foundation: Minutes of 15 February 2001 Meeting of Board of Directors of James Hardie Industries Limited', www.cabinet.nsw.gov.au/ publications.html, accessed 18 December 2004

Noonan G., 2004, 'James Hardie Faces Public Works Ban' in *The Sydney Morning Herald*, 3 August 2004, p. 3

Oliver S., 2004, *Public Relations Strategy*, The Institute of Public Relations in association with
　　Kogan Page Ltd, London, pp. 55–67

Pinsdorf M. K., 1999, *Communicating When Your Company is Under Siege: Surviving Public Crisis*,
　　3rd edn, Fordham University Press, New York

Priest M., 2004a, '"Beguiling" Media Strategy: The PR' in *The Australian Financial Review*,
　　29 July 2004, p. 7

Priest M., 2004b, 'Face Value is Worth Very Little' in *The Australian Financial Review,*
　　29 July 2004, p. 7

Prince P., Davidson J. & Dudley S., 2004, 'In the Shadow of the Corporate Veil: James Hardie
　　and Asbestos Compensation' in *Law and Bills Digest Section*, 10 August 2004, www.aph.gov.
　　au/library/pubs/rn/2004-05/05rn12.htm, accessed 1 August 2005

Quinlaven B., 2004, 'Asbestos: Powder Traces' in *Business Review Weekly*, 3 June 2004, pp. 28–9

Seeger M., Sellnow W., Timothy L. & Ulmer R. R., 2001, 'Public Relations and Crisis
　　Communication: Organizing and Chaos' in Heath R. L. (ed.), *Handbook of Public Relations*,
　　Sage Publications, CA, pp. 155–250

Sexton E., 2004, 'Hardie Pleads Good Faith on Asbestos Victims/We Didn't Set Out to Dud
　　Asbestos Victims: Company' in *The Sydney Morning Herald*, 30 July 2004, pp. 1 & 7

Susskind L. & Field P., 1996, *Dealing with an Angry Public: The Mutual Gains Approach to
　　Resolving Disputes*, Free Press, New York

Tench R. & Yeomans L., 2006, *Exploring Public Relations*, Pearson Education, Essex

Tossavainen A. & Takahashi K., 2000, 'Epidemiological Trends for Asbestos-related Cancers' in
　　People and Work Research Reports, FIOH, Helsinki,Vol. 36, pp. 26–30

Wilcox D., Cameron G., Ault P. & Agee W., 2005, *Public Relations Strategies and Tactics*, 8th edn,
　　Pearson Education, USA

Zawawi C., 2001, 'Feeding the Watchdogs—An Analysis of Relationships Between Australian
　　Public Relations Practitioners and Journalists', Doctorial Thesis, Faculty of Business,
　　Queensland University of Technology, Brisbane

Emergency Crisis Communication

14

Returning Power to Collinsville

Robina Xavier

AIMS OF THIS CHAPTER

- To demonstrate the importance of planning and response during emergency situations

- To outline key communication principles and practices for community relations during an emergency

INTRODUCTION

Physical crises such as natural disasters and accidents often hit quickly and require immediate action to ensure the safety of local communities. Lerbinger (1997) categorises such crises as those of the physical world, being caused by nature and technology. Unlike the James Hardie case (see Chapter 13)—which grew for many years before becoming public, and then involved a response that played out over many months—physical crises can happen in a matter of minutes, leaving little planning time for the organisations involved. Crisis managers must coordinate the operational crisis response with the communication response to stakeholders, and ensure that all partner organisations are working towards achieving an effective solution to the problem at hand.

As suggested by Fearn-Banks (1996), if your company is an important cog in the wheel of life as normal, it does not matter if you did not cause the disaster. People will look to you to restore their services and remove any inconvenience suffered.

Two major Queensland energy organisations experienced first hand the importance of immediate action and teamwork when crisis hit in March 2007. This case study outlines their response, and considers the important elements in maintaining stakeholder relationships and protecting organisational reputations during a crisis.

BACKGROUND

Collinsville is a small mining town in North Queensland with approximately 2600 residents. The surrounding area produces more than 1 million tonnes of coal each year, and many of the town's residents and businesses are linked to the mining sector.

Getting electricity to Collinsville residents is a joint affair. Powerlink Queensland, a government-owned corporation, operates Queensland's high-voltage electricity transmission network and supplies electricity to Ergon Energy, which then uses its distribution network to provide power to its customers. Both organisations have invested significant resources over the years in building their reputations as high-quality operators in the energy sector.

Powerlink operates two transformers at its Collinsville substation, each capable of supplying the entire electricity needs for the community. However an incident in January 2007 damaged one of these transformers, and highly specialised replacement components were still not on site when a severe electrical storm hit Collinsville at 4.30 p.m. one afternoon in March 2007. The storm damaged the only operating transformer at the substation, affecting electricity supply to around 1500 Ergon Energy customers. These customers were now facing not only the onset of nightfall in storm conditions with no power, but potential disruptions to their electricity supply for up to two weeks while complex technical repairs were undertaken.

ROBINA XAVIER

RESEARCH

The immediate nature of many physical crises leaves little time for new research to be undertaken. However organisations can draw on their past experience and emergency management plans to help guide their strategy selection.

Powerlink and Ergon Energy reviewed their emergency management handbooks, which had been prepared by both organisations as part of their pre-crisis planning. This helped them consider response processes, and evaluate the strengths and weaknesses of the available options. They also reviewed the handling of the earlier January 2007 incident at the Collinsville substation to assess the effectiveness of the organisational responses and to identify the key publics. They were aware that there would be some ongoing frustration among key publics that the town was being powered by a single transformer—given the repairs to the other damaged transformer had still not been completed—and that this would need to be addressed in the crisis response.

As both organisations were experienced operators in the area, staff were able to access and share their information about the local community and their knowledge of key issues that would need to be considered. Two key issues emerged from the research, which informed the subsequent communication strategy:

1 Collinsville is a remote location, which intensified the impact of the power loss for residents. Residents could not easily move to a different location to access services no longer available, so the communication strategy would have to directly address the physical concerns of living without power for a certain period of time.

2 There are no Collinsville-specific media outlets, so using the media as a primary communication method was not likely to achieve the results needed.

TARGET PUBLICS

Seven major groupings of publics were identified as important to the communication strategy for the crisis:

1 Internal publics including senior decision-makers, response teams and employees

2 Community publics in Collinsville, including the residents, influence groups, opinion leaders, local business and community associations

3 Local industry publics, including the major coal mine in the area and the major water provider

4 Government publics at both the local and state government levels, including elected representatives and bureaucrats

5 Electricity industry publics

6 Media publics at both a local and state level, as well as trade media

7 Supplier publics, which would support the delivery of service.

The crisis managers assessed the relationships with each of the groups and considered their particular needs.

GOALS AND OBJECTIVES

The overall goal of the crisis communication response was to communicate openly and effectively to all stakeholders that both Powerlink and Ergon Energy were committed to restoring power as quickly and safely as possible.

Specific objectives included:

- Educating target publics about the challenges of restoring power

- Empowering customers to make informed decisions about their own situation in relation to their power supply

- Mitigating negative perceptions about the incident and achieving balanced or favourable media coverage where possible

- Protecting Powerlink and Ergon Energy's reputations and brands.

COMMUNICATION STRATEGY AND TACTICS

The crisis communication strategy was underpinned by four main themes:

1 Be visible

2 Be available

3 Share information

4 Partner with and involve relevant groups in the process and outcome.

Following the advice of many crisis authors, Powerlink and Ergon Energy recognised the importance of being on the ground in the face of such a major event. They based senior executives in the crisis zone to ensure they were able to develop meaningful relationships with key local stakeholders. This accessibility demonstrated the human face of Powerlink and Ergon Energy, and helped to build organisational credibility and a shared understanding of the complexity of restoring power supplies.

ROBINA XAVIER

Emergency management protocols were in place for both organisations, and these were referred to throughout the planning and implementation stages. The restoration process involved close to 100 electricity workers and 90 back-up generators being brought in from surrounding towns and cities, to ensure critical community services such as medical facilities and the water plant maintained supply.

Having evaluated the needs of each of the stakeholders, the two organisations established a system of proactively communicating with these important groups via their preferred communication channels. This ensured not only that stakeholders were informed, but that they knew both Powerlink and Ergon Energy were on the ground, doing all they could to address the issue. Both organisations also ensured that important stakeholder groups understood what was involved in the restoration process, to help gain their support.

A number of communication tactics were used to ensure all stakeholders were kept informed during the six-day restoration period, including the following.

DEVELOPMENT OF KEY MESSAGES

As it was important to ensure consistency in all communication, key messages were prepared and used throughout the restoration period. These were targeted to address the main concerns of stakeholders, as well as to ensure the key organisational messages were communicated.

PROACTIVE MEDIA RELATIONS

Controlled and uncontrolled media were used to help inform key stakeholders. Media were invited to the substation site to report on the complex restoration activities, and media releases were distributed on a regular basis to provide information updates, as well as reinforce the campaign message strategy. Ergon Energy activated its web-based Storm Centre as a communication channel, with regular updates on restoration work and planned timelines. Radio community services and press advertisements were also used to keep stakeholders updated.

CUSTOMER ADVICE AND SERVICE

To assist customers in remote areas surrounding Collinsville, Ergon Energy's national contact centre proactively called more than 100 customers who were without power for the longest period of time, to ensure they were updated on restoration progress.

A public meeting on the first day was held to immediately update residents and interested parties, and to give advice to those without power. A community information centre was staffed by Powerlink and Ergon Energy at the Collinsville Workers Club to offer support and practical assistance, including providing food vouchers for those in need. To ensure residents were kept up to date, Powerlink and Ergon Energy arranged doorknocking, and used posters and community blackboards to communicate relevant information.

PARTNERING WITH LOCAL STAKEHOLDERS

Powerlink and Ergon Energy cultivated close partnerships with local community groups to assist with disseminating information; for example Lions Club members distributed flyers and doorknocked to ensure older residents in the area were supported and informed. Given this level of relationship building and information sharing, Powerlink and Ergon Energy were able to further build on established trust and meaningful relationships with key opinion leaders, who in turn became third-party advocates for communicating key messages about the emergency response.

STAKEHOLDER UPDATES

Key stakeholders were briefed in person onsite at the substation, as well as through formal progress reports. The organisations' websites also enabled interested parties to keep informed.

EMPLOYEE UPDATES

As an important part of the restoration process, organisational employees were emailed with relevant information and were also thanked for their efforts throughout the period.

ONGOING RELATIONSHIP BUILDING

Following the crisis, both organisations took the opportunity to thank those involved and to re-establish their links in the community. Staff were thanked and recognised for their efforts through tactics such as sending family movie passes to those who contributed to the response effort. Key stakeholders received thank you letters, and the wider community was thanked through newspaper advertisements and radio broadcasts. Powerlink also took the opportunity to sponsor a Family Fun Day and Golf Day in Collinsville shortly after the crisis.

Debriefing sessions were held at both communication and operational levels within and between the organisations. Emergency management protocols were updated and detailed information logs from the response were recorded.

Figure 14.1: Powerlink media release: March 2007

Friday, 16 March 2007 – 10.00 am   **MR7044**

Powerlink continues working with Collinsville community

Powerlink brought in people and equipment from across Australia yesterday to help with the restoration of high voltage electricity supply to the Collinsville community.

Powerlink Queensland Chief Operating Officer, Simon Bartlett, said Powerlink representatives also provided immediate support to more than 200 local residents by supplying food vouchers to people who had been affected by the extended power outage.

"We recognise that the loss of electricity supply to the area has caused hardship and we are aiming to minimise this by providing practical assistance where we can," Mr Bartlett said.

"We have been providing food vouchers redeemable at the local supermarkets to individuals and families whose food has perished as a result of the outage.

"Around 200 people came down to the Collinsville Workers Club to receive food vouchers to enable them to re-stock their fridges now that temporary electricity is being supplied to the majority of Collinsville via generators.

"Powerlink representatives, assisted by Bowen Shire Council and Ergon Energy staff, were on hand to assist community members who have been affected by the outage and provide information about compensation and insurance matters, and will be doing so again today.

"We thank the community for its ongoing understanding and patience," he said.

After talking to residents at the Collinsville Workers Club in the morning, Mr Bartlett went to the Collinsville Substation to inspect progress on the installation of the high voltage electricity transformer that will replace the transformer permanently damaged in Tuesday's storm [13 March].

"On-ground work at the substation is progressing on schedule. Lighting was installed yesterday to enable work to be carried out day and night," Mr Bartlett said.

"Yesterday, specially manufactured equipment and parts required to connect the transformer to the electricity grid arrived from across Queensland.

"In addition, a technical expert flew into Collinsville to work with our team of specialist substation experts to execute the complex connection of the replacement transformer.

Mr Bartlett acknowledged Ergon Energy staff for their ongoing efforts to provide temporary electricity supply via generators to much of the Collinsville community while the damaged transformer is being replaced.

After Friday, members of the community who wish to discuss any losses incurred as a result of the outage can contact Powerlink by calling Freecall 1800 635 369.

Enquiries: Melissa Azzopardi 0418 181 538
              Capital Works Communications Manager

About Powerlink Queensland:

Powerlink is a State Government-owned corporation, which owns, develops, operates and maintains a $3.4 billion high voltage transmission network that extends 1700km from north of Cairns to the New South Wales border. Powerlink's primary role is to provide a secure and reliable network to transport high-voltage electricity from generators to electricity distribution networks owned by Energex, Ergon Energy and Country Energy. Powerlink also transports electricity directly to large Queensland customers, such as aluminium South Wales via the NSW/Qld Interconnector.

33 Harold Street Virginia PO Box 1193, Virginia, Queensland 4014, Australia
Telephone: (07) 3860 2111 Facsimile: (07) 3860 2100 Website: www.powerlink.com.au

Figure 14.2: Powerlink 'thank you' advertisement: March 2007

Message to the Collinsville community
from Powerlink Queensland

Powerlink and Ergon Energy crews restored high voltage supply to the electricity grid in the Collinsville area on Thursday 22 March after working around the clock to replace a transformer which was damaged in a severe lightning storm on Tuesday 13 March.

The installation of the replacement transformer was one of the most complex emergency restoration projects Powerlink has ever undertaken.

Powerlink thanks the Collinsville community for its patience, understanding and support for Powerlink and Ergon Energy staff working locally to restore high voltage electricity supply to the area.

We would also like to thank the following people and organisations for their invaluable support during the substation restoration efforts:

- Bowen Shire Council, including Mayor Cr Michael Brunker, Cr Geoffrey Buckley and Cr Peter Ramage
- the Collinsville Workers Club
- the Collinsville Lions Club
- the local Collinsville business community
- Transfield Services Collinsville Power Station
- Ergon Energy staff for their work to restore temporary electricity supply via generators and their help with the installation of the replacement transformer.

Powerlink is continuing work at its Collinsville Substation to prepare to install a second transformer and will provide the community with regular updates on the progress of this work in the coming weeks.

ROBINA XAVIER

EVALUATION

The response was evaluated throughout the crisis period as well as at the end.

Media monitoring was used to assess the flow-through of key messages. Attendance at the community information centre was monitored, as was all communication from key stakeholders and customers.

Close to 150 media items were run in the ten-day period surrounding the crisis, with almost all reflecting positively on the organisations' actions. Key messages were well represented in the coverage. More than 700 residents visited the community information centre to receive vouchers, information and practical assistance.

The response was recognised by state and local government, with the organisations praised for their prompt action and open communication.

LESSONS LEARNT

The Collinsville power crisis demonstrates the importance of early planning and a quick response when faced with a physical crisis. Pre-planning allowed the organisations to swing into action immediately, as soon as they were notified of the issue, and to start proactively communicating with key stakeholders.

In a media- and technology-driven society, this case also shows the importance of more traditional and direct forms of communication in a time of crisis. Without electricity, communicators had to find innovative ways to get information to a diverse group of stakeholders who faced potential hardship and economic loss.

Bringing local key opinion leaders and community groups 'into the problem'—rather than talking 'at' them about solutions—was also an important strategy. This helped to further foster local community trust in Powerlink and Ergon Energy's approach, bring the community together to focus on common needs, and show that both organisations were doing all that they could to get power restored. The organisations also focused on practical advice and support, understanding that this would be highly valued by the community and would help mitigate any negativity felt towards the organisations for the inconvenience suffered.

Basing senior executives in the crisis zone helped cultivate a 'human face' for both organisations, and portrayed the message first hand that decision-makers were accessible and responding to the community's needs. The targeted, proactive and continued stream of communication ensured that accurate and appropriate messages were dispersed, thus protecting and even strengthening organisational reputations and brands.

REFERENCES

Fearn-Banks K., 1996, *Crisis Communications: A Casebook Approach*, Lawrence Erlbaum
   Associates, NJ

Lerbinger O., 1997, *The Crisis Manager: Facing Risk and Responsibility*, Lawrence Erlbaum
   Associates, NJ

Storm Centre, www.ergon.com.au/Storm_Centre/

Media Relations

Avian Influenza and the Press

Dr Richard C. Stanton

15

AIMS OF THIS CHAPTER

- To describe the key characteristics of building and maintaining relationships with media

- To identify how issues can be suitably framed to attract media attention

- To explore how different stakeholders in different countries framed the avian influenza issue

INTRODUCTION

Media relations usually attempts to define itself by what it is not—it is not propaganda, it is not lobbying and it is not advertising. Media relations describes the relationships with and between media, media relations practitioners and clients. Media relationships may not always be immediately evident, but there are certain tests we can apply to see if they are present. A story in *BRW*, Australia's leading business magazine—on innovative processes being used by GM-Holden to design internationally acclaimed motor vehicles and written by managing editor Peter Roberts—is seen as a story sourced by the journalist (Roberts 2006). But underlying the initial story idea are layers of stakeholders with interests the same as those of Roberts: Roberts wants to see the story because it sells magazines; Holden wants to see it because it sells cars; the designer around whom the story is written wants to see it because it will strengthen his design credentials among those readers most likely to employ him. For the story to 'get a run', relationships have to be built by and between the stakeholders: Holden, *BRW* and the designer.

This chapter describes the characteristics of building and maintaining relationships with the media. It outlines the way theories assist the building process, and how to frame a story so that it is more likely to get a run. It uses as a case study the issue of avian influenza and its potentially devastating effect on human health.

Avian influenza affects birds. It kills them. It also has the potential to kill millions of humans, not only in developing countries, but in western countries where there is less sense of urgency and a greater sense of immunity. Both of these senses are inaccurate, as avian influenza—or bird flu—has the potential to migrate from birds to humans with devastating effect.

The main stakeholders in the bird flu issue for our purposes are the New Zealand Government, the World Health Organization and the Australian Government. And, of course, the news media. We are interested in understanding how the issue of bird flu can, to use the vernacular, 'gain traction' with the media when other issues such as war, energy security and global warming occupy more important frames.

While significant aspects of contemporary media relations draw upon theory and practice derived from the US experience, media relations must—by its situational nature—adapt to specific social, political and economic variables and rituals in each individual location (see e.g. Page & Hazleton 1999). The media are acknowledged as being of primary importance to the campaign goals and objectives of all types of issues and events. Rare is the public issue or event that does not require support from some form of media.

Media relations is a subfield of public relations because the media are one of many stakeholders within the wider public relations field. It is through the media that the diverse range of stakeholders in the public sphere reach other stakeholders and what US scholar

Dean Kruckeberg calls 'stakeseekers' (Kruckeberg 1998). Stakeseekers are those groups and individuals who are looking to have a stake or a share in an issue or event, but who are not yet perceived to be a part of it. This does not mean the media is supplicant in delivering effective outcomes. The news media is generally hostile towards issues and events that seek to influence and persuade them of some virtue that might not normally make a contribution to news. So it is crucial for practitioners to build media relationships in which trust and integrity are the underlying elements. We are interested in *framing* issues and events as news so that they resonate with the media we are delivering them to.

FRAMING A MEDIA RELATIONS CAMPAIGN

In developing a media relations campaign we need to consider theoretical direction. We need to frame our campaign so that it makes sense to a number of stakeholders—notably, our client and the media to which we are pitching. Framing theory is the capacity of a media relationship builder to comprehend and interpret the agenda-setting policies and source selection processes employed by the media. It is the construction of a suitable ground onto which an issue or event can be projected as an elegant story (characterised by grace of form; simple and effective) relevant to specific media stakeholders (Stanton 2007b).

Framing theory requires SGI:

* Strategy (design)

* Ground (foreground/background)

* Image (story).

We will apply each of the elements of SGI to our case study.

Building strategies and tactics into our framing model

For our framing model to be effective, we must think about it in parallel with what sort of strategy and tactics we are likely to need. A strategy is more than a plan. It requires us to think competitively and to gain some advantage. We can gain an advantage from a successful strategy by the actions we take.

Strategy exists at all levels within all organisations. It is also something that is used by individuals. A person may say they have a strategy to further their career. This is more than a plan because it requires the individual to act competitively. A plan is not always strategic. A plan can be as simple as making a decision to go to the movies and acting out the sequence: gathering friends together, finding the money for the tickets, getting to the theatre, buying tickets and refreshments, watching the movie. Such a plan only becomes strategic when circumstances become competitive. The plan to go to the movies becomes strategic if the movie theatre decides to give free tickets to the first twenty people who arrive for the session. This decision is widely known, so it becomes strategic because the plan now has to compete against others if the free tickets are to be secured. This is a simple example, but it is important to understand that all media relations plans become strategies because they are in competition with others who have similar plans. In media terms a campaign proposal is strategic because our client is competing with everyone else's clients for finite media space.

Understanding the mechanics of the issue

Newspapers do not add extra pages to their daily run because they find an important news story that needs publishing. Newspapers only increase their page numbers when more advertising is sold, as news is not counted as being important enough to increase page numbers. So the important news story replaces a less important story, which gets pushed back in the hierarchy. News, as we will see shortly, is ranked according to its worthiness, so if there are insufficient pages on a given day, some news items may get dropped from the news schedule. A client's newsworthy story may be newsworthy for the client, but it may not make it into the news pages because it was outranked by more important news. So developing and designing a client's media campaign strategy requires us to keep in mind that we are always competing for limited news or feature space in newspapers, on radio and on television. In media relations terms, a strategy statement describes how, in concept, an objective is to be achieved, providing guidelines and themes for the overall campaign.

All media relations activity begins with a dialogic relationship between two interested parties:

• The media relations counsellor (agent)

• The primary stakeholder (client).

If an initial dialogue proceeds past a point of agreement, where the client perceives the need to engage the agent, it will be incumbent upon the agent to demonstrate to the client the most appropriate course of action to achieve media goals and objectives.

It is important to understand that the client is not a media relations specialist, so quite often they need 'convincing' that what they are about to engage in will be of great benefit. This is most often done by way of the agent preparing a proposal, or campaign strategy. A media campaign may be successfully completed by the relatively simple act of writing a letter to a newspaper editor. Or sending a one-off news statement. In these cases the strategy is simple, and the tactical objective cost-effectively achievable.

In theoretical terms a dialogic position can be described as a system, rather than monologic policies (Botan 1997). Media relations campaigns that begin from this premise have a much greater success rate than those that do not. Part of the reason concerns the informed nature of stakeholders. In historical terms, there was less information available to stakeholders who were asked to accept on faith the policies of governments, corporations and other organisations, which then frequently went about doing harm. The invention of the internet assisted the information process and its wider dissemination to disenfranchised stakeholders, with the result that those organisations or governments with poor policy goals had to change their ways.

A campaign is defined as an organised course of action that has boundaries or specific objectives. For media relations, campaigns are the central activity around which issues and events revolve. Campaigns are made up of particular elements that come together to present an image of an issue or event to media stakeholders, to encourage them to act in some way towards the issue or event to achieve a desired result (Stanton 2007b).

For media relations, the campaign is always pitched at the media as the primary stakeholder. Campaign proposals in media relations—like campaign planning in war, or any other time of action—require details that can be assembled in some specific and rational order so that they reflect what is proposed to happen in a linear fashion, from a beginning to an ending. They can be difficult to construct because they require balance between meaning ascribed by an agent and meaning ascribed by a client, and then the transference of the agreed meaning to stakeholders so that goals and objectives can be reached within mutually acceptable frames. While a client may have a limited knowledge of the technical skills required to run a campaign, nonetheless, from a narrow perspective, the client will have a definite understanding of the required outcomes. The campaign proposal reflects both the client's desires and the agent's capabilities (Stanton 2007a).

DEVELOPING A THEORY AND MODEL FOR EVALUATION

Just as they are in the wider field of public relations, evaluation and measurement are important elements in media relations. The development of measurement techniques has signalled the intentions of media relations practitioners to think and act in a serious way and to promote cost-effectiveness for clients. As we have seen in other chapters, evaluation is the fourth stage of the strategic development of a media relations campaign. But, as we will see in this chapter, it is not limited to the end of a campaign. If it is undertaken correctly, it provides valuable signals all along the campaign journey.

For campaign evaluation to be taken seriously it must be considered in a systematic way. There is always room for emotive evaluation—a crowd of journalists offering a standing ovation in response to a client's speech is a good emotive measure of success—but this should run parallel with rational evaluation if a client is to see it in terms of a return on investment (ROI). When thinking about evaluation, a media relations practitioner must always keep in mind the needs of the client and how the client's organisation measures its own success (Stanton 2007a).

While there is a variety of measurement techniques available for media relations evaluation, it remains a constant among Australian and New Zealand practitioners that the message exposure model is still the boss. When we think of media relations, we focus our attention on one stakeholder group—the media—so we are interested in the success of published, broadcast and narrowcast (internet) material.

There are three reliable and widely used methods of evaluation in media relations. We will refer to them together as *three M evaluation*, meaning the three 'M's of media relations:

- Metrics

- Message exposure

- Media impressions.

When used in conjunction with each other, these offer the most reliable set of formative and summative measurement tools presently available (Stanton 2007b).

METRICS

The use of metrics in media relations has been adapted from linguistics and psychology. It uncovers and interprets specific characteristics about groups of reporters, journalists or other media workers. It relies on the interpretation of characteristics associated with individuals that have been extrapolated from their written or spoken work. Metrics is most valuable as a method of interpreting a journalist's characteristics so that a media profile can be built of an individual or a group who may display similar characteristics. When used in conjunction with media impressions and message exposure, metrics provides a triangular frame on which to build a strong evaluation.

Metrics has its basis in content analysis. News databases provide the key to metric evaluation of large scale analyses. They may not play an important role in smaller metric analysis—for example psychological interpretation of a single reporter on *The Press* over a period of a few weeks—but their value when applying large-scale measurement is enormous. Metrics relies for its success on constants within the psychological functions of humans, and the capability to respond to persuasion and influence.

Media workers as a group may respond less positively to certain stimuli—gifts or gadgets attached to news releases, for example—because they have become inured through cynicism. But they exist within a state that Katz (1960) identified as needing to be pleasantly situated, while at the same time developing a defensive mechanism to protect them from issues within themselves and their environments that they do not wish to face.

MESSAGE EXPOSURE

Message exposure is the most widely used form of evaluation. It involves compiling clippings and mentions. This is also a good way to evaluate media acceptance of the message. Using this method we can evaluate message content against exposure. According to US scholar Richard Perloff (2003), exposure to all types of communication can influence stakeholders' attitude and behaviour. He suggests exposure is a 'strong, robust persuasion phenomenon' and he cites numerous advertising examples to support his argument.

We can extrapolate Perloff's argument out of the advertising field and apply it to media messages, with an additional feature that neutral issues—those for which we have no strong opinion—are most likely to resonate because stakeholders have yet to develop an attitude or opinion about them.

MEDIA IMPRESSIONS

A media impression is the measurement of the number of people who might realistically connect with the material in newspapers, television or radio. It can be determined by circulation or readership (audience) numbers.

BACKGROUND

The client we are interested in for this case study is the New Zealand Ministry of Health. But we are also interested in the media campaigns of other World Health Organization (WHO) stakeholders, including the Government of Australia. The Ministry of Health developed its initial campaign from the WHO model, so let us begin by looking at what WHO has done.

WHO (a not-for-profit global organisation) is monitoring bird flu around the world and attempting to raise the level of interest in the media (local and international) of the consequences to human health of a pandemic. Some western governments have 'talked it up', saying it has potential pandemic proportions, but generally, in the past few years, the issue has been overtaken in the western media by more immediate, 'sexier' issues such as war, climate change and Japanese whaling. But the problem of avian influenza and its potential disastrous human effects has been growing, along with the number of countries in which it has been detected. Media relations experts have been commissioned by a number of competing stakeholders to 'frame' the issue in terms that will benefit them specifically.

Some of the stakeholders and their frames are:

- **WHO**

  Big threat, keep monitoring

- **Australian Government**

  No threat because of strict quarantine policy

- **Chinese Government**

  No threat because bird flu has been contained to specific areas

- **Australian Medical Association (AMA)**

  Best to be safe, support production of antidote

- **New Zealand Government**

  Possible threat, manage issue.

When corporations, governments or individuals (clients) engage a media relations expert (agent) to frame an issue or event, they do it with different stakeholders in mind (Stanton 2007b). Most often, it is the news media stakeholder the client is interested in, because the news media can disseminate information far quicker and wider than any other stakeholder. At other times it might be a specific stakeholder group that the client is interested in, such as community groups or special interest groups. Whatever the nature of the stakeholders being pitched to, we can add to the definition of framing by suggesting that it is the process of imagining, in words and pictures, something that is meaningful to its source, whose meaning can be transferred to others through the construction of issues and events (Stanton 2007b). And this is where the media becomes a vitally important stakeholder in the dissemination of messages about bird flu for every conceivable reason. But there is another dimension to this. The media has a duty to investigate the political or non-political context of issues or events so that they can be reported or rejected in an equitable and meaningful fashion.

Part of the problem of bird flu getting on to the news media agenda in the western world is political. And part of the problem is caused by the way it is framed. A complex issue requires one or more frames to have legitimacy, as we can see by considering the following scenarios:

- A simple event, such as the launch of a television program showing fat people losing weight, may have one dominant frame *(univalent)*.

- A concert to raise money for India's poor may have two dominant frames *(bivalent)*, namely the donation of their performance by highly paid musicians and the issue of poverty.

- However an issue such as avian influenza, with many significant frames *(multivalent)*, requires meaning to be applied across a number of levels to a number of stakeholders.

RESEARCH

When we investigate the issue of bird flu, our research throws up some interesting material. According to WHO, since December 2003, highly pathogenic H5N1 avian influenza viruses have swept through poultry populations across Asia and parts of Europe. The outbreaks are historically unprecedented in scale and geographical spread. Their economic impact on the agricultural sector of the affected countries has been large. Up until July 2005, outbreaks of avian influenza in poultry occurred in nine countries (Cambodia, China, Indonesia, Japan, the Republic of Korea, the Lao People's Democratic Republic, Malaysia, Thailand and Vietnam). Since late July 2005, outbreaks in domestic poultry as well as in wild birds have been reported in the Russian Federation, Kazakhstan, Romania, Mongolia, Turkey and Croatia. In addition, during this period outbreaks in poultry have increased again in Indonesia, Thailand, Vietnam and China (WHO website).

Remember, in media relations we need to develop a specific strategy because everyone else is competing for the same space in the public sphere. New Zealand and Australia developed specific media strategies for avian influenza, bearing the following specifics in mind:

- The Australian Government Department of Health and Ageing puts the level of national security threat in Australia at medium and the level of pandemic threat at zero (Department of Health and Ageing website). (Note that WHO coordinates the global response to human cases of H5N1 avian influenza and monitors the corresponding threat of an influenza pandemic.)

- In New Zealand, the issue of avian influenza was seen as less important than global warming, terrorism or Japanese whaling.

So, let us start by breaking the bird flu campaign down into manageable strategies and tactics.

STRATEGIES AND TACTICS
New Zealand and Operation Cruickshank

The New Zealand Ministry of Health worked with the health sector and other government agencies to ensure New Zealand was as prepared as possible for a potential pandemic. New Zealand campaign strategies appeared to be more coordinated and provided more information than their counterparts in Australia. This was partly due to the smaller size of the land mass in which the government needed to operate, but it was also due to the government's concern that the disease would be potentially devastating to a relatively small population. For the six months leading up to February 2007 the Ministry of Health provided the following to the media:

SEPTEMBER 2006

- **Headline**

  'Latest Version of Plan to Respond to an Influenza Pandemic Released'

- **Lead paragraph**

  'A bigger and better version of New Zealand's plan for responding to an influenza pandemic was released by the Ministry of Health today.'

NOVEMBER 2006

- **Headline**

  'Ministry of Health Holding Nationwide Influenza Pandemic Exercise'

- **Lead paragraph**

  'The Ministry of Health is staging a nationwide influenza pandemic exercise tomorrow.'

FEBRUARY 2007

- **Headline**

  'Ministry of Health Confident with New Zealand's Level of Pandemic Preparation'

- **Lead paragraph**

  'The Ministry of Health says New Zealand's pandemic planning is among the best in the world and is confident the country will be ready when the big one hits.'

The New Zealand response to the potential for an avian influenza pandemic (in association with WHO) included a number of strategies concluding with a general total population inclusion response strategy codenamed 'Exercise Cruickshank' (New Zealand Government 2007).

Overall interest in the government's plans were generally encouraging in 2005–06, and this particular exercise received named media coverage in:

- *The Press* (metropolitan daily, Fairfax), 21 October 2006

- *The Marlborough Express* (regional daily, Fairfax), 8 November 2006

- *The Timaru Herald* (regional daily, Fairfax), 8 November 2006

- *Nelson Mail* (regional daily), 10 November 2006

- *Hawkes Bay Today* (regional daily, APN), 9 November 2006.

(Factiva database)

The Ministry of Health framed the issue in a particular way:

Strategy
Comprehend the policies of

- World Health Organization (primary stakeholder)
- International media (Western + Asian)
- National media (New Zealand)
- Local media (network television, talk-back radio)

Ground
- Foreground: widespread human infection
- Background: government action—mock crisis test

Image
- Impending doom (simple human disaster)
- Government management (control mechanisms)
- Reduced cause for alarm through crisis management.

(Factiva database)

Australia develops a different strategy

The Australian Government localised its strategy. It constructed a health management plan and ran a test of it in 2006. Its lead tactic was to use the skills of experts to present the image of avian influenza (Australian Government Department of Health & Ageing website). John Horvath, Australia's Chief Medical Officer, made a number of conference presentations in late 2006 on the Australian health management plan for pandemic influenza (Australian Government Department of Health & Ageing website). The strategy was designed to provide shock value by highlighting the number of deaths around the world from pandemics. Dr Horvath made some comparisons:

Deaths
1918–19 Spanish Influenza 20–50 million
1957 Asian Influenza approx. 1 million
1968–9 Hong Kong Influenza approx. 1 million

(Australian Government Department of Health & Ageing website)

The Australian Government's plan and associated strategies were covered by a number of important national and metropolitan newspapers including (some multiple times) *The*

Australian, The Herald Sun, The Canberra Times, The Australian Financial Review, The Age and *The Sydney Morning Herald* (Factiva database).

The Australian Government framed the issue in a slightly different way:

Strategy

Comprehend the policies of

- World Health Organization (primary stakeholder)
- International media (Western + Asian)
- National media (Australia)
- Local media (network television, talk-back radio)

Ground

- Foreground: management of issue by government
- Background: government action—provide expert comment

Image

- Impending doom (simple human disaster)
- Government management (control mechanisms)
- Reduced cause for alarm through crisis management.

Dateline Christchurch: The Press

Let us look at a particular journalist writing about the avian influenza case. (We can extract full texts of everything journalists have written from an archival database such as Factiva.)

Between 13 October 2006 and 10 November 2006, journalist Kamala Hayman wrote four stories on avian influenza that were published in *The Press* in Christchurch (averaging one a week) (Hayman 2006a–d). We can code these four stories against a predetermined scale, indicating for example the level of hostility the journalist may display towards the subject, or perhaps revealing the level of anxiety, dismay or hope that the journalist composes around the subject.

A simple content analysis will help us understand the way the journalist feels about the issue. To begin with, in the course of the four stories Hayman used the word 'pandemic' twenty-four times. Three of the stories (21 October, 31 October and 10 November) mentioned the Ministry of Health and quoted a spokesperson for the ministry. The source of these stories was the client, the Ministry of Health. The other story (13 October) was sourced from a *New Zealand Medical Journal* article.

The measurement and evaluation of psychological characteristics in humans is not new. What is relatively new for media relations is the application of psychometrics to investigate the work of journalists, reporters and other media workers, and to draw inferences and make predictions. By making accurate psychometric measurements of the work of certain journalists, we can argue it is almost impossible to create a media campaign that will fail (Stanton 2007a). In the bird flu case, we can find everything that is written by specific journalists and then analyse the content of the material. Or we can analyse the headlines to see whether the stories are going to be positive or negative.

The headlines in the four Hayman stories appearing in *The Press* were:

- 'Coin Toss may Rule Treatment' (13 October)

- 'Health Staff Practise for Pandemic' (21 October)

- 'Planners Prepare Quarantined Measures for Possible Pandemic' (31 October)

- 'Canterbury Readies for Pandemic' (10 November).

We can see immediately that three of the four use language that appears to be positive about the issue. (Headlines are written by a sub-editor but they usually reflect the tone of the copy.) The exception is the story on 13 October which, as mentioned above, was derived from a source other than the Ministry of Health, so there was an opportunity for the journalist to find a different angle.

For the purposes of this case study, the overall New Zealand coverage was more favourable for the client (the New Zealand Government) than the coverage in Australia of the Australian Government's involvement in the issue (Factiva database).

EVALUATION
Message exposure

For our evaluation, we will use the metrics that we discussed above. First of all, we collect all the material published and broadcast about our issue or event. (In the past, this was sufficient for media relations practitioners to bill clients.) In other words, we collect all the material appearing on the avian flu case in Australia. In Australia, for example, material appeared in *The Australian, The Bulletin, The Mercury, The Herald Sun, ABC, The Canberra Times, The Australian Financial Review, Northern Territory News, BRW, The Courier Mail, Townsville Bulletin, The Age, Australian Doctor, West Australian, Sunday Telegraph, Geelong Advertiser, The Sydney Morning Herald, The Knox Leader* and *The Whitehorse Leader*. The collection of all this material in all these media is in itself a measure of the success of the campaign, but it will be measurably more meaningful if this material is evaluated against a number of other criteria, which might include style and tone of language. Message exposure is a vital beginning for any type of evaluation.

A better way to evaluate our issue: media impressions

To enhance our evaluation further, let us calculate the impressions from the New Zealand newspapers we've collected for the specific campaign of Exercise Cruickshank by considering the circulation and readership numbers.

TABLE 15.1: EXERCISE CRUICKSHANK: CIRCULATION AND READERSHIP

NEWSPAPER	CIRCULATION	READERSHIP
The Press	89,027	234,000
Hawkes Bay Today	28,000	63,000
Nelson Mail	18,445	39,000
The Timaru Herald	14,329	31,000
The Marlborough Express	10,362	n/a

We have no available data on *The Marlborough Express* readership, so for this exercise we will use the circulation figures for each newspaper. Our actual impressions for Exercise Cruickshank therefore total 160,163.

Now we might decide to use what we call *gross impressions* as an additional method of analysis. To do this we take the circulation figures for our publications and multiply them by the number of times our material appeared. For Exercise Cruickshank, each newspaper ran one story with no follow-up. Therefore gross impressions in this case are the same as actual impressions.

We can then calculate *total effective impressions* if next we consider the percentage of the press coverage impressions that could be considered by our target audience—say 50 per cent of one hit in *The Press*—and this becomes our total effective impressions. In this case we might assume that the issue is of importance to 70 per cent of the population, so 49,857—or roughly 50,000—people absorbed the message of Exercise Cruickshank.

To give us an idea of how important the issue was in editorial terms, we might also measure the *actual column centimetres* appearing.

We can then assign an *individual content value* to each piece, relative to its position in the medium.

The best positions were p. 2 in the *Nelson Mail*, p. 3 in *The Timaru Herald* and *Hawkes Bay Post*, and front pages of special sections in *The Press* and *The Marlborough Express*. Our overall value might then be thirty-nine, from a potential total value of fifty (see Table 15.2).

TABLE 15.2: INDIVIDUAL CONTENT VALUE: ASSIGNABLE TO POSITION IN MEDIUM

VALUE	POSITION IN MEDIUM
10	Front page/cover/lead
9	Front page of section, issue-appropriate
8	Front page of less important section
7	Prominent page position inside a section
6	Neutral position, not immediately obvious
5	Short copy, buried
4	One paragraph or less, buried

We can now calculate an *average position value* by adding individual placement values together and dividing that total by the number of placements. This will give us an average position relative to our assumed values. Our average position value is 7.8/10.

Next we assign a *content value* for each placement, using a chosen scale. In this case we might use the following:

TABLE 15.3: CONTENT VALUE: ASSIGNABLE TO NUMBER OF KEY COPY POINTS

VALUE	KEY COPY POINTS
10	5
9	4
8	3
7	2
6	1
5	Negative angle (regardless of point coverage)

We can calculate an *average content value* by adding individual content values and dividing that total by the total number of placements.

This is a very good score, indicating a strong response by the press to the issue of avian influenza in general and Exercise Cruickshank in particular. It also provides evidence of a generally positive image of the issue from newspapers within the Fairfax organisation (*The Press, The Marlborough Express* and *The Timaru Herald* are all Fairfax newspapers).

TABLE 15.4: CALCULATING AVERAGE CONTENT VALUE

NEWSPAPER	NO OF POINTS	VALUE
The Press	7	12
Hawkes Bay Today	2	7
Nelson Mail	3	8
The Timaru Herald	3	8
The Marlborough Express	6	11
Average content value		9.2/10

We can use similar methods to calculate *average airtime* by dividing the total minutes of airtime by the total number of placements. As an additional overlap measure, we can calculate a *total equivalent advertising value* by multiplying the ad rate by the amount of space or time given to the placement. We can then sum the individual ad values to reach a total equivalent ad value. (This assumes advertising space has the same meaning as editorial space in the mind of the stakeholder public.)

There is, however, considerable debate in Australia and New Zealand on the ethical and professional value of using advertising equivalencies as a measure of success and the Public Relations Institutes of Australia and New Zealand (PRIA and PRINZ) suggest their members should avoid using it. If the client wants an additional overlap, we can instead calculate a *gross cost per impression* by dividing the total cost of the campaign by the total gross impressions.

We can also calculate an *effective cost per impression* by dividing the total cost of the campaign by the total effective impressions. This is a post-campaign evaluation, but if we had conducted it pre-campaign we would have been in a better position to make a pre–post campaign comparison, and therefore be in a better position to document the impact of the campaign. If we repeated this methodology each month we would have a time-series research design that would be even better. It is equally important to be able to measure failure, so that we do not repeat it.

LESSONS LEARNT

Our client, the New Zealand Ministry of Health, should be very happy with the results of the media coverage for avian influenza. It appears the client has framed the issue in such a way that it resonated with the press, fitting in with the ideology of the media: the well-being of its readership. The results also reflect a positive use of strategy, ground and image within the campaign.

But there is another important lesson. Even when we use the same campaign strategies, tactics and research, different clients will get different results. As we can see, this is dependent upon the way the client views the issue and the media relationship. In the Australian case, we could make the comment that the outcome was not as clear as it was for New Zealand because the New Zealand Government took a much more 'holistic' approach to the issue. Additionally, we could say that even though they appear to have similarities, the governments and the media of both countries had different views of the issue and how it was framed. And in the framing, the result was always destined to be different.

REFERENCES

Australian Government Department of Health and Ageing, www.health.gov.au/, accessed 2007

Botan C., 1997, 'Ethics in Strategic Communication Campaigns: The Case for a New Approach to Public Relations' in *Journal of Business Communication*, Vol. 34, pp. 187–201

Botan C. & Hazleton V. (eds), 2006, *Public Relations Theory II*, Lawrence Erlbaum, Mahwah, NJ

Broom G. & Dozier D., 1990, *Using Research in Public Relations: Applications to Program Management*, Prentice Hall, Englewood Cliffs, NJ

Cornelissen J., 2004, *Corporate Communications Theory and Practice*, Sage, London

Entman R., 1993, 'Framing: Toward Clarification of a Fractured Paradigm' in *Journal of Communication*, Vol. 43, No. 4, pp. 51–8

Factiva (current affairs and company information database), www.library.usyd.edu.au/subjects/projectmanagement/factiva.html, accessed February 2007

Goffman E., 1974, *Frame Analysis*, Harper & Row, NY

Grunig J., 1992, *Excellence in Public Relations and Communication Management*, Lawrence Erlbaum, Hillsdale, NJ

Hallin D. & Mancini P., 2004, *Comparing Media Systems: Three Models of Media and Politics*, Cambridge University Press, Cambridge

Hayman K., 2006a, 'Coin Toss May Rule Treatment' in *The Press*, 13 October 2006, p. 5

Hayman K., 2006b, 'Health Staff Practice for Pandemic' in *The Press*, 21 October 2006, p. 14

Hayman K., 2006c, 'Planners Prepare Quarantine Measures for Possible Pandemic' in *The Press*, 31 October 2006, p. 3

Hayman K., 2006d, 'Canterbury Readies for Pandemic' in *The Press*, 10 November 2006, p. 4

Heath R. (ed.), 2001, *Handbook of Public Relations*, Sage, Thousand Oaks, CA

Hendrix J., 1998, *Public Relations Cases*, Wadsworth, Belmont, CA

Ihlen Ø., 2005, 'The Power of Social Capital: Adapting Bordieu to the Study of Public Relations', in *Public Relations Review*, Vol. 31, No. 4, pp. 492–6

Katz D., 1960, 'The Functional Approach to the Study of Attitudes' in *Public Opinion Quarterly*, Vol. 24, pp. 163–204

Kruckeberg D., 1998, 'The Future of PR Education: Some Recommendations' in *Public Relations Review*, Vol. 24, pp. 235–48

Marston J., 1963, *The Nature of Public Relations*, McGraw-Hill, NY

Moloney K., 2005, *Rethinking Public Relations: The Spin and the Substance*, Routledge, London

Nelson Mail, 2006, 'Pandemic Tests Health Response', 10 November 2006, p. 2

Neuendorf K., 2002, *The Content Analysis Guidebook*, Sage, Thousand Oaks, CA

New Zealand Government Ministry of Health, www.moh.govt.nz/moh.nsf

Newton K., 2006, 'Pandemic Readiness Put to the Test' in *Hawke's Bay Today*, 9 November 2006, p. 3

Page K. & Hazleton V., 1999, 'An Empirical Analysis of Factors Influencing Public Relations Strategy Selection and Effectiveness' in *International Communication Association (ICA)*, San Francisco, CA

Perloff R., 2003, *The Dynamics of Persuasion: Communication and Attitudes in the 21st Century*, Lawrence Erlbaum, Mahwah, NJ

Roberts P., 2006, *BRW*, February 2006, John Fairfax, Sydney

Seib P. & Fitzpatrick K., 1995, *Public Relations Ethics*, Harcourt Brace, Forth Worth, TX

Shen F., 2004, 'Effects of News Frames and Schemas on Individuals' Issue Interpretations and Attitudes' in *Journalism and Mass Communication Quarterly*, Vol. 81, pp. 400–16

Sparrow B., 1999, *Uncertain Guardians: The News Media as a Political Institution*, Johns Hopkins Press, Baltimore, MD

Sriramesh K. & Vércîc D., 2003, *The Global Public Relations Handbook: Theory, Research and Practice*, Lawrence Erlbaum, Mahwah, NJ

Stanton R., 2007a, *All News is Local: The Failure of the Media to Reflect World Events in a Globalized Age*, McFarland & Co., NC

Stanton R., 2007b, *Media Relations*, Oxford University Press, Melbourne

Stanton R., 2006c, *Towards Public Relations Liberalization: An Australian Contribution*, 1st Asia Pacific Public Relations Conference, Seoul

Timaru Herald, 2006, 'Pandemic Exercises for Health Officials', 8 November 2006, p. 3

Tymson C. & Lazar R., 2006, *The New Australian Public Relations Manual*, Tymson Communications, Sydney

World Health Organization, 2007, www.who.org, accessed 2007

Index